The Archaeology of Everyday Life at Early Moundville

A Dan Josselyn Memorial Publication

The Archaeology of Everyday Life at Early Moundville

Gregory D. Wilson

THE UNIVERSITY OF ALABAMA PRESS
Tuscaloosa

Manufactured in the United States of America

Typeface: AGaramond
∞
The paper on which this book is printed meets the minimum requirements of American National Standard for Information Sciences-Permanence of Paper for Printed Library Materials, ANSI Z39.48-1984.

Library of Congress Cataloging-in-Publication Data

Wilson, Gregory D., 1969–
The archaeology of everyday life at early Moundville / Gregory D. Wilson.
p. cm.
Includes bibliographical references and index.
ISBN-13: 978-0-8173-1579-5 (cloth : alk. paper)
ISBN-10: 0-8173-1579-9 (alk. paper)
ISBN-13: 978-0-8173-5444-2 (pbk. : alk. paper)
ISBN-10: 0-8173-5444-1 (alk. paper)
1. Moundville Archaeological Park (Moundville, Ala.) 2. Mississippian culture—Alabama—Black Warrior River Valley. 3. Mississippian pottery—Alabama—Black Warrior River Valley. 4. Social archaeology—Alabama—Black Warrior River Valley. 5. Black Warrior River Valley (Ala.)—Antiquities. I. Title.
E99.M6815W55 2008
976.1′43—dc22

2007026077

For Amber

Contents

Illustrations

Figures

Tables

Acknowledgments

First and foremost I would like to thank my wife, Amber VanDerwarker, for years of unwavering support. I could have never made it this far without her. Thanks in particular to Vin Steponaitis for his advice on all things anthropological. Special thanks to Margie Scarry and John Scarry for their help in selecting this research project. I also extend my gratitude to Steve Davis for his substantial contribution to the Moundville GIS map. Finally, I wish to thank Brian Billman for sharing his insights into household archaeology.

A great number of other individuals and institutions also facilitated this research. Thanks to my peers Tony Boudreax, Kandi Detwiler, Scott Hammerstedt, Hunter Johnson, Jon Marcoux, Mintcy Maxham, Scott Meeks, Chris Rodning, and Bram Tucker for their friendship and scholarly feedback. Hats off to Anna K. Bauguess, Catherine V. Brooks, Tara Miranda, and Jessica Newman for being great research assistants. I also thank those senior scholars who have generously provided me with advice and guidance: John Blitz, Bill Iseminger, John Kelly, Vernon J. Knight, Jr., Brad Koldehoff, and Timothy Pauketat. Major thanks to Eugene Futato and the staff at the Office of Archaeological Research in Moundville, Alabama, for providing access to collections and analysis space during the early stages of this research. Finally, I would like to thank my family for their love and support. Thanks, Dad, for introducing me to archaeology all those years ago.

The Archaeology of Everyday Life at Early Moundville

1 Introduction

How complex were Mississippian polities and in what ways were they complex? What role did small-scale social groups play in the emergence of regionally organized political hierarchies? These issues are the focus of this archaeological investigation of the Moundville site in the Black Warrior Valley of west-central Alabama. Between the twelfth and fifteenth centuries, the Moundville site was the political and ceremonial center of a regionally organized Mississippian polity. The Moundville site encompasses 75 ha and consists of 29 mounds grouped in pairs around a rectangular plaza (Figure 1.1). There is a very orderly arrangement of these earthen monuments (Peebles 1971, 1978). The largest mounds are located on the northern edge of the plaza and they become increasingly smaller going either clockwise or counterclockwise around the plaza to the south (Figure 1.1). Knight (1998) has interpreted this community plan as a sociogram, "an architectural depiction of a social order based on ranked clans" (Steponaitis and Knight 2004:168). According to this model the Moundville community was segmented into a variety of different clan precincts, the ranked position of which was represented in the size and arrangement of paired earthen mounds around the central plaza. The largest earthen mounds on the northern portion of the plaza were associated with the highest-ranking clans while smaller mounds to the south were associated with lower-ranking clans.

There has been a general acceptance of Knight's (1998) interpretation, which is grounded in both archaeological analysis and ethnohistoric analogy. Still unclear is the kind of hierarchy this network of ranked clans at Moundville entailed. Did a corporate group's ranked place and space in the Moundville sociogram involve notable differences in status and wealth? If so, how were these inequalities materialized and what kinds of corporate-group strategies served to produce them?

Previous investigations of Moundville's Mississippian occupation portrayed a complex chiefdom that was highly differentiated politically, socially, and economically. It has been argued that substantial organizational differences not only characterized mound and off-mound residential contexts but also crosscut the broader community and regional polity (Peebles 1971, 1987a, 1987b; Peebles and Kus 1977; Steponaitis 1978; Welch 1991a, 1991b, 1996; Welch and Scarry 1995). This model of Moundville's political economy has become an oft-cited example of how Mississippian polities were organized and compare to other middle-range

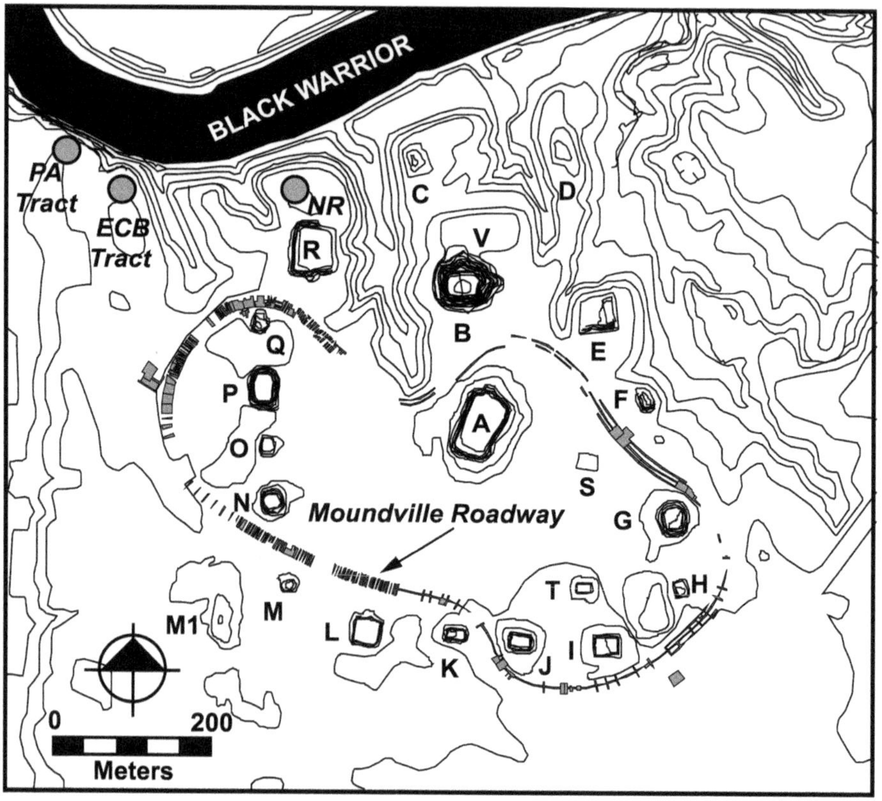

Figure 1.1. The Moundville site (geographic information system [GIS] representation), featuring the Roadway (1939–1940), Riverbank (Picnic Area [PA] and East Conference Building [ECB] tracts), and North of Mound R (NR) excavations.

societies around the world (Cobb 2003; Earle 1987; Price and Feinman 2001; Scarry and Fish 1999). In recent years, however, there has been increasing debate concerning the organization of Moundville's political economy (Marcoux 2000; Maxham 2000, 2004; Welch 1996; Wilson 2001). These disagreements stem from a broader scholarly debate regarding the complexity of Mississippian polities throughout the southeastern United States (Blitz 1999; Milner 1998; Muller 1984, 1986, 1997; Pauketat 1994; Welch 1991b). Over the past decade different scholars have generated contrasting arguments based on the examination of the same regional datasets (Anderson 1994; Blitz 1999; Emerson 1997a, 1997b; Mehrer 1995). In many cases it appears that these disparate interpretations are linked to different perspectives about the organizational dynamics that define "chiefdoms" as a societal category.

I believe that investigations of Moundville's political economy would benefit from the implementation of an agent-centered household archaeological approach.

By focusing on the everyday practices and interactions among small-scale social groups, I hope to sidestep many of the a priori assumptions about macroscale organizational dynamics that fuel ongoing debates about Mississippian political complexity. I begin by documenting and describing the different residential groups at early Moundville and the kinds of routine activities that formed everyday Mississippian domestic life. Second, I consider how the everyday practices and interactions among these groups contributed to the emergence of social complexity in the Black Warrior Valley of west-central Alabama. The data for this research include 140 Mississippian buildings and 14,320 pottery sherds from throughout the Moundville site (Appendixes 1 and 2). These data derive primarily from the 1939 and 1940 Moundville Roadway excavations conducted by the Alabama Museum of Natural History.

Agency and Structure in the Archaeological Record

Agency theory and practice theory are broad, interrelated approaches for examining the relationship between the actions of individuals and broader social phenomena. These theoretical approaches were developed, in part, as a reaction against top-down models that seek to explain human behavior as a direct result of structural forces like social institutions, cultural norms, and the environment (Dobres and Robb 2000). Structure can be loosely defined as beliefs, environmental conditions, or infrastructures that condition, constrain, or enable human behavior (Scarry 2001). The notion of reflexivity between structure and agency is a cornerstone to theories of practice (Dornan 2002; Giddens 1979). Structure conditions behaviors and beliefs but individuals also produce and alter structure through their actions. Structure is not external to the individual but internalized in the form of pragmatic understandings about the world and everyday routines and behaviors (Bourdieu 1977). It is through these day-to-day routines that social norms and institutions are generated and maintained.

What is the relationship between everyday practices and broader social phenomena? Simply put, our everyday practices and commonsense understandings are charged with deeper meanings. As Shennan (1993) has argued, these seemingly mundane behaviors are surface phenomena that relate to more deeply structured notions about how we perceive and act in the world. Thus, the gendered organization of domestic space and labor (Bourdieu 1977; Whitridge 1999), technological choices in tool manufacture (Pauketat 2001), food-preparation techniques (Atalay and Hastorf 2006), and even methods of trash disposal (Walker and Lucero 2000) serve to produce cultural norms about the position of individuals in society.

Throughout their lifetimes individuals acquire knowledge about their social positions by observing and participating in everyday routines. Because such routines are steeped in tradition, their relationship to the social system often goes unquestioned. This nonexplicit and unquestioned collective of understandings and practices is termed "doxa" by Bourdieu (1977) and "ideological" by Jean and John Comaroff (1991:22–27). This is not to say that individuals are automatons destined to unconsciously accept and reproduce traditional values and relationships. Individuals have the ability to critically and reflexively monitor past conduct in light of new situations that arise (Dornan 2002; Giddens 1979). Moreover, traditional practices may be altered or abandoned in light of structural problems and contradictions within the social system.

The unquestioned and taken-for-granted nature of many everyday practices and beliefs makes them well suited for those aspiring to produce and maintain relations of social inequality. A common strategy employed by aspiring elites is to co-opt widely held traditions for their own political purposes. Archaeologically documented transitions from egalitarian to hierarchically ascribed societies are replete with examples of this political and cultural dynamic. Puebloan religious specialists co-opted traditional forms of domestic architecture in the construction of ceremonial facilities known as kivas (Walker and Lucero 2000:143). Earthen platform mounds in the late prehistoric Southeast were traditional communal ceremonial facilities that the Mississippian elite co-opted to legitimize their elevated social positions (Knight 1989; Steponaitis 1986).

An important principle guiding practice-centered research is that the actions of individuals and small groups must be examined in order to determine how broader social arrangements were generated. The goal of such an endeavor is to first identify the different social groups that existed and consider the strategies they pursued that served to reproduce or alter (intentionally or not) the existing social order. Through cooperative labor projects, cost sharing, and communal ritualism, small-scale social groups negotiate relationships by which more inclusive social entities are formed. Thus, from a practice approach, society writ large is the outcome of negotiations that take place among a network of individuals.

A structuralist interpretation might contend that nonelite members of a society paid tribute to central administrators in the form of corvée labor or the mobilization of surplus foodstuffs because they lived in a hierarchical society like a chiefdom. In contrast, a practice-centered interpretation would contend that a hierarchical society existed because some individuals provided others with tribute in the form of corvée labor or surplus foodstuffs. The difference between these theoretical approaches is that within certain structuralist models, tribute payments are considered to be an intrinsic quality of hierarchical societies. Societal members are then assumed a priori (and sometimes in the absence of supportive data) to have behaved in accordance with this cross-cultural norm. Rather than assume, on the basis of a preassigned societal category, that certain structural qualities existed, practice theorists contend that it is necessary to begin with small-scale social groups and follow out the network of relationships that were negotiated to generate the broader social order.

Household Archaeology

Household archaeology refers to a number of loosely related methodological and theoretical approaches to understanding social, political, and economic organization. Household archaeology is not practice theory. Many of the goals and interests of household archaeologists, however, overlap with those of practice theorists. First and foremost is an interest in microscale organizational dynamics (Rogers 1995; Wilk and Rathje 1982). Archaeological approaches to households differ on the basis of theoretical interests in production, consumption, gender, health, and social status (Wilk and Netting 1984). There have been nearly as many definitions for the household as have been offered for the concept of culture. For my purpose here I use the term *household* to refer to the minimal, coresidential social group present in a given society.

Households vary greatly in terms of the number and composition of their constituents (Ashmore and Wilk 1988). It is this intrahousehold organizational variation and the network of interhousehold relationships that is of interest here. In order to properly account for intrahousehold variation in artifact assemblages and architectural features, it is necessary to consider a suite of issues that archaeologists have traditionally referred to as middle-range theory.

Making sense of archaeological data from domestic contexts requires reconstructing households and examining differences and similarities in the ways they organized themselves. Reconstructing household organization requires consideration of the following factors: (1) occupation span and dates of occupation, (2) household size and structure function, (3) the life cycle of the household, and (4) feature formation processes.

Occupation Span and Dates of Occupation

Ceramic seriation combined with radiocarbon dating is a common approach to dating Mississippian archaeological sites. While such techniques provide data about when a site was occupied, they often do not have the resolution by which to determine length of occupation. Analyses of structure use life and ceramic-accumulation studies provide the means by which occupation span can be more precisely estimated (Pauketat 1986, 2003; Schlanger 1986; Varien and Mills 1997; Varien and Potter 1997; Ward and Davis 1991). Ethnoarchaeological and experimental studies have produced estimates of structure use life that can be applied to archaeological cases in which people used similar building materials and structures were subject to similar environmental conditions (Warrick 1988:37). Occupation span is also an important factor in the composition of discard assemblages, as different artifacts have variable use lives and replacement rates (Varien and Mills 1997).

In Chapter 3 I employ several different seriation techniques to date the ceramic assemblages in this study. Calibrated radiocarbon dates from previous studies are used to anchor this seriation in real time (Knight et al. 1999). Data on architectural rebuilding techniques are used in Chapter 4 to estimate the occupation span of Moundville's early Mississippian community.

Household Size and Structure Function

One of the most fundamental axioms of household archaeology is that houses are not the same as households (Wilk and Netting 1984; Wilk and Rathje 1982). Households are people whereas houses are the structures within which they live. A single household may occupy one or more houses, storage buildings, kitchens, and outbuildings. Different kinds of structures may be occupied seasonally. Moreover, the function of individual structures may change through time, beginning their use lives as sleeping and eating quarters and ending their use lives as kitchens, work sheds, or storage rooms (Bailey 1996; Rothschild et al. 1993). Thus, to understand household organization it is critical to properly ascertain the function of different buildings and how these functions may have changed through time.

Differences in household size and composition greatly contribute to the architectural and artifactual variation observable in the archaeological record (Shapiro 1984; Turner and Lofgren 1966). Understanding why these differences in household size and composition existed in the past is a separate but related issue to documenting the differences in the first place. Household organizational variation may be a result of differences in social status and wealth, but it is also linked to site function and to a household's stage in the cycle of life (see below).

Power asymmetries are often built into the spatial structure of communities (Knight 1998; Nielsen 1995). Thus, proximity of households to monumental architecture, plazas, and other politically important areas forms an important spatial axis through which intercommunity differences in power relations can be manifested (Herndon 1995). Variation in the sizes, types, and spatial arrangements of domestic architecture provides an important source of information about intercommunity power relations (Nielsen 1995). House size is a common method used by archaeologists to infer household wealth and status (Kramer 1982; Netting 1982; Wilk 1983). Big houses require more resources in terms of building materials and labor investment than small houses. Larger houses may also indicate larger households, as social groups will create architectural spaces of the appropriate size for the number of people who use those spaces (Naroll 1962). As a result of their greater access to or control over certain resources, wealthier households not only attract more kin to residential locations than poorer households but may also experience higher reproductive success (Netting 1982:642). Larger and wealthier households may also possess a greater number and variety of architectural features such as storage structures and ceremonial facilities. Amassing large stores of surplus foodstuffs provides wealthy households with a competitive edge over their more modest neighbors.

In Chapter 4 data on architectural style, size, and methods of rebuilding are considered to evaluate the function of Mississippian buildings at Moundville. I also consider the distribution, arrangement, and proximity of buildings to one another and public architecture. This architectural information provides important insight into the organization of and relationships among early Mississippian households at Moundville.

The Life Cycle of the Household

Household size and composition change through time. A household may begin as a young married couple living in a small house with few material possessions. When that couple has children they may need to enlarge their house or build another one altogether. With time the couple may also acquire more material possessions and increase their social status in the greater community (Smith 1987:322). Eventually the couple's children move away, marry, and begin families of their own. Elderly family members may ultimately come to reside with the couple.

All of these life-changing events are part of the household life cycle (Fortes 1958; Goody 1958, 1972). This cycle varies for every household but they all pass through it in one way or another. The relevant point here is that a household will have a different archaeological signature based on its stage in the life cycle. Moreover, considerable interhousehold organizational variability documented by archaeologists is in some way related to the household life cycle. As discussed in Chapter 4 there are notable differences among early Mississippian structures in terms of their use lives. Some structures were rebuilt as many as four times while others were not rebuilt at all. These data provide insight into the ebb and flow of Moundville's nucleated occupation.

Feature Formation Processes

An understanding of feature formation processes is critical to archaeological interpretation. All items of material culture, whether they be artifacts or buildings, pass through a series of formational stages referred to here as use, abandonment, and postabandonment (LaMotta and Schiffer 1999; Schiffer 1977, 1987). It is important to understand that artifacts recovered from archaeological features may not directly reflect the activities that took place in or near those features. A whole series of factors structure the rate at which certain items are broken and replaced, where they are discarded, and how long they preserve after being discarded.

Much of what has been recovered from archaeological excavations at Moundville is refuse. Discard assemblages recovered from refuse contexts differ considerably from artifact assemblages recovered from primary-use contexts (DeBoer 1983). Different artifacts and buildings have variable use lives based on their function, frequency of use, and the materials from which they are constructed. Mississippian vessel assemblages provide a good example of this phenomenon. Cooking jars that are repeatedly exposed to the thermal stress of cooking fires have very short use lives compared with large storage jars that are moved infrequently and kept away from fires (David 1972; Foster 1960). Although there may have been an equal number of cooking and storage jars in use at any one time in any Mississippian household, the higher breakage and replacement rates for cooking jars would have generated discard assemblages in which cooking jars are disproportionately represented relative to storage jars. As noted in Chapter 5 this appears to be the case with early Mississippian ceramic materials in the Moundville study assemblage, the majority of which were recovered from the excavation of midden deposits.

Theoretical Summary

This study is informed by a long tradition of research in which scholars have examined the origins of social inequality. I benefit directly from ongoing and previous research on chiefly politics and regional developments of political complexity. We have much to learn from a cross-cultural approach to chiefdom political economy. That being said, I have embraced a healthy skepticism concerning an overreliance on organizational categories and societal models. In recent years a number of Southeastern archaeologists have charged that the use of ethnographic models from other times and places has obscured archaeological understandings of Mississippian political and economic organization (Blitz 1993b:21, 1999:579; Muller 1997). While it is important to look broadly at chiefly strategies of control, we should not lose sight of the historical particularities of regional political complexity.

On the basis of this perspective I have adopted a bottom-up approach to examining chiefdom political organization. Households and other small-scale social groups serve as the starting place for this endeavor. By examining the organization of and relationships among small-scale social groups, I hope to arrive at an understanding of broader social phenomena that is less structured by top-down assumptions about what chiefdoms are and how they function. At the same time I understand that no anthropological investigation can be truly objective. My interpretations are necessarily, and I hope positively, influenced by the research of others. With this in mind I have attempted to follow the lead of an increasing number of Southeastern archaeologists who have consulted ethnohistoric information on indigenous social organization from the protohistoric and historic southeastern United States (Blitz 1993b, 1999; Knight 1986, 1998; Muller 1997).

Examining the emergence and maintenance of political complexity through the everyday practices of small groups is a complex endeavor. My investigation of this issue is divided into five chapters. Chapter 2 is devoted to providing an ethnohistorical and archaeological background on Southeastern household and community organization. I begin by summarizing ethnohistorical information on Southeastern kinship systems as it relates to Mississippian social organization. I also consider archaeological case studies of Mississippian residential groups in order to identify general trends in the spatial layout and organization of Mississippian households. This is followed by a review of previous archaeological investigations about Moundville community organization and Mississippian occupation in the Black Warrior Valley of west-central Alabama.

The data for this study are presented in Chapters 3, 4, and 5. I begin in Chapter 3 by providing background on the excavations that generated the archaeological data analyzed in this study. Chapter 3 also includes a ceramic and architectural seriation that chronologically situates the different residential groups that are the focus of my analyses. In Chapter 4 these different residential groups are defined and discussed. A number of architectural analyses provide the data that inform my investigation of Moundville's community formation, occupation span, and household wealth and status. An analysis and discussion of domestic pottery assemblages in Chapter 5 helps broaden my investigation of Mississippian household organization at Moundville by providing information on domestic foodways. Finally, in Chapter 6 I summarize the results of my analyses and discuss the role that small-group interactions played in the emergence of the Moundville polity.

2 Mississippian Communities and Households

Mississippian peoples throughout the southeastern United States drew from a common suite of architectural elements to build and organize their communities. Mounds, plazas, courtyards, palisades, and cemeteries were basic components of a Mississippian architectural grammar that defined major settlements throughout the greater Southeast and Midwest (Lewis and Stout 1998). There was also considerable variation among Mississippian communities in regard to scale and composition. On one end of the organizational spectrum there were densely populated, multimound civic-ceremonial centers. On the other end of the spectrum there were small, dispersed villages.

Examples of the largest Mississippian communities include sites like Etowah, Cahokia, and Moundville. Each of these sites consists of multiple, contemporaneously used platform mounds and residential areas arranged about one or more plazas (King 2003; Knight and Steponaitis 1998; Fowler 1989). These sites were also fortified by the construction of palisade walls and/or moats at some point in each of their occupational histories. While larger and more complex than many other communities in the Southeast, these three mound centers also differed considerably from one another (Wilson et al. 2006). In the case of Cahokia, multiple plazas are present, each of which is surrounded by numerous mounds and residential areas. Both Etowah and Moundville, on the other hand, consisted of fewer mounds and one main plaza. At its peak Cahokia also had a population several magnitudes larger than either Etowah or Moundville (Pauketat and Lopinot 1997; Steponaitis 1998). The vast majority of Mississippian communities had significantly smaller populations and fewer mounds (Payne 1994). Sites like Town Creek Indian Mound in North Carolina and Cardin Farm II in Tennessee consisted of only about a dozen houses arranged around a central plaza (Coe 1995; Schroedl 1998).

The differences between Mississippian communities were not all scalar in nature. Individual communities were uniquely shaped by their developmental histories. Just as there were organizational differences between communities, individual communities also changed dramatically over time. For instance, a nucleated village organizational pattern characterized many Mississippian communities only for a restricted portion of their occupational history and for some communities never at all (Knight and Steponaitis 1998; Pauketat and Lopinot 1997; Rogers 1995). Patterns of nucleation tend to correspond well with periods of political consolidation or warfare (Knight and Steponaitis 1998; Morse 1990; Pauketat 1994; Stanish 1999). In periods of regional consolidation, a nucleated population provides an emerging elite with a centralized source of labor. In times of war it is necessary to relocate large portions of the regional populace behind palisade walls. In other times and situations, however, a more dispersed pattern of settlement with vacant ceremonial centers appears to have been more commonplace (Rogers 1995; Steponaitis 1998).

This chapter provides archaeological and ethnohistoric background on the organization of Mississippian communities and households. I begin by discussing historic Southeastern kinship systems to identify the different corporate groups that made up native towns and villages. I argue that a better understanding of these historically documented kin groups can inform archaeological research on Mississippian household and community organization. Next, I consider archaeological research on Mississippian household organization. I present case studies from eastern Tennessee and southwestern Illinois to illustrate similarities and differences in the organization of Mississippian households and multihousehold groups. In the final portion of this chapter I provide an overview of Mississippian culture history in the Black Warrior Valley of west-central Alabama and summarize previous models of Moundville community organization.

Kin Groups and Community Composition

The entities that archaeologists identify as Mississippian towns, villages, and communities were composed of numerous, smaller social and residential groups. A community's developmental history is a chronicle of the interactions among these groups. Thus, a better understanding of Mississippian community organization requires an examination of the network of interactions among households. Another reason to study small-scale Mississippian social groups is that household organizational schemes were employed on the community level. Muller (1997:185) argues that the Mississippian "public square replicated the household on a grander and promoted scale. Indeed, so did the location of mounds around plazas." Likewise, Sullivan (1987:27–28) has argued that late Mississippian Mouse Creek phase (A.D. 1400–1600) townhouse-and-plaza community arrangements in eastern Tennessee mimicked the pairing of household winter and summer structures. From this perspective Mississippian villages and civic-ceremonial centers were founded upon the organizational principles of the household rather than the other way around.

Great strides have been made in understanding Mississippian chiefdom organization by relating archaeological data to ethnohistoric information on Southeastern kinship organization. This approach has been directed primarily at the study of regional settlement patterns and broad-scale community organizational characteristics such as mound-and-plaza arrangements (Blitz 1993b, 1999; Knight 1990,

1998; Rodning 2005). However, I believe there is also utility in considering households and other small-scale residential groups from this perspective. It is not always possible to directly equate historically documented kin groups with the residential groups we identify archaeologically. Nevertheless, an understanding of the basic mechanics of historic Southeastern kinship can provide a heuristic framework for investigating Mississippian domestic organization.

Knight (1986, 1990, 1998) has been a prominent contributor to this ethnohistorically informed research, offering a coherent model of Southeastern kinship and social organization based on the works of Swanton (1922, 1928, 1931), Speck (1907), and other early scholars. In his synthesis Knight (1990) discusses three primary social categories—a society-wide dual division, clans, and subclan groups or lineages. I will briefly discuss each of these social groups.

Clans were exogamous kin units in the early historic Southeast. Property and land were not owned or controlled by the clan. Moreover, clans were not territorial groups, as members often lived in numerous villages and rarely assembled as a unified group (Knight 1990). Individual clans within any society would have belonged to one of two social divisions (Swanton 1922, 1928). In some cases these divisions were exogamous and functioned as moieties. Each of the two divisions was assigned different and often opposing social and ceremonial responsibilities. Historically such divisions were referred to as red towns and white towns (Hudson 1976). One town or division sometimes administered issues of warfare and the other issues of peace. Knight (1990:6) has argued that an ingrained notion of hierarchy was fundamental to the relationship between these dual social groups as well as between the clans that comprised them (see also Speck 1907). In some cases this hierarchy was merely ceremonial but in other cases resulted in a formal ranking of social groups.

Subclan units differed from clans in that they were often coresidential domestic groups, tied to an estate, which produced and consumed in common (Knight 1990). Swanton (1922) refers to these subclan units as local groups or house groups, and there appears to have been some intrasocietal diversity in their size and organization. Some of the most detailed descriptions of local groups are provided by Swanton (1922) and Speck (1907) for the Chickasaw. Chickasaw house groups bore names such as "high corn crib," "little corn crib," "having a red house," "double hill," "a little round hillock," "broken post oak," "behind a tree," "a lot of weeds in the crop," and "a grown over field" (Swanton 1922). Thus, Chickasaw subclan group names generally correspond with localized geographic features or the character of a particular group's houses, outbuildings, or fields. This naming convention is important, as it highlights the corporate and localized organization of house groups. This contrasts with the naming convention for Chickasaw *clans,* which included totemic designations such as Bear, Fish, and Wildcat (Swanton 1922).

These descriptions of Chickasaw house groups bear some resemblance to local groups among the Creek known as *huti* (Knight 1990). Both Chickasaw house groups and Creek *huti* had hereditary names and titles, with a house chief appointed by a council of elders. In terms of size and composition, Swanton (1928:79) describes a typical Creek local group as consisting of "a man and woman, their children, one or more sons in law, some grandchildren, some aged or dependent individuals of the same clan group, and perhaps an orphan or two or one or more individuals taken in war." In reference to the spatial layout of Creek local groups Swan (1855:262) notes that "[t]hese houses stand in clusters of four, five, six, seven, and eight together." Although vague, these descriptions indicate that Creek domestic groups may have consisted of 10 to 20 people occupying four to eight buildings. It is unclear how closely local groups among other Southeastern peoples corresponded to the Chickasaw or Creek pattern. Timucuan clans were also subdivided by a number of hereditary local groups, but the specific nature of their corporate organization is less understood (Knight 1990). Indeed, the specific size and corporate organization of local groups among different Southeastern social entities probably varied on the basis of political, economic, and historical factors. This review of the ethnohistorical record provides an important basis by which to consider archaeologically documented domestic groups in the Mississippian Southeast.

Mississippian Household Archaeology

After a century of Southeastern archaeology scholars are still addressing the nuts and bolts of Mississippian domestic organization. In part this situation is a result of the importance assigned to the excavation of mounds and burials. Domestic artifact assemblages are less ornate than burial assemblages and nonelite houses are less elaborate than mound-summit architecture. However, with increasing interest in small-scale social dynamics and the practices of everyday life, Southeastern archaeologists have taken new interest in examining Mississippian households and the organization of domestic space (Emerson 1997b; Hally and Kelly 1998; Mehrer 1995; Rogers 1995; Scarry and McEwan 1995).

Houses are but one portion of a constellation of archaeological features often associated with households. Winter (1976) used the term *household cluster* to refer to the set of archaeological features associated with individual households in Formative period Oaxaca. As a general trend, Winter found that Oaxacan household clusters consisted of houses, storage pits, earth ovens, midden deposits, and burials. Household clusters within a single community were typically separated from one another by 20 to 40 m of empty space. Archaeologists have identified similar clusters of archaeological features within Mississippian communities throughout the southeastern United States. These feature clusters typically consist of some combination and arrangement of houses, storage facilities, midden deposits, burials, and work space. To be sure, not every Mississippian household cluster was identical in terms of its composition and spatial layout or in its relationship with the broader community. The archaeological signatures of Mississippian households varied on the basis of social status, stage in the domestic cycle, population density, the local environmental context, and regional political dynamics (Rogers 1995).

Here I summarize Mississippian household organizational patterns from eastern Tennessee and the American Bottom region of southwestern Illinois. Examples from both regions are discussed in terms of the spatial arrangement of buildings, storage facilities, activity areas, and methods of refuse disposal. The primary goal of this exercise is to identify trends in the spatial layout and organization of Mississippian households.

Eastern Tennessee

Archaeological research in eastern Tennessee has provided important insight into Mississippian community and household organization (Lewis and Kneberg 1946; Polhemus 1987; Schroedl 1986, 1998; Sullivan 1987, 1995). The late Mississippian and Historic period occupation in this region can be divided into the Dallas phase (A.D. 1300–1600), Mouse Creek phase (A.D. 1400–1600), and Overhill Cherokee phase (post–A.D. 1600). Differences in community organization, mortuary patterns, and mound construction indicate that these three archaeological complexes differed in terms of political complexity (Schroedl 1998:91; Sullivan 1995:120). Sullivan (1995) has argued that ascribed status differences were more rigorously defined in the Dallas phase than in the Mouse Creek phase. Overhill Cherokee communities, on the other hand, appear to have been relatively egalitarian compared with earlier Dallas phase and Mouse Creek phase communities. There is no evidence of Overhill Cherokee platform mound construction, and the arrangement of mortuary complexes and public buildings suggests that achievement and not ascription was the primary avenue to social status (Sullivan 1995:120).

Despite these differences in social organization there was considerable continuity among these eastern Tennessee groups in terms of household organization. As a general trend, household clusters from all three eastern Tennessee phases consist of a winter house, a summer house, some kind of cleared activity space, and storage facilities (Sullivan 1995). Polhemus (1987:1240) also identified small-scale Dallas phase multihousehold groups that consist of two or more household clusters situated around a central yard or open space. Similar household aggregates appear to have been missing from Mouse Creek and Overhill Cherokee phase communities (Schroedl 1998). Other organizational differences among Dallas, Mouse Creek, and Overhill Cherokee household clusters relate to house size, storage, and refuse disposal.

Sullivan (1995:114–115) has identified a larger range of house sizes in both Dallas phase (27–86 m^2) and Mouse Creek phase (28–89 m^2) sites than in Overhill Cherokee sites (29–42 m^2). She interprets this pattern as evidence of more pronounced status distinctions in Dallas and Mouse Creek phase communities than in Overhill Cherokee phase communities (Sullivan 1995; see also Polhemus 1987). There are also phase-specific community differences in the location and sizes of public buildings. The Dallas phase occupation at the Toqua site included two categories of public buildings, located on and adjacent to mounds (Sullivan 1995:116). Both Mouse Creek and Overhill Cherokee sites lacked mounds and included fewer public structures (Sullivan 1995:117).

Other more basic differences existed among Dallas, Mouse Creek, and Overhill Cherokee households. Deep storage pits are rare in both Dallas and Mouse Creek phase communities. Instead, surplus foodstuffs were primarily stored in aboveground structures (Schroedl 1998:82). There was a shift toward the use of belowground storage in the Overhill Cherokee period (Polhemus 1987). Why this shift took place is unclear. However, the increasing importance of sweet potato cultivation may have figured prominently in these changes (Brett Riggs, personal communication 2003). For preservation purposes maize is best stored above ground. Sweet potatoes, on the other hand, require cool and damp conditions to keep them from sprouting or dehydrating (Riggs 1999). These changes in storage were accompanied by changes in domestic refuse disposal. Extensive sheet middens identified at the Toqua site reveal that Dallas phase villagers primarily deposited refuse in trash dumps or toft areas. Overhill Cherokee households, on the other hand, took advantage of abandoned pit features for refuse disposal (Polhemus 1987).

American Bottom

Considerable household organizational variation has been documented in the early Mississippian (A.D. 1050–1200) American Bottom. At least three different modes of early Mississippian domestic organization have been identified in the region. These three organizational patterns correspond with mound centers, upland villages, and rural farmsteads. Household clusters associated with rural farmsteads typically consist of one to three structures, several storage pits, and cleared activity areas (Finney 1985; Jackson 1980; Mehrer 1995; Milner 1983). Abandoned storage pits and house basins were used as receptacles for domestic refuse disposal. There are, however, small rural sites that include ceremonial architecture, mortuary complexes, larger-than-average storage pits, and an overrepresentation of serving-ware pottery containers (Emerson 1997b). While some of these sites may simply represent older and more affluent households, others appear to have served to integrate politically and ceremonially a dispersed community of rural farmsteads (Emerson 1997a, 1997b).

Pauketat's (1994, 1998) analysis of the Tract 15A and Dunham tract excavations at the Cahokia site revealed an early Mississippian community consisting of a number of multihousehold groups arranged around a rectangular plaza. Early

Mississippian architecture in this portion of the Cahokia site included a variety of building sizes, styles, and functions. A wide assortment of domestic activities probably took place in the plaza and in cleared activity spaces between buildings. Surplus foodstuffs were primarily stored in subterranean pit features but may have also been placed inside small buildings (Pauketat 1998; see also Mehrer and Collins 1995). Once abandoned, these features were used for refuse disposal.

A more or less continuous distribution of houses, ceremonial structures, and pit features within these multihousehold group residential areas has hindered attempts to identify individual household clusters (Pauketat 1998). However, there are organizational differences between multihousehold groups that point to differences in social status. Pauketat (1994, 1998) has identified a bimodal distribution of early Mississippian structure sizes in this portion of the Cahokia site. Moreover, there also exists in this area a class of ceremonial circular buildings known as sweatlodges. Multihousehold groups on the northern end of the plaza include many examples of the larger-size class of houses. These large houses, however, are scarce in or absent from multihousehold groups on the southern edge of the plaza (Pauketat 1994, 1998). This pattern also correlates with the distribution of circular sweatlodges: multihousehold groups on the northern end of the plaza include a number of these ceremonial buildings while those to the south have relatively few (Pauketat 1994, 1998).

The uneven distribution of larger houses at the Cahokia site indicates that some multihousehold groups included larger and higher-status households than others (Netting 1982; Pauketat 1994). It is also significant that some multihousehold groups included sweatlodges and others did not. Those groups who more directly participated in sweatlodge ceremonialism probably enjoyed elevated positions of status in the greater Cahokian community.

The final domestic organizational mode corresponds with a number of early Mississippian upland villages immediately east of the American Bottom. These communities consist of clusters of domestic structures and storage pits arranged around central courtyards (Alt 2001; Bareis 1976; Pauketat 2003; Wilson 1998). As with the Tract 15A case it is difficult to isolate individual household clusters, suggesting that the courtyard group itself represents the basal social and residential unit at these upland sites. The central portions of courtyards were primarily devoid of features and were probably used for communal work and ritual (Wilson 1998). Midden deposits located between and behind houses suggest that these central spaces were regularly swept clean of refuse. Refuse was also deposited in abandoned house basins and pit features.

Regional Comparison

There are broad similarities between the American Bottom and eastern Tennessee cases in terms of household composition. Household clusters in both regions consisted of some combination of buildings, storage facilities, and cleared activity spaces. One important difference relates to architectural style. Early Mississippian household clusters from the American Bottom lacked clear evidence of the seasonal (summer/winter) houses identified in the eastern Tennessee case studies. As will be discussed in Chapter 4, this difference relates to technological changes in domestic architecture that occurred in the late Mississippian period Southeast. The nature of domestic refuse disposal also varied on the basis of the kind of storage technology used. In the American Bottom and Overhill Cherokee cases, household members took advantage of abandoned storage pits for refuse disposal. Above-ground midden deposits were minimized as a result. In the Dallas and Mouse Creek phase communities surplus goods were primarily stored above ground and refuse was dumped in toft areas that later formed extensive sheet middens. This difference affects the formation of domestic artifact assemblages. In the American Bottom and Overhill Cherokee cases individual pit deposits form relatively discrete discard assemblages while in the Dallas and Mouse Creek cases (and in the Moundville case examined in this work) archaeological analyses must sample from sheet midden deposits.

These case studies have also revealed the presence of domestic coresidential groups organized on a scale intermediate between the household and the community. The members of these small-scale coresidential groups often shared cleared work space and in some cases appear to have pooled agricultural surpluses (Kelly 1990; Polhemus 1987). The courtyard groups and other clusters of domestic structures have been interpreted as representing corporate kin groups (Kelly 1990; Pauketat 2003; Polhemus 1987). The smaller examples of these coresidential groups may simply represent extended families. Larger multihousehold groups, however, may represent kin groups such as the historically documented subclan groups discussed earlier.

Finally, this comparison has provided several potential archaeological correlates of interhousehold status variation. Mississippian communities characterized by ascribed status distinctions appear to have included a wider range of house sizes than less hierarchically organized communities (Pauketat 1994, 1998; Sullivan 1995). Intercommunity status distinctions also appear to be represented in the location and size of public buildings and other ceremonial facilities. The American Bottom case revealed that ceremonial buildings were part of some household clusters and not others. Moreover, the Dallas phase Toqua site case displayed a variety of public building sizes and locations that were not present at less hierarchical Mouse Creek and Overhill Cherokee communities.

Moundville Culture History and Community Organization

Now that I have provided a general background on the organization of Mississippian and Historic period Southeastern households and communities, I turn my attention to the Mississippian occupation of the Black Warrior Valley. In the remaining portion of this chapter I provide an overview of the terminal late Woodland and Mississippian occupation of the region and summarize previous investigations of Moundville community organization. In the final portion of the chapter I summarize recent Moundville archaeological investigations and define important research questions that will be examined in Chapters 4 and 5.

The Moundville site is located in west-central Alabama on a high, flat terrace where the Black Warrior River cuts close to the Fall-Line Hills (Knight and Steponaitis 1998; Peebles 1978). The Moundville site and other affiliated settlements are located within a portion of the Black Warrior River valley starting below the fall line just south of Tuscaloosa, Alabama, and extending 40 km downriver (Figure 2.1; Peebles 1978; Welch 1991b:25). Below the fall line, the valley widens and the uplands consist of rolling hills dissected by intermittent streams (Scarry 1986:92). This region corresponds with the transition between the Piedmont and Coastal Plains and encompasses considerable physiographic and ecological diversity (Peebles 1978; Scarry 1986:67). Environmentally this portion of the Black Warrior Valley was an ecotone that had floral and faunal characteristics of temperate oak-hickory, maritime magnolia, and pine forests (Peebles 1978).

Today the Moundville site consists of 29 mounds arranged around a rectangular plaza (Knight and Steponaitis 1998:3). Figure 2.2 displays the estimated location of the palisade wall that surrounded the site. In all, the Moundville site was about 75 ha in size (Knight and Steponaitis 1998:3). The primary areas of residential occupation are located between the plaza and the palisade wall. Much of the central plaza appears to have been unoccupied. However, a number of small residential areas have been identified along the outside edges of the plaza as well as outside the limits of the palisade (Chapter 4).

West Jefferson Phase

Moundville emerged from a terminal late Woodland period occupation known as the West Jefferson phase. The West Jefferson settlement system consisted of small villages ranging from .2 to .5 ha in size scattered up and down the floodplain terraces and adjacent uplands of the Black Warrior River valley (Bozeman 1982; Welch 1990:211). Welch (1981) has outlined a shifting seasonal settlement model for the West Jefferson phase based in part on the location of many floodplain sites at elevations below the five-year flood line. When flooding occurred during the late winter to early spring these floodplain communities would have had to be abandoned (Welch 1981, 1990). In this model upland sites would have been occupied in the cold season with floodplain sites being occupied in the warm season. This model is also supported by seasonality data from faunal and botanical materials recovered from upland and floodplain sites (Welch 1990).

In terms of subsistence, early West Jefferson communities had a wide resource base composed primarily of wild gathered plants and animals (Scarry 1993a,

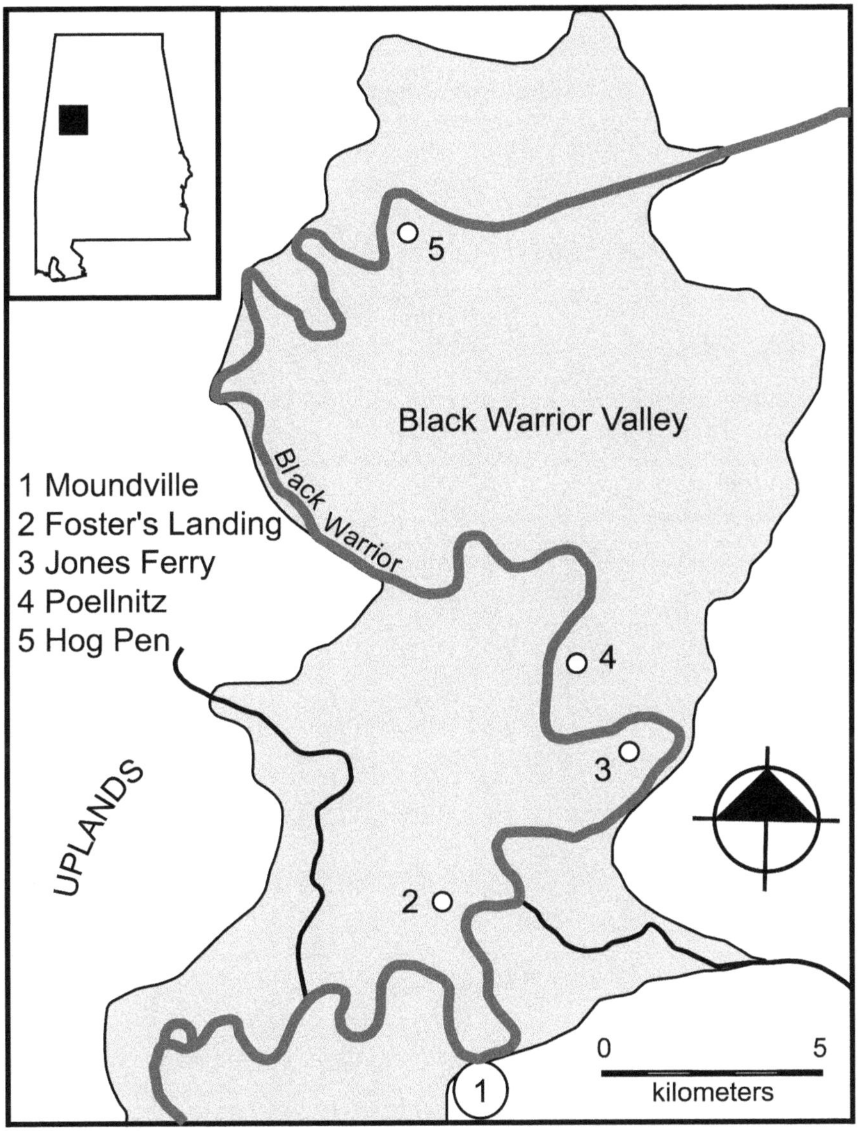

Figure 2.1. Early Mississippian mound centers in the northern Black Warrior Valley.

1993b). Maize production intensified in the later portion of the West Jefferson phase, though regional inhabitants still relied upon a variety of wild plants and animals (Scarry 1993a). Similar landforms and loam series soil types appear to have been repeatedly targeted by West Jefferson phase peoples as indicated by the identification of multiple, overlapping sites, particularly on floodplain terraces (Hammerstedt 2000; Hammerstedt and Myer 2001).

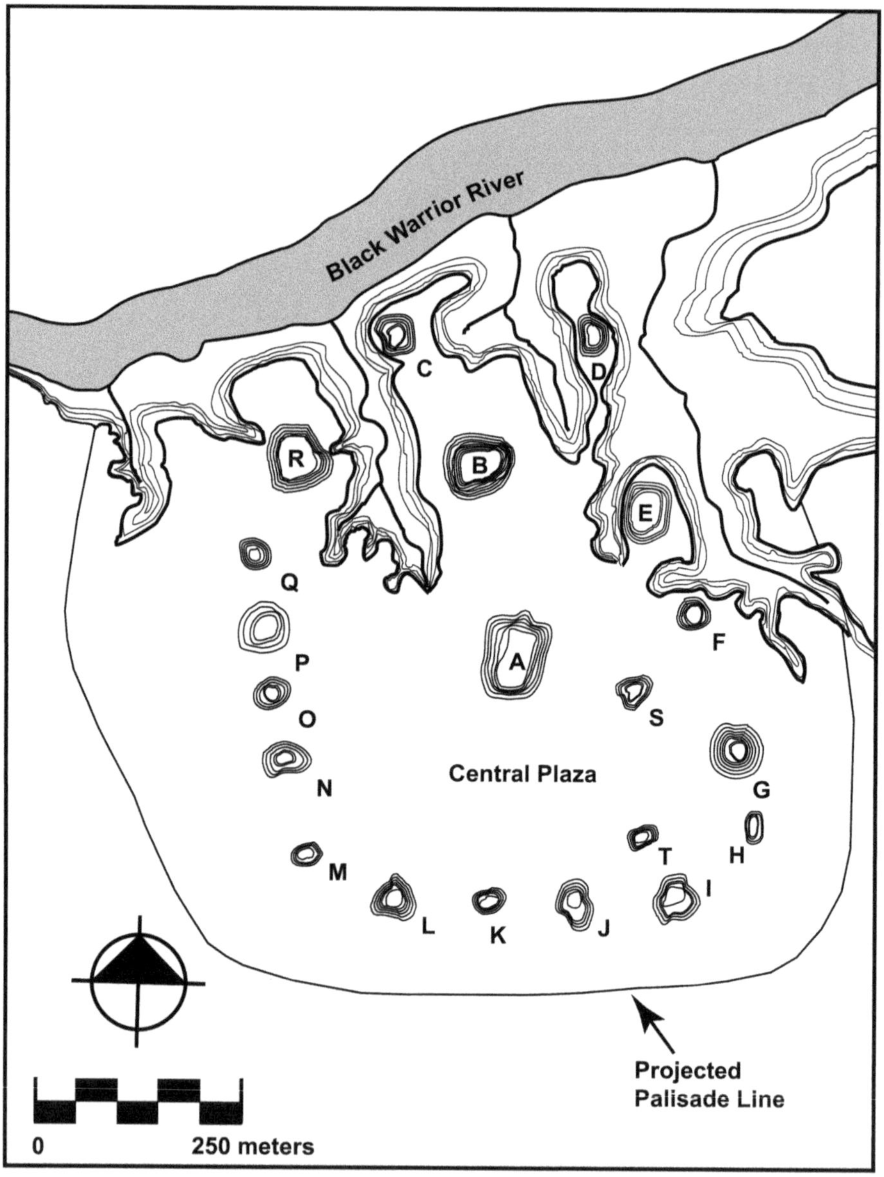

Figure 2.2. The Moundville site, showing the mounds, central plaza, and palisade wall.

Very little is known about West Jefferson phase community and household organization. Only one West Jefferson phase house has thus far been excavated. The house was a single-post structure with a central hearth. The excavation of several West Jefferson phase bell-shaped pits indicates that surplus foodstuffs were stored below ground. On the basis of surface surveys and limited excavations there is little evidence to suggest the presence of social ranking in the West Jefferson phase Black Warrior Valley (Welch 1990). With the exception of greenstone and small amounts of Fort Payne chert, regional inhabitants relied primarily on local lithic materials. Tuscaloosa chert is abundant in the gravel bars of the Black Warrior Valley (Pope 1989; Welch 1990). Collected primarily in the form of small river-worn pebbles, Tuscaloosa chert was commonly heat treated prior to being knapped into projectile points and a wide variety of expedient flake tools. Also present in West Jefferson phase lithic assemblages are specialized tools known as microdrills. Pope's (1989) use-wear analysis of microdrills revealed they were used primarily for the manufacture of shell beads. Marine-shell beads have been interpreted as wealth items, the production of which may have been related to increasing competition between tribal leaders in the region (Pope 1989; Steponaitis 1986). In addition to the intensification of maize production, the introduction of this shell-bead industry points to important political-economic changes that foreshadowed the development of the Moundville chiefdom.

Early Moundville I

The early Moundville I phase marks the emergence of Mississippian culture in the Black Warrior Valley. At around A.D. 1200 a suite of highly visible and sudden changes in settlement patterns, community organization, and material culture took place. Village life in the region was abandoned for a settlement system consisting primarily of dispersed farmsteads and small administrative centers with earthen platform mounds (Ensor 1993; Knight and Steponaitis 1998; Michals 1998; Mistovich 1988). Several politically autonomous simple chiefdoms may have existed in the region at this time. However, the only two platform mounds in the region were built at the site of Moundville (Steponaitis 1992). Thus, in the era immediately preceding regional consolidation Moundville appears to have been a locus of unequaled political importance. On the basis of available survey data it would also appear that there was a higher density of early Moundville I households along the Moundville riverbank than elsewhere in the region (Knight and Steponaitis 1998).

Limited research has taken place at the two early Moundville I phase mounds. In 1975 the University of Alabama Field School conducted excavations at the Asphalt Plant mound (1TU50) located immediately northeast of the Moundville site. The materials recovered from these excavations were later analyzed by Steponaitis (1992). The results of this research revealed a small mound center with an artifact assemblage composed of an unusually high percentage of nonlocal materials. Steponaitis (1992) concludes from his analysis that the abundance of exotic materials in what was presumably an elite context reveals the importance of craft production and long-distance exchange in the early development of the Moundville polity.

Considerably less is known about the mysterious Mound X located just east of Mound G on the southeastern corner of the Moundville site. Limited excavations conducted in 1984 revealed that the mound was partially truncated during the late Moundville I phase by the construction of several palisade lines (Vogel and Allan 1985). This early mound was essentially abandoned and destroyed during the construction of the regional political center of Moundville in the late Moundville I phase.

Our current understanding of early Moundville I household organization comes from a handful of small-scale excavations. C. Margaret Scarry's (1995, 1998) analysis of the maps and artifact assemblages generated from the excavation of two areas along the northwest riverbank at the Moundville site has yielded the most coherent picture of Moundville I domestic life.[1] The excavation of these two areas, dubbed the Picnic Area (PA) tract and the East Conference Building (ECB) tract, uncovered eight buildings, four of which date to the early Moundville I phase. Three different architectural styles are represented among the early Moundville I buildings from these Riverbank excavations (Scarry 1995, 1998). One style is characterized by a rectangular building with four wall-trench foundations. Also present are rectangular houses constructed with walls built from single-set posts. The final house style is represented by one house that displayed a combination of both wall-trench and single-post construction techniques. The walls of this building were also set in a shallow, rectangular basin. Aside from central hearths these early Moundville I buildings typically lack interior features such as benches, support posts, and partitions.[2]

Stylistically similar early Moundville I phase buildings have been identified elsewhere at the Moundville site and in the surrounding countryside (Scarry 1986; Steponaitis 1992). One early Moundville I building excavated north of Mound R is particularly worthy of mention (Scarry 1986). In addition to having its foundation set in a shallow basin this building also had on its floor a raised clay platform immediately adjacent to a wall. The building was not fully excavated so the shape and size of this interior feature are unclear. It is noteworthy that the basin house from the Moundville Riverbank also had a raised platform composed of yellow sand adjacent to one of its walls.[3] Similar features have been identified on the floors of several domestic buildings at the Bessemer site (DeJarnette and Wimberly 1941). These small, mound-like features have been interpreted as benches or platforms for social activity (Blitz 1993b:79). How frequently these features occur inside early Moundville I houses is uncertain. However, they appear to be absent from later Mississippian structures in the Black Warrior Valley.

Overall, there appears to have been considerable architectural variation and experimentation in this era (Lacquement 2004). Notably missing from early Moundville I domestic contexts are the bell-shaped storage pits commonly associated with West Jefferson phase residential areas. The absence of subterranean storage facilities has been interpreted as indirect evidence that surplus foodstuffs were stored in above-ground facilities such as granaries (Scarry 1995, 1998).

Local Tuscaloosa gravel still makes up a large part of the early Moundville I flaked stone assemblages (Scarry 1995). Notably present, however, are Mill Creek chert hoes from southern Illinois (Steponaitis 1992). The appearance of these agricultural implements corresponds with the intensification of maize agriculture in the region (Scarry 1998). Also present are both Fort Payne and Bangor cherts from northern Alabama, used primarily for the manufacture of expedient flake tools (Scarry 1995; Steponaitis 1992). As noted earlier the presence of these nonlocal materials reveals an expansion of regional trade networks negotiated in part by aspiring Mississippian leaders attempting to consolidate political control over the region (Steponaitis 1992).

Pottery assemblages from early Moundville I contexts contrast sharply with preceding West Jefferson assemblages. Shell-tempered wares predominate in these early Mississippian assemblages (Scarry 1995, 1998). However, the presence of small amounts of grog-tempered sherds in early Moundville I assemblages reveals that potters continued to manufacture minor amounts of grog-tempered pottery. Elsewhere in the nearby uplands these late Woodland pottery traditions were apparently retained for a century or more (Jackson 2004; see also Seckinger and Jenkins 1980).

A number of new vessel shapes were introduced during the early Moundville I phase (Steponaitis 1983). Many of these vessels were serving wares, embellished with a variety of slips and incised design fields that were not present in earlier West Jefferson phase assemblages. The lack of a clear stylistic transition from West Jefferson to early Moundville I phase pottery assemblages has fueled arguments for an intrusive origin for Mississippian culture in the Black Warrior Valley (Jenkins 2003; Seckinger and Jenkins 1980). Intrusive origin explanations were all but rejected over the past two decades. However, new evidence of intrusive Mississippian settlements in the nearby Chattahoochee River valley (Blitz and Lorenz 2002) has reasserted the possibility that Mississippian settlement in the Black Warrior Valley somehow involved nonlocal populations. Most scholars still argue for a local developmental scenario for the Moundville chiefdom (Knight and Steponaitis 1998). Currently there is not enough evidence from this transitional period to disprove either scenario.

Late Moundville I–Early Moundville II

The late Moundville I phase marks the establishment of the Moundville chiefdom as a regionally consolidated Mississippian polity (Knight and Steponaitis 1998). The dynamics of regional consolidation transformed socioeconomic relationships throughout the Black Warrior Valley. A regional administrative center was established at the Moundville site, where many polity members settled to form a nucleated community (Steponaitis 1998). Diachronic settlement studies have revealed that the Mississippian emergence in the Black Warrior Valley was marked by a sharp decrease in the population of the rural countryside (Maxham 2004:126). This rural population decrease corresponds with the influx of people at the Moundville site (Maxham 2004; Steponaitis 1998). Preexisting mound sites were abandoned, and at least four second-order mound centers were established (Knight and Steponaitis 1998). Tribute relationships developed that required the planting, harvesting, and processing of maize at lower-order settlements and its transport to higher-order settlements (Scarry and Steponaitis 1997; Welch and Scarry 1995).

The residents of this greatly expanded Moundville community participated in a variety of large-scale labor projects. A palisade was erected around the perimeter of the site. This fortification was rebuilt a minimum of six times before being dismantled around A.D. 1300 (Knight and Steponaitis 1998; Scarry 1998; Vogel and Allan 1985). The Moundville ceremonial precinct was also constructed during the late Moundville I phase. This endeavor involved the construction of at least 29 mounds arranged around a rectangular plaza (Knight 1992, 1998). Portions of the plaza were also artificially filled to create a level surface (Knight 1998).

Late Moundville II–Early Moundville III

Starting in the late Moundville II phase dramatic organizational changes took place at Moundville and throughout the Black Warrior Valley. What was once a nucleated and fortified town became a vacant ceremonial center occupied by a small number of Moundville's elite (Knight and Steponaitis 1998:17–21). This outmigration corresponds with increasing population densities in the rural countryside of the Black Warrior Valley (Maxham 2004:129). Somewhat paradoxically this is the era in which there is the strongest evidence of an administrative elite group in the region, represented in the emergence of chiefly cult symbolism and high-status burials at Moundville with elaborate mortuary regalia (Knight and Steponaitis 1998:17–21). It seems the symbolic distancing of the Moundville elite from the nonelite corresponded with the physical distancing of these groups in the region.

At this time Moundville became a necropolis where regional inhabitants buried their dead in numerous cemeteries throughout the site (Knight and Steponaitis 1998; Steponaitis 1998). Although the Moundville site continued to be used for many ceremonial activities, it ceased being a residential locus for much of the regional populace. The palisade surrounding the site also fell out of use (Scarry 1998). On the household level a new hipped-roof architectural technology was adopted, replacing the traditional flexed-pole style of buildings. Analysis of lithic assemblages from mound contexts indicates a decline in long-distance exchange and certain crafting activities from the Moundville II to the Moundville III phase (Knight 2002:148–150). Relatively little is known about nonelite domestic contexts in this era of Moundville's culture history.

Late Moundville III–Moundville IV

The late Moundville III–Moundville IV era in Moundville's culture history is characterized by regional trends of political collapse and reorganization (Knight and Steponaitis 1998). Only three mounds at Moundville show evidence of occupation and construction at this time. All three earthworks, Mounds P, B, and E, are located in the northern portion of the site (Knight and Steponaitis 1998). The only area of off-mound occupation that has been dated to this period is located in an area to the southwest of Mound G.

Outlying mound sites show considerable evidence of continued residential occupation, mound construction, and mortuary ceremonialism (DeJarnette and Peebles 1970; Knight and Steponaitis 1998; Rees 2001; Welch 1991b). Moreover, Steponaitis (1983) reports that mortuary mounds at Moundville were no longer used for the interment of elite burials (Knight and Steponaitis 1998:21). Collectively, these organizational changes indicate an increasing political autonomy of outlying centers with a diminished importance of Moundville as a regional political and ceremonial center (Knight and Steponaitis 1998).

Previous Perspectives on Moundville Community Organization

Christopher Peebles's (1974, 1978, 1981, 1983, 1987a) model of Moundville as a ranked society is one of the best-known archaeological case studies of Mississippian political organization (Peebles and Kus 1977). In this model the Moundville polity consisted of elite and nonelite classes; membership in each was genealogically based. Peebles also argued that the organization of the Moundville polity was highly differentiated politically, socially, and economically.

Support for this model derived from Peebles's (1974) mortuary analysis of over two thousand burials at Moundville, through which he divided the Moundville burial population into superordinate (elite) and subordinate (nonelite) classes. The superordinate class comprised approximately 5 percent of the population and was defined on the basis of burial location in or near mounds and the presence of distinctive artifacts and human retainers (Peebles and Kus 1977). The rest of the burial population was interred with artifacts "associated with particular ages and one or the other of the sexes" (Peebles 1987a:29). The social standing of these subordinate-class burials was further delineated by their placement in non-mound portions of the Moundville community.

As further evidence of social ranking Peebles (1971) pointed to a highly structured use of space at the Moundville site. Moundville's ceremonial precinct consists of at least 29 mounds arranged in functional pairs around a rectangular plaza. Each pair consists of a smaller elite mortuary mound and a larger elite residential mound. Peebles (1971:82) observed a bilateral symmetry to this spatial arrangement such that the eastern and western portions of the Moundville site mirror one another (see also Knight 1998). Peebles argued that aspects of this bilateral symmetry were also represented in the distribution of effigy vessels and mineral pigments at the Moundville site. Frog, turtle, bat, clam, and fish effigy vessels were found to be associated with the eastern and duck effigy vessels with the western portion of the site (Peebles 1971:83).

Peebles also observed important distinctions between the northern and southern portions of Moundville. Mounds in the north are appreciably larger than those in the south. Moreover, two of the northernmost earthworks, Mounds C and D, included the most elaborate, high-status burials at Moundville. He interpreted these spatial patterns as indicating an underlying status gradient built into the layout of the Moundville community. Peebles argued that further evidence of this intercommunity differentiation is represented in non-mound architecture. He identified a high-status residential area in the northeastern portion of the site (Peebles and Kus 1977:435). Moreover, he identified large public buildings and areas for ritual game playing (chunkey) at the northern corners of the plaza (Peebles 1987a:27; Peebles and Kus 1977:435). A sweatlodge and charnel houses were also located along the margins of the plaza (Peebles and Kus 1977:435).

Peebles's argument for an economically differentiated Moundville was based primarily on the identification of craft workshops and other evidence of specialized production activities. From an analysis of records and artifact assemblages from depression-era excavations at Moundville, Peebles identified three specialized craft industries: pottery production, hide processing, and shell-bead manufacture (Peebles and Kus 1977). Specialization in the manufacture of pottery vessels was represented in the presence of large firing areas and caches of mussel shell, clay, and fuller's earth in the northwestern portion of the site (Peebles and Kus 1977:442). Peebles also argued that a high level of stylistic standardization among Moundville pottery vessels indicates "their manufacture was not a household craft" (Peebles and Kus 1977:443). Evidence for hide processing derives from a large area in the northeastern portion of the site where "hundreds of large bone awls and the stones which were used to sharpen [them]" were recovered (Peebles and Kus 1977:442). The shell-bead production area was also located in the northeastern portion of the site. Evidence for this industry consisted of "a large quantity of finished shell beads, unworked shell, and beadworking tools" (Peebles and Kus 1977:442).

Welch (1991b, 1996) further developed Peebles's model of Moundville's political economy. He examined the regional production and distribution of craft items and subsistence goods. Welch (1991b:179) argued that Moundville's economy was characterized by the centripetal mobilization of agricultural foodstuffs and venison from the rural nonelite to the chiefly elite living at mound centers in the Black Warrior Valley. Balancing this inward mobilization of subsistence goods was the outward distribution of prestige goods from Moundville to the elite at outlying mound sites (Welch 1991b:180).

On the basis of the identification of greenstone production debris in the northeastern portion of the site and the presence of greenstone celt preforms in the Moundville Roadway assemblage, Welch (1991a:164–165, 1996:81) also argued that the production of utilitarian greenstone celts was centralized at Moundville. This argument for centralized production has important implications for Moundville's political economy. By controlling access to greenstone celts, the Moundville elite would have effectively controlled the ability of commoners to clear agricultural fields and conduct other basic tasks like house construction. Thus, in dominating the production and distribution of greenstone celts, the Moundville elite could have exerted control over the agricultural means of production in the Black Warrior Valley.

Welch also identified variation in the organization of foodways represented in pottery discard assemblages (Welch and Scarry 1995). Comparisons among pottery assemblages from farmsteads, rural mound sites, and different portions of the paramount center of Moundville revealed considerable variation in ratios of service ware to cooking ware. These pottery assemblages also varied in terms of the relative frequencies of different kinds of serving wares. Welch linked this interassemblage variation to status distinctions between the different social groups that made up the Moundville chiefdom.

Recent Investigations

A number of recent archaeological investigations have contributed to a more fine-grained understanding of Moundville community organization and of Mississippian political economy in the Black Warrior River valley in general. Some of these studies have supported aspects of both Peebles's and Welch's arguments while others have contradicted them. Here I briefly summarize several of these investigations by subject of inquiry.

Knight's (1998) research on Moundville's ceremonial precinct has supported Peebles's argument that Moundville was a planned community with a spatial layout corresponding to an underlying social organization. Through comparison with an ethnographic example of Chickasaw community organization, Knight (1998) argues that each of the paired mound groupings at Moundville served as political and ceremonial facilities for distinct social groups such as matrilineal clans. The political ranking of these social groups is represented in the variable sizes of these earthen monuments, the largest of which are in the north and the smallest in the south (Knight 1998).

C. Margaret Scarry's paleobotanical research has supported Welch's argument that the Moundville elite received tribute in the form of agricultural goods. Scarry's analysis and comparison of paleobotanical assemblages have revealed that rural, nonelite farmsteads conducted more on-site processing (shelling) of maize cobs than did residents of the Moundville site and other mound centers in the Black Warrior Valley. Moreover, there was more on-site maize processing at lower-status than higher-status residential areas of the Moundville site (Welch and Scarry 1995). Scarry interprets these variable patterns of food production as evidence of tribute mobilization in the form of shelled maize provided to the Moundville elite from nonelite residents of the Black Warrior Valley (Welch and Scarry 1995).

Issues of economic centralization and social differentiation at Moundville have been debated in recent years. Marcoux (2000) recently conducted a distributional study of display goods manufacturing debris in the Black Warrior Valley. Surprisingly, Marcoux's examination of artifacts and excavation records did not confirm the existence of the four off-mound special production loci previously identified at Moundville by Peebles, Kus, and Welch. Only a small number of display goods in an incomplete stage of manufacture were identified. Moreover, these incomplete specimens and two concentrations of craft-related artifacts were recovered either from mound-summit contexts or from contexts immediately flanking the mounds (see also Astin 1996; Wilson 2001).

Perhaps of greater import to this study was Marcoux's (2000) conclusion that much of the evidence for craft production appears to postdate the early Mississippian period. With the exception of a small cache of unworked mica found in a Moundville I phase house, the evidence discussed above was recovered from contexts that are thought to date to the late Moundville II and early Moundville III phases (ca. A.D. 1300–1450).[4] It is important to note, however, that no excavations have been conducted on mound summits dating to the early Mississippian period. Nevertheless, the timing and evidence of craft production suggest that this activity was a relatively small-scale affair restricted to elite households within the Moundville site.

I also have taken issue with aspects of Welch's economic model in an expanded study of the Mississippian greenstone industry at Moundville (Wilson 2001). My analysis of greenstone tool production, use, and recycling revealed little evidence of celt production at Moundville. Many of the greenstone artifacts Welch previously identified as production related were in fact finished celts that were broken in use and had been subsequently recycled into other tools. On the basis of this evidence, I argued that most utilitarian greenstone tools must have been either crafted at the greenstone outcrops in northeastern Alabama or transported to the Black Warrior Valley as late-stage preforms (Wilson 2001). The upshot of this study is that there is little direct evidence that the Moundville elite exerted a high degree of control over the economic means of production in the Black Warrior Valley.

Summary and Discussion

Evidence of tribute mobilization (Welch and Scarry 1995), ascribed mortuary patterns (Peebles 1971, 1974), and large-scale labor projects indicate that the Moundville polity was politically centralized with an ascribed social hierarchy. The spatial layout of the Moundville site suggests that Moundville comprised multiple, ranked social groups (Knight 1998). Clearly Moundville was one of the most politically complex polities in the Mississippian Southeast. However, important questions remain unanswered. What kinds of coresidential social groups made up early Moundville? What status-based differences existed between these groups and how were these differences produced and maintained? How did social ranking play out in the daily lives of Moundville community members? Did membership in a higher-ranked clan entail special privileges for all of its members or only for the elite? I submit that finding answers to these questions requires a more inductive, household-centered, theoretical approach combined with the analysis of large-scale midden assemblages from Moundville's residential areas. This theoretical approach is outlined in Chapter 1. The data for this research are discussed and analyzed in the following two chapters.

3 Moundville Households in Space and Time

There is a rich, untapped dataset on Mississippian households from the Moundville site. During the late 1930s and early 1940s the Alabama Museum of Natural History conducted excavations throughout the site, uncovering hundreds of Mississippian buildings along with thousands of artifacts. The vast majority of these archaeological materials have not been systematically analyzed. The Moundville Roadway excavations and two associated projects dubbed the Administration Building (ADM) and Museum Parking Area (MPA) excavations are the primary focus of the current research. This chapter describes these excavations and presents a seriation to date the associated architectural and artifactual materials.

The Roadway excavations were conducted in 1939 and 1940 at the Moundville site within a winding corridor, 50 ft wide and 1.5 miles long, that was to be disturbed by the construction of the road that now encircles portions of the plaza and areas east, west, and south of the mounds (Peebles 1971). In conjunction, several large block excavations occurred prior to the construction of an entrance building (Administration Building excavations) and site museum (Museum Parking Area excavations). These excavations were divided into 147 50-×-50-ft blocks. Each of these blocks was subdivided into 10 5-×-50-ft blocks (Figure 3.1). Most ceramic artifacts were assigned to these excavation units. However, many nonceramic materials (copper, shell, bone, pigments, greenstone celts and pendants, projectile points, discoidals, and nutting stones) and large ceramic vessel fragments were piece-plotted on the original excavation maps. Excavated soil was not screened. Moreover, stratigraphic information was not recorded. However, excavators collected all ceramic and greenstone artifacts they encountered. Other archaeological materials were less systematically collected; only a small portion of the faunal, botanical, and chipped stone artifacts recovered from these excavations was collected.

The excavation and mapping of the Moundville Roadway was supervised by Maurice Goldsmith. Goldsmith's excavation system involved first uncovering individual 5-×-50-ft blocks. These blocks were expanded upon the identification of architectural features or midden deposits. Ultimately, close to one-third of the 362,000 ft^2 of the Moundville Roadway was excavated (Peebles 1979). These excavations uncovered the archaeological remains of hundreds of Mississippian buildings and associated architectural features, a total of 289 burials, and over 100,000 artifacts.

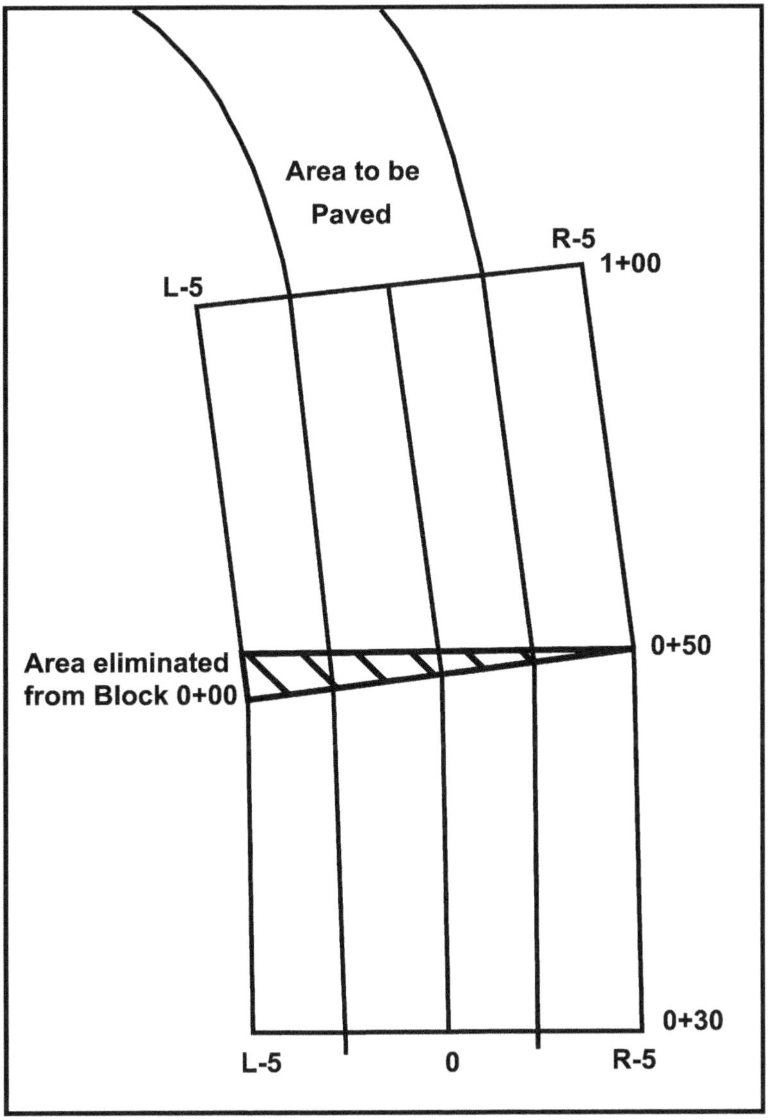

Figure 3.1. Drawing of the relationship between excavation blocks and the Roadway.

There has been no comprehensive analysis of the Roadway collections to date. However, several scholars have both sampled from Roadway artifact assemblages and summarized excavation field notes and maps. McKenzie (1964a, 1964b) gathered basic data on Roadway ceramic materials, lithic materials, and maps. On the basis of his analysis of these data, McKenzie (1964a, 1964b) offered a general functional analysis of Mississippian pots, stone tools, and buildings at Moundville. Moreover, he highlighted cultural similarities between Moundville and other Mississippian period sites. Peebles (1971, 1974) later provided an extensive description of the Roadway maps and excavation forms and a summary of mortuary artifacts. He also used Roadway architectural and mortuary datasets to evaluate Moundville's organization as a ranked society (Peebles 1979). More recently, Welch (1989) examined portions of the Roadway collections and reported on the distribution of certain chronological markers and imported items.

The Study Assemblages

All the subsurface features from the Moundville Roadway were examined in this study. This dataset consists of thousands of post molds, wall trenches, burials, and other features. The ceramic study assemblage for this project consists of a total of 14,320 sherds from five widely separated and discrete portions of the Moundville Roadway (Figure 3.2). I also examined published ceramic and architectural data from the Moundville Riverbank and North of Mound R excavations at Moundville (Scarry 1995, 1998; Steponaitis 1983). The five contexts from which the Roadway ceramic assemblages derived are marked on Figure 3.2 and consist of Roadway blocks 30+00 to 31+50, 43+50 to 46+00, 70+50 to 72+05, the Administration Building, and the Museum Parking Area excavations. The Moundville Riverbank and North of R excavations are also plotted on the map.

These assemblages were chosen on the basis of their large sample sizes, associations with residential architecture, and locations in widely separated portions of the Moundville site. Each of these assemblages derives from midden contexts that were formed through the successive dumping of refuse near residential areas. These deposits consist primarily of secondary refuse deposits, based on the recovery of large and generally well-preserved vessel fragments and other artifacts. A lack of crossmends between sherd assemblages indicates a low degree of postdepositional disturbance. While these midden assemblages are qualitatively similar in terms of their formation, they vary in sample size with 43+50 to 46+00 being the largest sample and 30+00 to 31+50 being the smallest (Table 3.1).

Seriation

A seriation was conducted to define the chronological relationships among the different archaeological contexts examined in this study. Domestic ceramic assemblages provide the principal evidence for this analysis. Ceramics are the most abundant archaeological materials recovered from the Moundville site. Moreover, domestic cooking and serving vessels had a high breakage and replacement rate relative to other examples of Mississippian material culture. The frequent replacement of Mississippian domestic wares, particularly cooking jars, created an enhanced possibility for stylistic changes in their manufacture over time. Tracking these stylistic changes has allowed archaeologists to define four primary chrono-

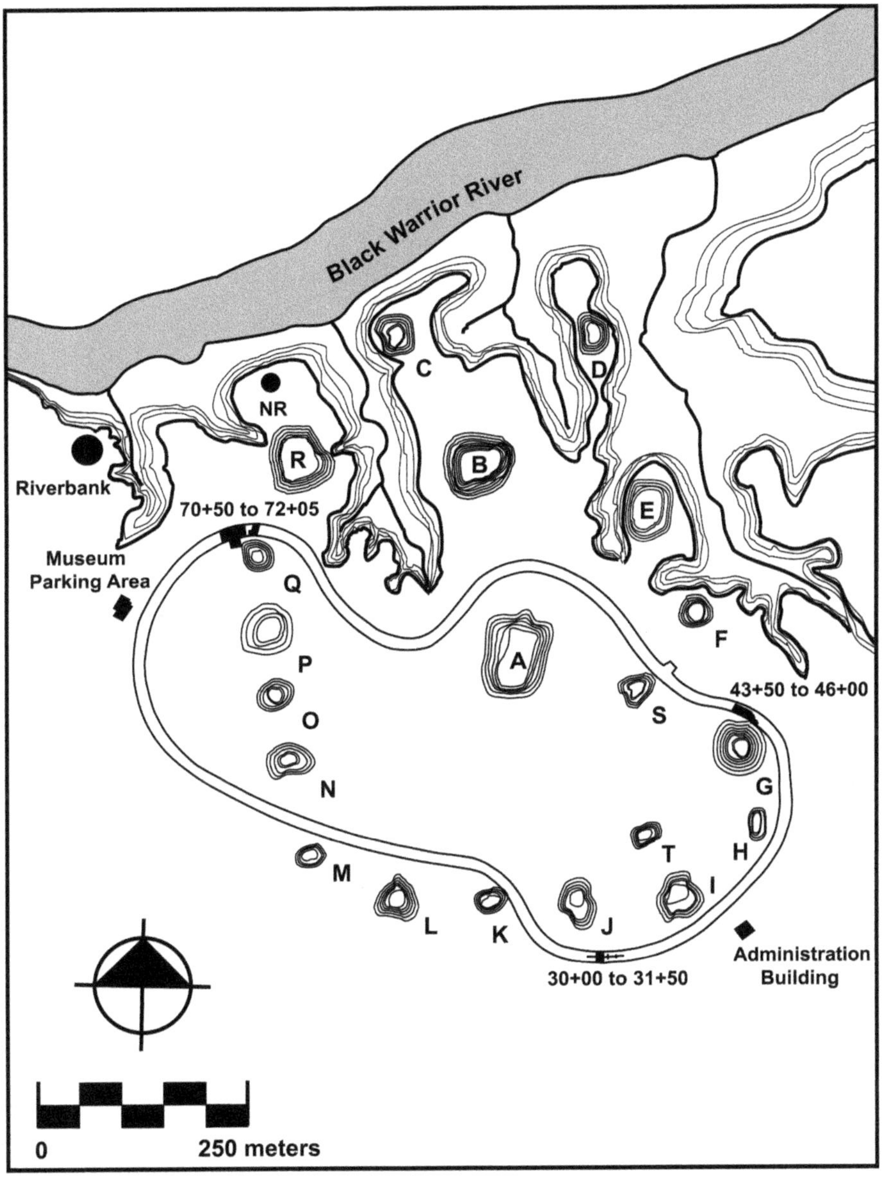

Figure 3.2. The Moundville site, featuring contexts from which pottery assemblages were examined.

logical periods or phases in Moundville's occupational history (Figure 3.3; Knight and Steponaitis 1998; Steponaitis 1983). Each of these phases, in turn, can be subdivided on the basis of statistical differences in the presence of certain ceramic variables (Knight and Steponaitis 1998; Scarry 1995; Steponaitis 1983).

Domestic architecture provides another line of chronological information for

Table 3.1. Counts and frequencies of sherds per area

Area	Sherds N	Sherds %
30+00–31+50	552	3.85
43+50–46+00	5,928	41.40
70+50–72+05	2,649	18.50
ADM	2,182	15.24
MPA	3,009	21.01
Total	14,320	100.00

Key: ADM, Administration Building; MPA, Museum Parking Area.

this analysis. As discussed in Chapter 2, there are chronological changes in the ways Mississippian community members manufactured their houses at Moundville (Lacquement 2004; Scarry 1995, 1998). Although houses had longer use lives than pots they provide a useful means by which to date different archaeological contexts at Moundville and to estimate their occupation spans.

I begin by providing background on previous ceramic seriation research at the Moundville site. In doing so I introduce the important ceramic attributes on which my seriation of the Moundville Roadway assemblages will focus. Next, I present a seriation of the Moundville Roadway, Administration Building, and Museum Parking Area ceramic assemblages. Several steps were required to establish this seriation. First, I present an incidence matrix for the Moundville Roadway ceramic assemblages, noting the presence or absence of temporally sensitive ceramic attributes from different phases of Moundville's occupation. Then I present an abundance matrix comparing the counts and relative frequencies of various ceramic attributes from the Moundville Roadway with those in well-dated assemblages recovered from the Moundville Riverbank and North of Mound R excavations. Third, I compare metric data on unburnished jar handles from the Moundville Roadway assemblages with data from mortuary assemblages from various well-dated contexts from the Moundville site and elsewhere in the Black Warrior Valley. This step provides important information on the degree of chronological mixture in the Moundville Roadway ceramic assemblages.

As a final step in this ceramic seriation I perform a nonmetric multidimensional scaling of the Moundville Roadway assemblages and those from the Moundville Riverbank and North of Mound R excavations. This step presents the finalized chronological sequence on which all further analyses are based in this study.

After completion of the various methods of ceramic seriation, I use Ford's (1962) method to further evaluate the occupation span and degree of chronological mixture in the Moundville Roadway and Riverbank contexts.

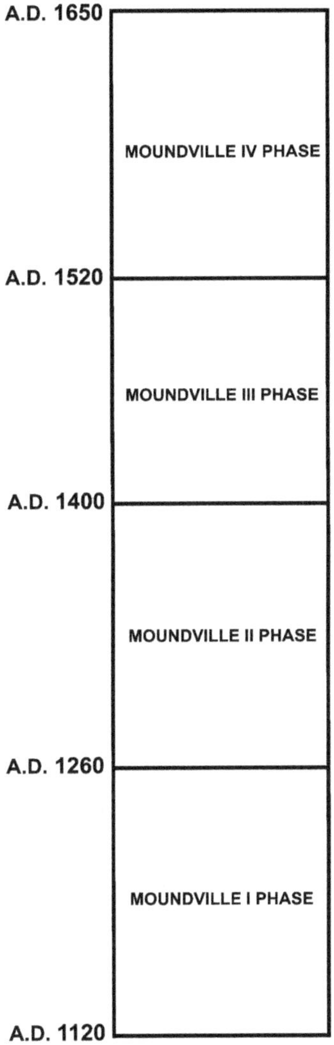

Figure 3.3. Mississippian period chronology for the Black Warrior Valley.

Background on Moundville Ceramic Seriation

The seriation presented here benefits greatly from previous analyses of Woodland and Mississippian ceramic assemblages from west-central Alabama (DeJarnette 1952; DeJarnette and Wimberly 1941; Jenkins 1980, 1981; Jenkins and Nielsen 1974; McKenzie 1966; Scarry 1995; Steponaitis 1980, 1981, 1983, 1998). Several projects in particular provide well-dated benchmarks that help to chronologically situate the Moundville Roadway assemblages. These projects include the University of Michigan's excavations north of Mound R and the University of Alabama's excavations at the Picnic Area (PA) and East Conference Building (ECB) tracts along the Moundville Riverbank (Scarry 1986, 1995; Steponaitis 1983). Also relevant is Steponaitis's (1998) ceramic research on diachronic trends in population density at the Moundville site.

Excavations North of Mound R

The University of Michigan's 1978 and 1979 excavations north of Mound R consisted of two 2-×-2-m squares that were excavated from surface to subsoil through approximately 2 m of cultural deposits (Scarry 1986). These deposits were systematically excavated and screened in natural levels. Steponaitis's (1984) analysis of the ceramic assemblages from North of Mound R, along with an assemblage of whole pots from Moundville burial contexts, produced the first comprehensive, fine-grained ceramic seriation for the Moundville site. On the basis of his seriation efforts, Steponaitis stratigraphically divided the midden deposits into Moundville I, II, and III phases (Figure 3.3). The lowest strata produced virtually unmixed Moundville I artifact assemblages (Steponaitis 1983). Moundville II and III deposits, however, did exhibit an increasing mixture with earlier materials.

Steponaitis (1983) defined six dimensions by which to characterize different attributes of Moundville ceramic assemblages: types and varieties, representational motifs, painted decoration, basic shapes, secondary shape features, and effigy features. I use this classification system in my seriation of the Moundville Roadway ceramics, and I focus on types and varieties, basic shapes, and secondary shape features. These dimensions proved to be the most robust indicators of temporal change in the study assemblage. I summarize each dimension below.

- Types and varieties are units within a hierarchical classification system based on differences in vessel paste, surface treatment, and decorative technique. Types represent broad units of classification. Varieties are more specific classification units, the identification of which is based on minor differences in vessel characteristics.
- The basic shape dimension refers to the overall shape or profile of a vessel. General categories within the basic shape dimension include jars, bowls, and bottles. Each of these general categories can be subdivided into a number of more specific subcategories. Table 3.2 lists and describes a number of chronologically sensitive basic shape classes as defined by Steponaitis (1983:64–70).
- Secondary shape features consist of elaborations of form found on Moundville pots. A list of relevant secondary shape features is provided in Table 3.3.

Riverbank Excavations

The University of Alabama, Alabama Museum of Natural History's 1991 and 1992 excavations targeted two areas where erosion threatened portions of the Moundville site near the riverbank (Scarry 1995:1). The areas excavated during this project include the ECB tract and the PA tract. Radiocarbon dates from both

Table 3.2. Selected chronologically sensitive Moundville basic shape classes

Vessel Shape	Phase	Description
Neckless jar	EMI	Jars with in-slanting lip shapes; jar lips do not reach a point of vertical tangency
Carinated bowl	EMI–MII	Wide and shallow vessels with vertical or slightly in-slanting rims that join a relatively flat base at a corner point
Out-slanting bowl	MII	Bowls with relatively straight upper walls and lips that slant outward at an angle greater than 20 degrees
Short-neck bowl	LMIII	A restricted bowl shape with the addition of a short vertical neck

Key: EMI, Early Moundville I; MII, Moundville II; LMIII, Late Moundville III.

Table 3.3. Selected chronologically sensitive secondary shape features

Feature	Phase	Description
Folded rim	MI	A jar rim that has been thickened by adding a coil strip beneath the lip
Folded-flattened rim	MI	A jar rim with a folded rim that has a flattened lip
Gardrooning	MI	A modeled decoration in which a vessel (usually a bottle) has vertical grooves evenly spaced around its body
Beaded rim	MIII	A notched appliqué strip encircling the rim of a vessel

Key: MI, Moundville I; MIII, Moundville III.

tracts revealed that most of the occupation in these areas dated to the Moundville I phase (Scarry 1995:91–94). On the basis of differences in the ceramic assemblages and architectural features from these areas, Scarry (1995) concluded that the PA tract occupation dated primarily to the *early* Moundville I phase and that the ECB tract occupation dated primarily to the *late* Moundville I phase. Deposits in both tracts exhibited minor amounts of mixing with later Moundville II and III materials.

Steponaitis's Least-Squares Regression

Recently, Steponaitis (1998) employed a least-squares regression technique developed by Kohler and Blinman (1987) to sort out chronological mixing in midden pottery assemblages from Moundville. Using well-dated assemblages from the

Bessemer site and from stratified deposits north of Mound R at Moundville, Steponaitis (1998) was able to generate model assemblages from different periods in Moundville's culture history. These model assemblages provided the baseline for analyzing the mixed assemblages. An important source of data for this research was Wimberly's (1956) basic tabulation of ceramic type varieties in the Moundville Roadway. The results of the least-squares regression revealed that approximately 73.4 percent of the total Moundville Roadway assemblage dates to the Moundville I phase, 25.5 percent dates to the Moundville II and III phases, and the remaining 1.1 percent dates to the Woodland period West Jefferson phase (Steponaitis 1998:Table 2.2).

Methods of Seriation

My first step in seriating the study assemblage entailed documenting the presence of chronologically sensitive types and varieties, basic shapes, and secondary shape features. Table 3.4 shows the presence of many Moundville I diagnostics in the study assemblage but also reveals the presence of a number of diagnostics from the Moundville II and III phases. Thus, while the study assemblage includes a substantial Moundville I component, there also appears to be some degree of mixing with later materials.

Sorting out this mixing is not an easy task. The Moundville Roadway artifact assemblages were not consistently provenienced by stratigraphic level. As a result, it is not possible to sort out earlier and later occupations by separating assemblages from natural or arbitrary levels in midden deposits. Moreover, there are few clear indicators of Moundville II and III ceramic assemblages that can be used to sort out the degree of chronological mixture. The primary diagnostics of Moundville II and III ceramic assemblages consist mostly of serving wares such as Moundville Engraved, pedestaled bottles, a number of effigy forms, and beaded-rim bowls. Not only do these serving wares represent a small amount of the total variation in post–Moundville I assemblages, but their relative abundance in refuse deposits may also be strongly influenced by social and economic factors such as status, ceremonialism, and duration of occupation (Maxham 2000, 2004; Varien and Potter 1997; Welch and Scarry 1995; Wilson 1999).

As an initial step in sorting out this mixing I compare the relative frequency of Moundville I chronological markers from the Roadway assemblages with that in the well-dated Moundville Riverbank and North of Mound R assemblages. The variables used in this comparison consist of standard, folded, and folded-flattened unburnished jar rims and the ceramic type Moundville Incised. On the basis of his seriation of stratified North of Mound R assemblages Steponaitis identified a temporal trend in which folded-flattened rims were the most popular jar rim type in the early Moundville I phase. This rim type was gradually replaced by folded rims during the Moundville I phase. By the Moundville II phase, standard or unmodi-

Table 3.4. Distribution of selected types and modes in the study assemblage

	EMI	LMI	EMII	LMII	EMIII	LMIII
Short-neck bowl						X
Carthage Incised, *var. Carthage*					X	X
Moundville Engraved, *var. Hemphill*				X	X	X
Beaded-rim bowl				X	X	X
Carthage Incised, *var. Akron*	X	X	X	X	X	
Out-slanting bowl			X	X		
Moundville Incised, *var. Snows Bend*		X	X			
Moundville Incised, *var. Carrollton*	X	X	X			
Moundville Incised, *var. Moundville*	X	X	X			
Carinated bowl	X	X	X			
Gardrooning	X	X				
Moundville Engraved, *var. Elliot's Creek*	X	X				
Carthage Incised, *var. Moon Lake*		X				
Carthage Incised, *var. Summerville*	X	X				
Folded rim	X	X				
Folded-flattened rim	X					
Neckless jar	X					
Moundville Incised, *var. Oliver*	X					

Key: EMI, Early Moundville I; LMI, Late Moundville I; EMII, Early Moundville II; LMII, Late Moundville II; EMIII, Early Moundville III; LMIII, Late Moundville III.

fied jars were the most common jar rim type. Moundville Incised is a ceramic type that was most common during the Moundville I phase and that continues into early Moundville II (Scarry 1995; Steponaitis 1983:108).

As revealed in Table 3.5, the Moundville Roadway assemblages are comparable to the late Moundville I Riverbank and North of Mound R assemblages in terms of the relative frequency of these ceramic variables. In nearly every case the relative frequencies of Moundville Incised sherds, folded rims, and folded-flattened rims are higher than or equal to those from late Moundville I assemblages from North of Mound R and the ECB tract (Table 3.5). Moreover, the Roadway assemblages have lower relative frequencies of standard jar rims than the North of Mound R and ECB tract assemblages (Table 3.5). The only explanation for these patterns is that the vast majority of sherds in the Moundville Roadway assemblages date to the Moundville I phase with only a slight Moundville II and III admixture.

Unburnished Jar Handles

An analysis of jar handles provides another means of evaluating the degree of chronological mixture in the Moundville Roadway assemblages (Steponaitis 1983). Changes in jar handles relate to differences between the top (near the lip of the

Table 3.5. Counts and percentages of selected ceramic attributes by assemblage

Assemblage	Standard Rims		Folded and Flattened Rims		Folded Rims		Moundville Incised	
	N	%	N	%	N	%	N	%
Late Moundville I								
ECB tract	50	60.98	11	13.41	21	25.61	112	2.92
NR	30	43.00	3	4.00	40	53.00	84	2.98
ADM	10	10.99	23	25.27	58	63.74	137	7.51
MPA	24	10.91	44	20.00	152	69.09	145	5.28
30+00–31+50	14	31.82	7	15.91	23	52.27	21	7.43
43+50–46+00	72	12.65	145	25.48	352	61.86	241	5.02
70+50–72+05	27	6.91	156	39.90	208	53.20	144	6.23
Early Moundville I								
PA tract	6	10.71	29	51.79	21	37.5	32	1.36

Key: NR, North of Mound R; ADM, Administration Building; MPA, Museum Parking Area.

jar) and the bottom (where the handle is attached to the vessel shoulder) widths of handles. The top and bottom of strap handles from Moundville I phase jars tend to be very similar in width. Throughout the Moundville II and III phases, however, Moundville potters increasingly made jars with strap handles that were wider on top relative to handle bottoms. This chronological trend can be expressed as a ratio of the top width divided by the bottom width.

Figure 3.4 compares the distribution of top-to-bottom width ratios for jar handles from each of the Moundville Roadway assemblages with a sample assemblage of Moundville I, II, and III whole vessels from the Moundville, Lubbub, and Bessemer sites (Steponaitis 1983:Tables 22, 24, 25, and 26). I chose this sample assemblage because it was used by Steponaitis (1983) in his original seriation of Moundville jar rim handles. I use boxplots for the purpose of graphically comparing these assemblages. Boxplots facilitate the visual representation of values within an archaeological assemblage through the use of a number of graphical elements. The outer edges (hinges) of the box represent the twenty-fifth and seventy-fifth percentiles of the distribution. The median value of the distribution is represented by a notch at the center of the box. The vertical lines (whiskers) on opposite sides of the box represent the tails of the distribution. Outlier values in the distribution are represented as asterisks and far outliers as open circles or dots (McGill et al. 1978). It is possible to compare the distribution of values within different assemblages by superposing them on the same graph. The outer portion of the notched section of the box represents the 95-percent confidence interval around the median. The medians of the two assemblages are significantly different at the 0.05 level when their notched sections do not overlap.

The results of this exercise revealed a very similar distribution of top-to-bottom width ratios for all of the Moundville Roadway assemblages and for the Moundville I phase sample assemblage. The notched confidence intervals for each of these assemblages overlap, indicating that they are not significantly different. The maximum and minimum scores for each assemblage are also very similar. The Moundville II assemblage overlaps with the Moundville Roadway assemblages and the Moundville I sample assemblage. However, it also exhibits a larger distribution of jar handle width ratios than the Roadway assemblages. Moreover, the Moundville II assemblage contains numerous jar handles with higher width ratios than any of the Roadway assemblages. Finally, the Moundville III sample assemblage exhibits a much larger distribution of jar handle width ratios than any of the other assemblages. Its mean value, however, is the highest among all the assemblages compared in Figure 3.4. This analysis indicates that the Moundville Roadway ceramic assemblages consist primarily of Moundville I sherds with little mixing with later Moundville II and III materials. If there was significant mixing with later sherds, then the handle width ratio distributions would be much higher than exhibited in Figure 3.4.

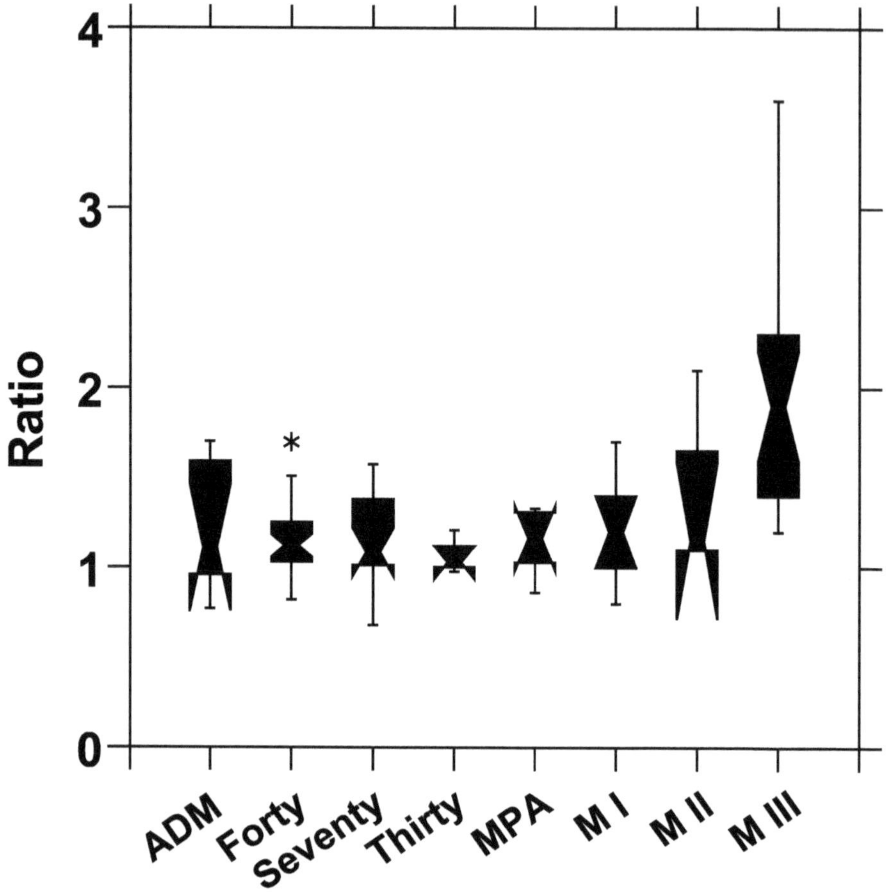

Figure 3.4. Boxplots of unburnished jar handles from Moundville contexts, displaying the distribution of handle width measurement ratios. Forty, Roadway blocks 43+50 to 46+00; Seventy, Roadway blocks 70+50 to 72+05; Thirty, Roadway blocks 30+00 to 31+50; MI, Moundville I; MII, Moundville II; MIII, Moundville III.

Nonmetric Multidimensional Scaling

Here I use nonmetric multidimensional scaling (MDS) to seriate ceramic assemblages from the five Roadway contexts, the PA and ECB tracts, and the Moundville I and Moundville II and III assemblages from North of Mound R. When used for the purposes of ceramic seriation, MDS graphically represents the relationships among various assemblages in two-dimensional space (Marquardt 1978). Thus, the MDS technique generates a rank ordering of intra-assemblage dissimilarities by reducing the number of dimensions in which the data are represented. The spatial distance between graphed assemblages indicates their degree of dissimilarity. Widely spaced assemblages reveal notable intra-assemblage compositional differences while closely spaced assemblages indicate similarities. Stress is a numerical index that denotes how successful an MDS seriation was achieved. Successful seriations can be generated with a low degree of stress. MDS seriations for assemblages characterized by well-demarcated temporal differences are commonly represented in chronological order along an arc or curve.

Vessel attributes used in this MDS seriation include the relative frequency of folded-flattened, folded, and standard unburnished jar rims and Moundville Incised sherds. These particular attributes were selected because they have proven to be useful temporal indicators in Mississippian ceramic assemblages from the Black Warrior Valley (Steponaitis 1983). As a first step to conducting this analysis I created a dissimilarity matrix of distance coefficients between these attributes using the city-block coefficient (see Cowgill 1972; Steponaitis 1983:85–88). Next, I used nonmetric multidimensional scaling to arrange these coefficients into a relative sequence. These procedures were performed using the statistical software application SYSTAT 9.0 (Wilkinson et al. 1992). As shown in Figure 3.5, this analysis produced a configuration in the shape of an elongated arc. The chronological ordering of assemblages in Figure 3.5 is presented right to left beginning with the early Moundville I assemblage from the PA tract and ending with the late Moundville I assemblage from the ECB tract. The stress of this configuration is very low at .016 with the two dimensions capturing 99 percent of the variation in the dissimilarity matrix.

This seriation confirms that all five Moundville Roadway assemblages date to the Moundville I phase. There is also some obvious clustering in this configuration. Assemblages from Roadway blocks 43+50 to 46+00, the Administration Building, and the Museum Parking Area comprise a tight cluster while those from Roadway blocks 70+50 to 72+05 and 30+00 to 31+50 fall earlier and later in the sequence, respectively (Figure 3.5). Moreover, the late Moundville I assemblage from North of Mound R falls between the Roadway blocks 30+00 to 31+50 and the ECB tract. Thus, while all the Moundville Roadway assemblages date to the Moundville I phase, there appear to be chronological differences in their occupation within the Moundville I phase.

One possible explanation for this pattern is that the clustered assemblages from 43+50 to 46+00, the Administration Building, and the Museum Parking Area date to one portion of the Moundville I phase while the remaining assemblages date earlier and later in the sequence, respectively. Another possibility is that the seriation presented in Figure 3.5 represents assemblages characterized by the differential mixing of early and late Moundville I sherds. If the latter possibility is correct then the contexts I examine in this study essentially represent contemporaneous late Moundville I occupations that were preceded by larger or smaller early Moundville I occupations. To distinguish between these two possibilities I turn to architectural data.

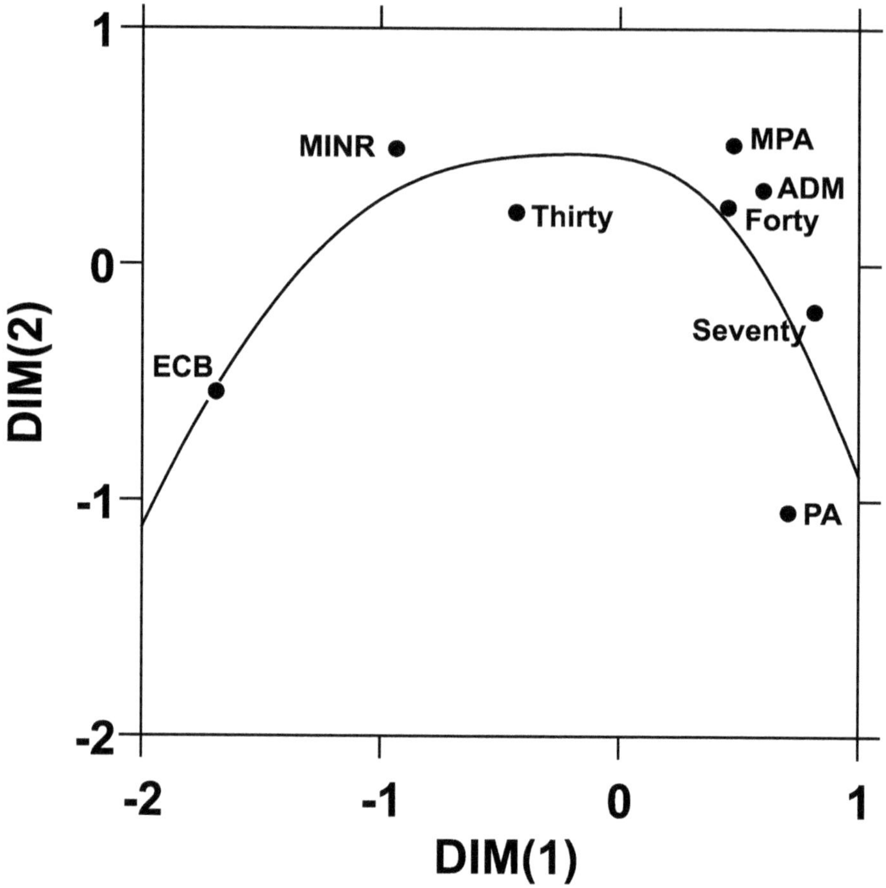

Figure 3.5. Multidimensional scaling of Roadway, Riverbank, and North of Mound R (NR) assemblages. DIM, Dimension; Forty, Roadway blocks 43+50 to 46+00; Seventy, Roadway blocks 70+50 to 72+05; Thirty, Roadway blocks 30+00 to 31+50; MI, Moundville I.

Architectural Seriation

Changes in architectural style provide an important means of evaluating occupational history that is independent of ceramics. As discussed in Chapter 2, archaeologists have identified three distinct architectural building techniques used at Moundville during the Mississippian period (Knight and Steponaitis 1998:18; Lacquement 2004; Scarry 1995, 1998). During the early Moundville I phase, inhabitants of the Black Warrior Valley primarily built structures using a single-set-post technique in which wall posts were bent over and interwoven to form a rounded roof (Lacquement 2004; Scarry 1995, 1998:91). A minority of early Moundville I structures consisted of a combination of single-set-post and wall-trench technologies. These "hybrid" structures may represent a transitional form between single-post and wall-trench architecture (Scarry 1995, 1998:91). By the late Moundville I phase, the regional populace primarily built structures using a wall-trench architectural design. After around A.D. 1300, residents built structures using a large-diameter, rigid-set-post technology involving internal support posts and separate wall and roof components (Knight and Steponaitis 1998:18).

Using Ford's method, I conducted a seriation of buildings by frequency of architectural style for each of the five Moundville Roadway areas and for the PA and ECB tracts.[1] Ford's method is based on the assumption that different stylistic attributes of material culture wax and wane in popularity through time (see Ford and Quimby 1946; Ford and Willey 1940). In other words, a particular style is introduced, gains popularity, and eventually is abandoned for a new style. By tabulating the relative frequencies of particular stylistic attributes from one context and comparing them with a set of diagnostics from earlier or later contexts it is possible to get a relative idea of how the popularity of a particular diagnostic changed through time. Horizontal bars representing the relative frequencies of different diagnostics from each context can be ordered vertically to graphically depict these changes. Each column of bars should ultimately depict the chronological waxing and waning of individual diagnostics. Such graphical trends are often referred to as "battleship curves," as they narrow and widen to represent a particular attribute's changing popularity. For the purpose of this analysis, single-post and hybrid structures are aggregated to represent the early Moundville I phase. Wall-trench structures represent the late Moundville I and early Moundville II phases. In addition, rigid-set single-post buildings represent post–A.D. 1300 occupations.

On the basis of the results of this seriation, it appears that both early Moundville I and late Moundville I to early Moundville II architecture is present in all contexts considered (Figure 3.6, lower section). Early Moundville I architecture, however, represents a minority of the total structures in all contexts except for the PA tract. The PA tract has a much higher percentage of single-post and hybrid structures (66.7 percent) and a lower percentage of wall-trench structures (33.3 percent) than any other context. In fact, wall-trench architecture predominates in Roadway contexts and the ECB tract but represents only a minority of the total structures in the PA tract.

This architectural seriation is important as it provides an independent line of evidence dating the Moundville Roadway study areas to the Moundville I phase. For purposes of comparison I juxtaposed this architectural seriation with Ford's graph of unburnished jar lips from the same contexts (Figure 3.6, top section). The results of both seriations and the nonmetric multidimensional scaling are very similar. The exceptions are Roadway blocks 30+00 to 31+50 and the Administration Building, which are reversed in the architectural and ceramic seriations. The reasons for this are unclear but may be a result of small architectural sample sizes

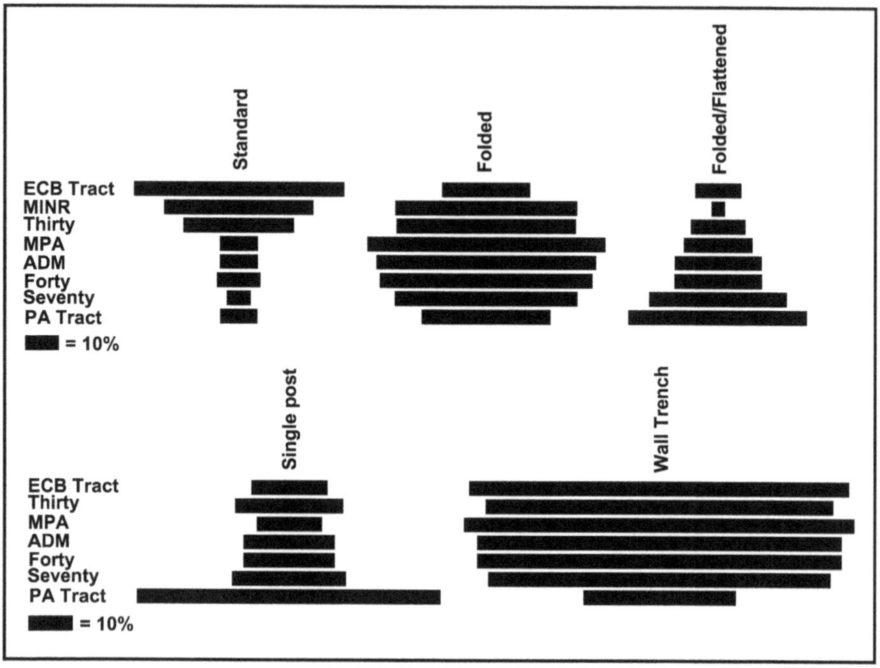

Figure 3.6. Ford's method seriation of Roadway structures by architectural style (bottom) and unburnished jar rims by context (top). MI, Moundville I; NR, North of Mound R; Thirty, Roadway blocks 30+00 to 31+50; Forty, Roadway blocks 43+50 to 46+00; Seventy, Roadway blocks 70+50 to 72+05.

for both of these areas. It is also noteworthy that the architectural data indicate a much sharper distinction between the PA tract and other contexts than revealed in any of the ceramic seriations presented above. Solely on the basis of these results it appears that the PA tract consists primarily of an early Moundville I occupation with a minor late Moundville I occupation, while all other areas possess a minor early Moundville I occupation followed by a much larger late Moundville I to early Moundville II occupation.

Summary of Seriation Evidence

All the seriation techniques employed in this chapter indicate the same general pattern: each of the Roadway areas was primarily occupied during the middle to late Moundville I phase (Table 3.5). When compared with the MDS seriation, the architectural data provide more specific information about the residential histories of each of the five Moundville Roadway contexts. Each area under consideration is marked by a minor early Moundville I phase occupation followed by a more intensive middle to late Moundville I occupation. The PA tract is somewhat unique in that it appears to date primarily to the early Moundville I phase (Scarry 1995, 1998). There is also ceramic admixture from later Moundville II and III occupations in each of these areas. The extent of this admixture, however, appears to be minor, as suggested by the MDS ceramic seriation, the scarcity of late Mississippian architectural styles, and the scarcity of post–Moundville I jar handle styles in the Roadway assemblages. This chronological information will facilitate my architectural and ceramic analyses in the following two chapters.

4 Architecture and Community Organization

This chapter presents an analysis of the architectural and mortuary features of the Moundville Roadway and Riverbank excavations. I begin by providing background on the architectural techniques used to construct Mississippian structures and on the purposes that these buildings served. Next, I describe the way the Moundville Roadway was originally mapped and the procedures used to create a geographic information system (GIS) map for Moundville. The rest of the chapter is devoted to a discussion of how Moundville's early Mississippian residential occupation was organized. Specifically, I consider when Moundville was first occupied, how long that occupation endured, and how kin groups organized themselves in relation to community space over the long term.

Architectural Construction Techniques and Functions

Despite major innovations in excavation methods and the expansion of regional datasets, Lewis and Kneberg's (1946) research in eastern Tennessee is still the yardstick against which any study of Mississippian architecture must be measured. Indeed, much of what is currently known about architectural construction techniques, building materials, form and function, and chronology can be traced back to the heyday of culture history. The details of these technological studies were primarily related to time-space systematics rather than issues of political organization or domestic economy. Nevertheless, these earlier investigations have proven invaluable to contemporary researchers throughout the southeastern United States. Future refinements or applications of architectural data would contribute greatly to studies of Mississippian household archaeology.

In the 1940s Lewis and Kneberg excavated several burned Mississippian structures in which the charred remains of walls, roofs, and other construction materials like thatch and matting were preserved. Architectural floor plans provided an additional source of data for their analyses. On the basis of the excavation and analysis of numerous Mississippian buildings from Hiwassee Island and other eastern Tennessee sites, Lewis and Kneberg (1946) identified a basic chronological distinction between early and late Mississippian architectural styles. Early Mississippian buildings were constructed using a flexed-pole technique with small, closely spaced wall posts that were bent over and interwoven to form a rounded roof. Wall posts were set in linear trenches or individually excavated postholes. In contrast, late Mississippian buildings were constructed using a rigid-post technique with large and widely spaced wall posts to which additional beams were attached to form a hipped or gabled design.

Polhemus's (1987) research at the Toqua site in eastern Tennessee built upon Lewis and Kneberg's earlier investigations in the region. The Toqua investigation represents one of the most comprehensive analyses of Mississippian architecture to date. The Toqua site project is relevant to the current study of the Moundville community in that much of the architectural variation documented by Polhemus is also present at the Moundville site. In all, Polhemus analyzed 133 buildings excavated by the University of Tennessee. Present in the Toqua sample are a variety of different structure shapes, styles, and functions. Most structures appear to have been of a wattle construction with either bark or thatch-covered roofs (Polhemus 1987). Rectangular, square, and circular building shapes were identified. Both flexed-pole and rigid-post structures were present, indicating a long-term occupation for the site. Many structures had interior hearths, and some also included benches and internal wall partitions.

Polhemus (1987:Figure 5.1) assigned a suite of different functions to Toqua site buildings on the basis of an analysis of variable structure sizes, construction techniques, and the presence or absence of certain internal features. In general, many of the smaller square and rectangular buildings appear to have been dwellings. The smallest of these were likely used for domestic food storage and/or special processing tasks. The largest square or rectangular buildings are interpreted as public buildings. Circular buildings dating to the early Mississippian period may have also had public uses. In the historic Overhill Cherokee period, circular buildings were winter houses often paired with elongate, rectangular domestic buildings that were used in the summer.

Creating a GIS Map for Moundville

A GIS map for the Moundville Roadway excavations was generated as part of a larger project to create a base map for the Moundville site (Wilson and Davis 2003). This system was generated with the use of ESRI ArcView, a software package that facilitates linking tabular data with georeferenced raster and vector images. Creating the final ArcView map of the Moundville Roadway involved several steps. First, the original field maps from the Roadway excavations were photocopied and scanned at 150 dpi. Next, each of these maps was loaded into DesignCAD, a vector drawing program. Different kinds of features (e.g., postholes, wall trenches, hearths, burials, and piece-plotted artifacts) were traced in different colors so that they would be distinguishable when exported into ArcView.

In order to fit together individual excavation maps, it was first necessary to plot the centerline of the Roadway. This was accomplished by using the Fosters, Alabama, 7.5-minute U.S. Geological Survey map (1969) as a guide. This quad map was chosen because it depicts the location of the modern Roadway and the old Administration Building. Once the centerline was plotted, it was possible to fit individual excavation maps together in DesignCAD. When this was completed, the total accumulated error along the entire length of the Roadway was found to be less than 2 m (Wilson and Davis 2003). The final step in this process was to export the DesignCAD drawing into ArcView and generate individual color-coded maps for excavation blocks, burials, hearths, wall trenches, postholes, and piece-plotted artifacts (Figure 1.1).

Structure Identification

One of the main objectives of generating a GIS map for the Moundville Roadway was to identify and gather data on domestic structures and other excavated features. This task was accomplished in several steps. As discussed above, different feature types were color coded for easy identification. Individual structures were then marked by shading their architectural floor areas. Once a structure was identified, all the features associated with it (e.g., wall trenches, postholes, and hearths) were temporarily removed from the map. This procedure allowed me to peel apart palimpsests of superimposed structures. Moreover, these methods facilitated the identification of many previously undocumented structures.

I identified a total of 140 structures in the Moundville Roadway. An additional 12 structures from the Moundville Riverbank are also included in my analysis (Scarry 1995). All but one of the structures identified in the Moundville Roadway and Riverbank excavations were of an early Mississippian (early Moundville I–early Moundville II) flexed-pole architectural style. These buildings have rectangular or square floor plans that typically lack internal features, with the exception of prepared clay hearths. One rigid-post structure stands out as the only example of late Mississippian architecture in the entire Moundville Roadway.

For analytical purposes I sorted all flexed-pole structures into two chronological groups (early Moundville I and late Moundville I–early Moundville II) on the basis of differences in wall-foundation construction (Chapter 3). The early Moundville I group includes single-post structures as well as "hybrid" structures that were built using a combination of single-post and wall-trench construction techniques. The late Moundville I–early Moundville II group, on the other hand, consists of structures that were built using only a wall-trench construction technique. I gathered the following eight kinds of architectural data for each complete structure: area (location), length, width, floor area, class, building episodes, status, and type (Appendix 1). A more limited set of data was gathered from structures that were incompletely excavated or mapped.

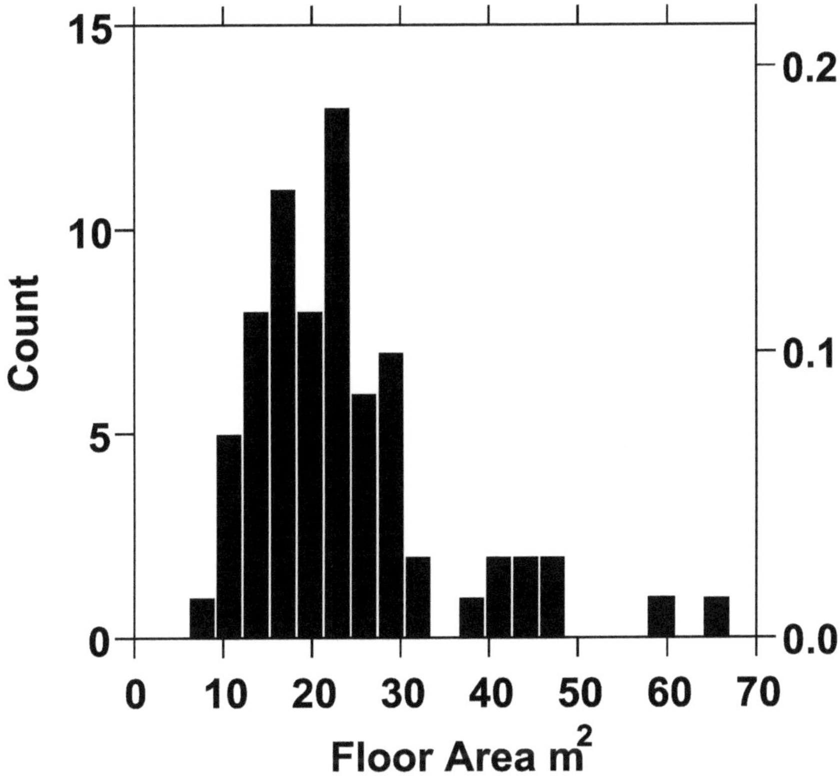

Figure 4.1. Histogram of structure floor areas from the Moundville Roadway and Riverbank.

Variation in Structure Size and Function

Floor areas for structures in the study assemblage varied from 8 m^2 to 64 m^2. As illustrated in Figure 4.1, there is a trimodal distribution of floor areas for these buildings. The structures in these three size modes, which I refer to as Class I, Class II, and Class III, have average floor areas of 21 m^2, 43 m^2, and 62 m^2, respectively. Possible explanations for this trimodal pattern include synchronic differences in structure function, household size, and household status and diachronic changes in household organization. Interpretation of this pattern is complicated by a low degree of chronological control for Roadway architecture. However, it is possible to gain some insight into structure size differences through a consideration of architectural style, frequency, shape, spatial distribution, and the presence or absence of certain internal features.

Figure 4.2 presents a boxplot comparing the floor areas of structures from both the early Moundville I and the late Moundville I–early Moundville II architectural

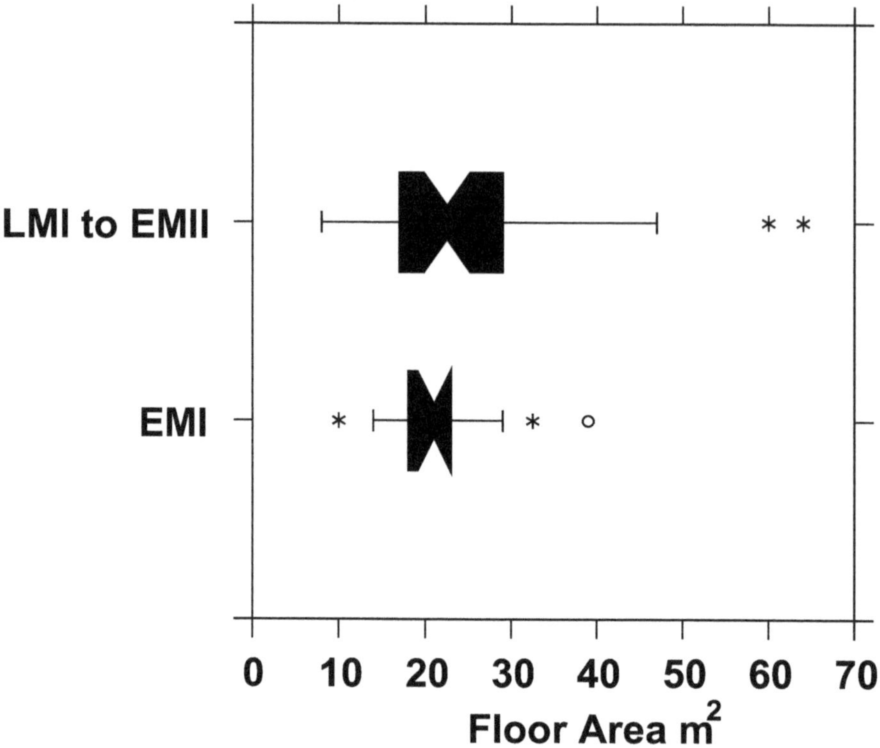

Figure 4.2. Boxplot comparing structure floor areas from early Moundville I and late Moundville I–early Moundville II architectural groups.

groups. This comparison reveals that the early Moundville I group has a smaller size range of floor areas than the late Moundville I–early Moundville II group. Specifically, the early Moundville I group includes only two examples of Class II buildings. Examples of Class III structures are absent from this group. Thus, there do appear to be diachronic changes in structure size at early Moundville. As I argue below, these changes represent the introduction of new functional structure types and increasing differences in household size during the late Moundville I phase. A better understanding of these differences in structure size can be achieved by examining each of the three structure size classes individually.

Class I Structures

Sixty-one Class I structures were identified in the study assemblage. This structure size class comprises most of the buildings in densely packed residential areas of the Moundville Roadway and Riverbank. On the basis of their high frequency and ubiquity, I argue that most Class I structures were dwellings. The small size (8–32.5 m^2) of these structures would have precluded many indoor activities. For this reason, I argue that Class I structures were primarily used as sleeping quar-

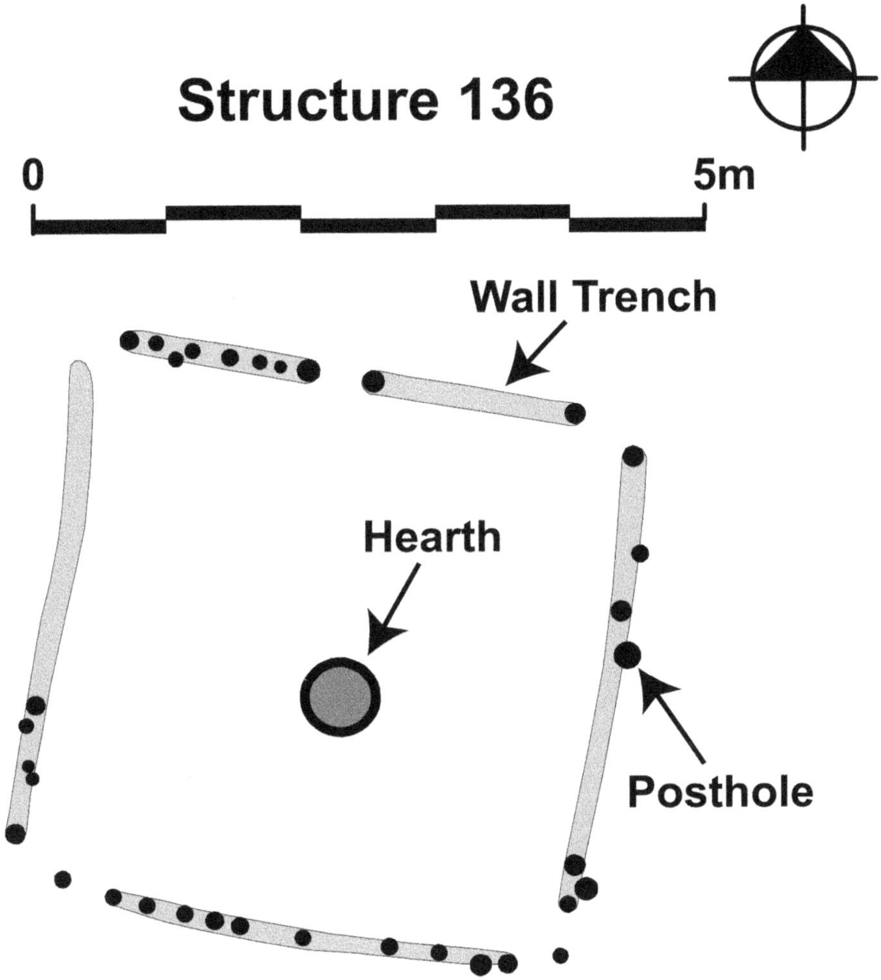

Figure 4.3. A Class I structure from the Museum Parking Area.

ters, as well as for a limited number of other domestic activities such as domestic cooking tasks, indicated by the presence of prepared clay hearths (Figure 4.3).[1] It is possible that Class I structures lacking hearths were used for different domestic purposes than those with hearths. It is more likely, however, that deep plowing disturbed the floors of some structures, thus removing evidence of hearths. Floor preservation would have depended on the depth of sheet middens deposited over abandoned houses. Structure floors blanketed by only thin midden deposits had poor chances for preservation.

Class II Structures

Only eight Class II structures were identified in the Moundville Roadway and Riverbank excavation areas. These buildings have floor areas that range from 39 m^2

Table 4.1. Counts of buildings by size class and area

Residential Group	Area	Class I	Class II	Class III
1	2+50–7+50 and MPA	21		2
2	12+00–14+00	5		
3	15+00–15+50		1	
4	17+50–24+50	5	1	
5	26+00–34+00	6	2	
6	35+50–37+60			
7	ADM	3		
8	43+50–46+50	2		
9	47+50–49+00	8	2	1
10	66+00–72+00	3	2	1
11	PA	6		
12	ECB	2		
Total		61	8	4

to 47 m^2. Although rare, Class II structures are widely distributed at Moundville, being present in over half of the residential areas identified in the Roadway excavation (Table 4.1). In addition to being larger, Class II structures also have more rectangular floor plans than Class I structures (Figure 4.4). This makes sense architecturally as increasing structure length while maintaining a standard width limits the need for longer wall/roof members to only two sides of the building. Otherwise, the floor plans of Class II structures are fundamentally similar to Class I structures in that they lack internal features aside from centrally placed hearths. Thus, despite differences in size and shape, many Class II structures were probably used for domestic purposes similar to those of Class I structures, though probably by larger households.

Three Class II structures (93, 94, and 96) require special consideration. These structures are part of a palimpsest of superimposed buildings located between Roadway blocks 48+00 and 48+50 on the western edge of a small cluster of domestic buildings (Figures 4.5 and 4.6). Structure 96 is the only building in this palimpsest that exhibits both wall-trench and single-post construction techniques. This structure has wall-trench foundations along its long walls and single-set posts along its short walls. It superimposes or is superimposed by at least two (Structures 94 and 95) and possibly a third (Structure 93) structure. Because of ambiguities in the original excavation maps, however, it is impossible to accurately determine the chronological order of superimposition.

Structure 93 is an unusually long and narrow (11 × 4 m) wall-trench building. Its dimensions roughly correspond with two and a half (average-sized) structures in length by one (average-sized) structure in width. A line of small widely spaced

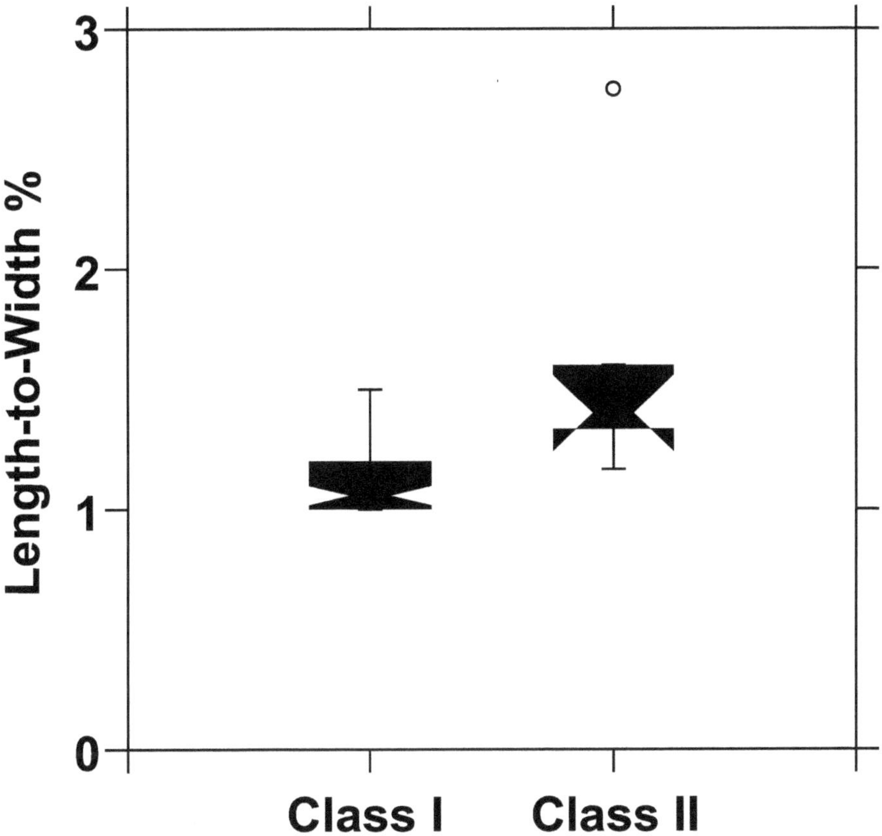

Figure 4.4. Length-to-width ratios for Class I and Class II structures.

posts a meter outside the eastern short wall represents a single rebuilding episode for this structure. No hearths or other internal architectural features were associated with this building. Structure 93 was superimposed by at least two other structures (94 and 95). Structure 95 is a 64-m^2, Class III, wall-trench building that appears to have been an expansion of Structure 94, an earlier Class II wall-trench building (Figure 4.5). On the basis of their large size and unusual architectural characteristics, I suggest that all the superimposed buildings in this palimpsest represent different stages of a special-purpose building associated with the adjacent multihousehold group.

An examination of small rectilinear arrangements of burials associated with three Class II structures (Structures 16, 25, and 89) suggests these buildings were contemporaneous with most of the Class I buildings in the Moundville Roadway and Riverbank. Figure 4.7 illustrates the location of two of these burial clusters in relation to Structures 16 and 25. At first glance it is tempting to conclude that the burials that make up these small cemeteries were placed beneath house floors while

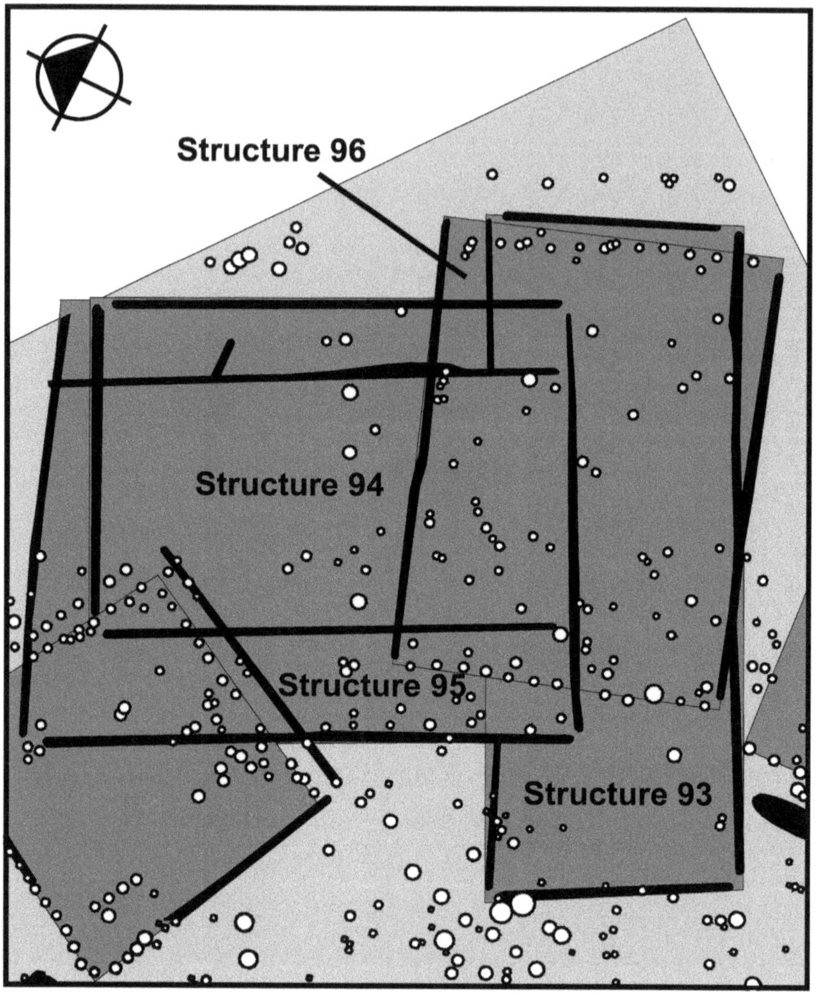

Figure 4.5. Palimpsest of Class II and III structures between Roadway blocks 47+50 and 49+00.

the structures were in use. Like the houses with which they are associated, most of the burials in each cemetery are oriented in the cardinal directions, creating a rectilinear spatial arrangement. Closer examination, however, reveals that several burials superimpose the wall-trench foundations of these houses (Figure 4.7). Thus, it is clear that these cemeteries postdate the wall-trench structures that they superimpose. Indeed, Steponaitis's (1983, 1998) analysis of the pottery vessels interred with these burials reveals most date to the late Moundville II and early Moundville III phases, which indicates their interment after the abandonment of these earlier domestic structures.[2]

Figure 4.6. Excavation photograph of superimposed structures between Roadway blocks 47+50 and 49+00.

Class III Structures

Class III structures have floor areas between 60 m² and 64 m² and represent the largest buildings in the Moundville Roadway. I identified only two examples of completely excavated and mapped Class III structures (85 and 95). However, there are two other partially excavated Roadway structures (131 and 135) with floor areas greater than 60 m². I will describe each of these structures individually.

Structure 95 has a floor area of 64 m² and is the largest completely excavated wall-trench structure in the Moundville Roadway (Figures 4.5 and 4.6). It is located southwest of Mound F between Roadway blocks 48+00 and 48+50. As discussed earlier, Structure 95 is the largest in a palimpsest of superimposed structures situated on the western edge of a small cluster of domestic structures. In addition to being very large, Structure 95 is characterized by a number of other unusual architectural features. Four large posts placed in a row down the middle of the structure's short axis may represent internal roof supports. Moreover, excavators identified a number of shallow pit features along its inner walls (Peebles 1979). These unusual characteristics led Peebles (1979) to interpret this structure as a public building. Indeed, Structure 95 and the palimpsest of structures with which it is associated all appear to be different stages of a special-purpose facility maintained by the same residential group.

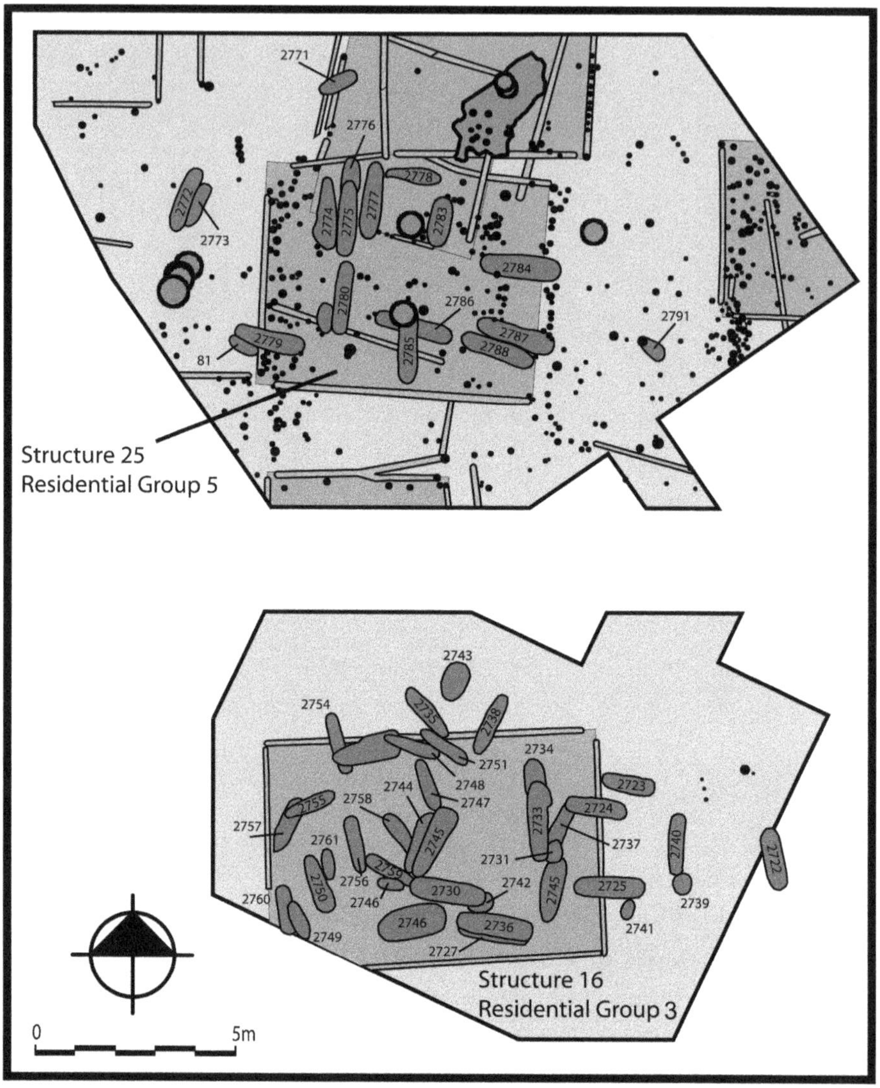

Figure 4.7. Two Class II structures superimposed by Moundville II and III burials.

Structure 85 is a square wall-trench building located immediately north of Mound Q between Roadway blocks 71+00 and 72+00. This Class III building represents one stage of at least five buildings rebuilt in the same location. On the basis of its large size and proximity to Mound Q, it is unlikely that Structure 85 was an ordinary domestic structure. Like Structure 96, it may have served as a public building for an adjacent residential group.

The two remaining Class III structures (131 and 135) were not completely excavated, which makes it impossible to determine their exact shapes and sizes. Structure 135 is located between Roadway blocks 4+50 and 5+00 west of Mound P. The distance along one axis of this structure measures 10.85 m. Had it been completely excavated it would have likely been the largest building in the Moundville Roadway. Structure 131, the final Class III structure, is located in the Museum Parking Area (MPA). Only a small portion of this large wall-trench structure was excavated and mapped, making it difficult to assess fully. On the basis of their large sizes it is likely that both of these structures served nondomestic functions. Like Structures 85 and 95, they may have been public buildings associated with an adjacent residential group.

Residential Group Organization

The construction of the GIS map for the Moundville Roadway facilitated the identification of a variety of household and community organizational trends. One of the most important discoveries is that early Moundville was characterized by a highly segmented residential organization. Moundville's residential areas consist of well-defined clusters of buildings, burials, and postholes separated by areas devoid of features. In some cases these residential areas appear to consist of several smaller clusters of domestic, public, and mortuary features.

The identification and analysis of these residential areas involved several steps. First, I calculated the ratio of post-mold density to excavation area for each of the 50-×-50-ft blocks of the Moundville Roadway. Wall trenches were converted into post molds for the purpose of this analysis. This was accomplished by calculating the average number of post molds per meter of wall trench for several early Mississippian structures.[3] Differences in post-mold density per excavation block are visually represented in Figures 4.8 and 4.9 by a scheme of graduated shades of gray overlain on the Roadway GIS map. This analysis revealed 10 discrete residential areas divided by areas where excavators uncovered little or no evidence of subsurface features (Figure 4.10). Two additional areas are represented by the Picnic Area (PA) and East Conference Building (ECB) tracts on the Moundville Riverbank. These residential areas (labeled 1–12) are listed in Table 4.1 and will be discussed individually.

Residential Group 1

Residential Group 1 is located 105 m west of Mound P in the northwestern portion of the Moundville site. This area represents the largest and most densely occupied portion of the Moundville Roadway. It consists of Roadway blocks 2+50 to 7+50 and the Museum Parking Area. I tentatively divided this residential group into three feature clusters on the basis of the uneven distribution of buildings, postholes, and burials (Figure 4.11). The narrow boundaries of the Roadway and Museum Parking Area excavations make it impossible to determine the exact size

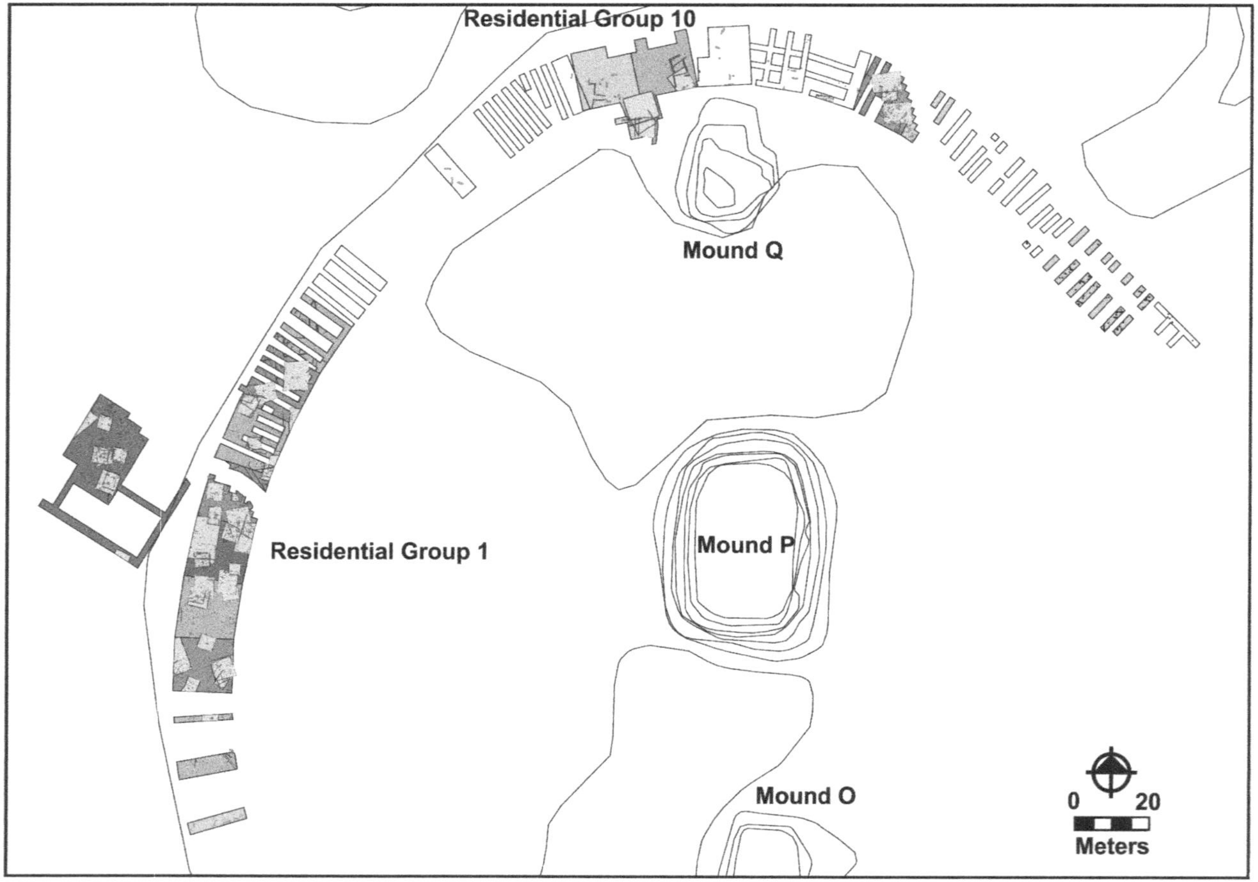

Figure 4.8. Post-mold density display highlighting Residential Groups 1 and 10.

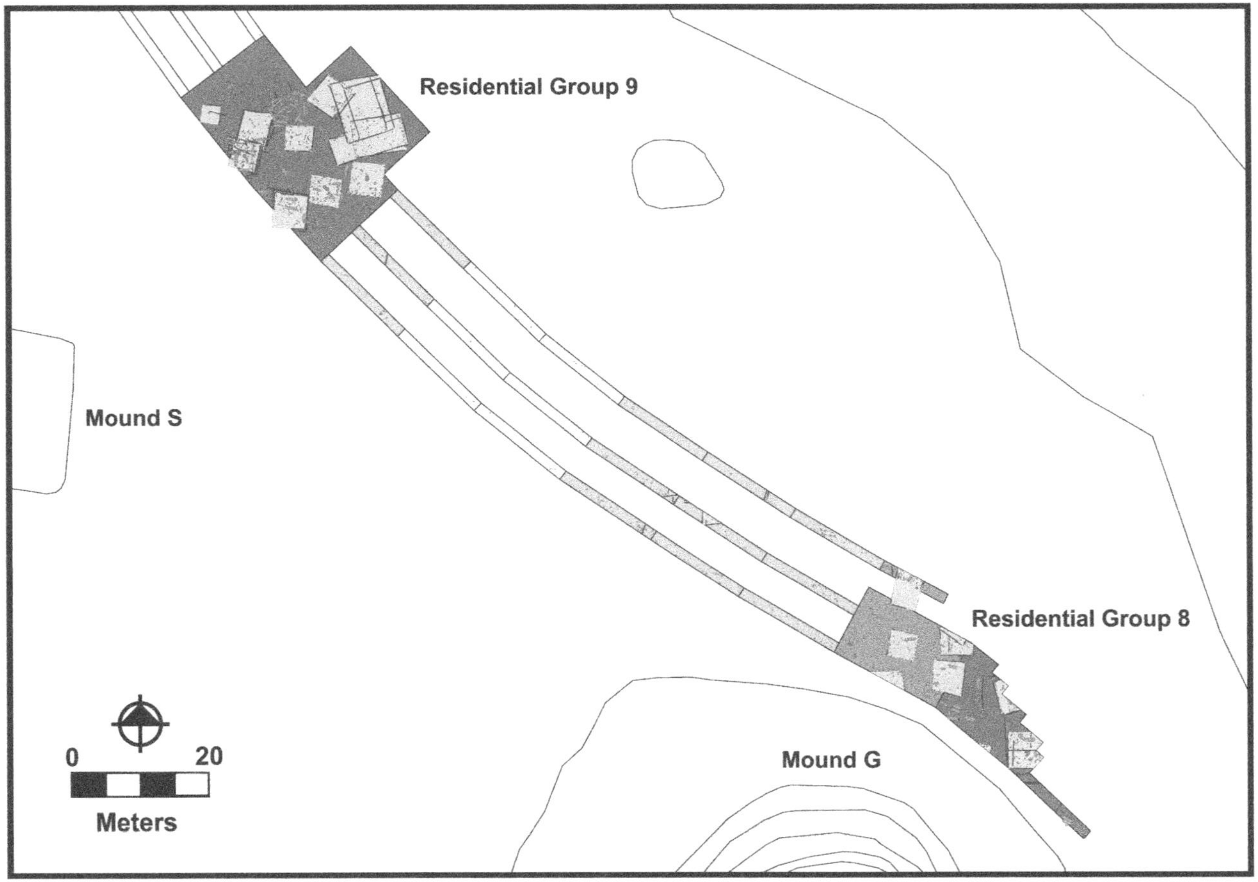

Figure 4.9. Post-mold density display highlighting Residential Groups 8 and 9.

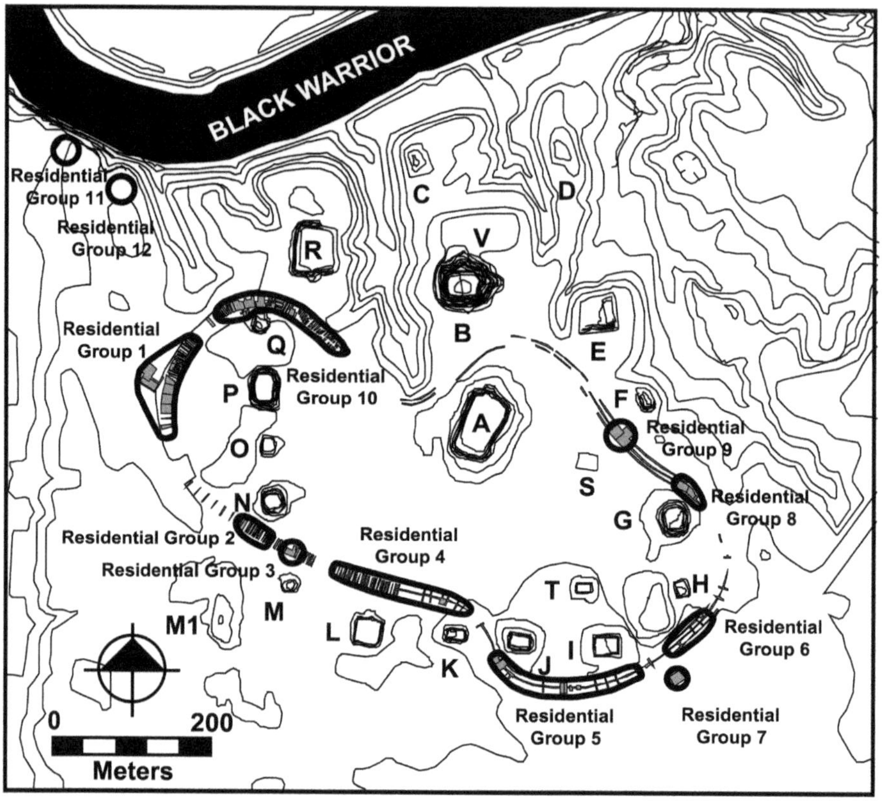

Figure 4.10. Residential groups identified in the Moundville Roadway and Riverbank excavations.

and composition of these clusters. Nevertheless, an examination of the number, location, and size of buildings within them reveals several generalized organizational trends. First, it appears that each of the feature clusters consists of small, nucleated arrangements of an estimated 10 to 20 buildings. Most of the buildings in each cluster are Class I domestic structures. However, two of these clusters also include a large Class III structure that may have served a public function. Finally, scattered throughout this residential group are a number of burials that date to the Moundville II and III phases.

Residential Groups 2 and 3

Residential Group 2 is situated in Roadway blocks 12+00 to 14+00, located immediately southwest of Mound N. It consists of a small, nucleated cluster of Class I domestic structures superimposed by several burials dating to the Moundville II and III phases (Figure 4.12). One small structure (with a floor area of 10 m^2)

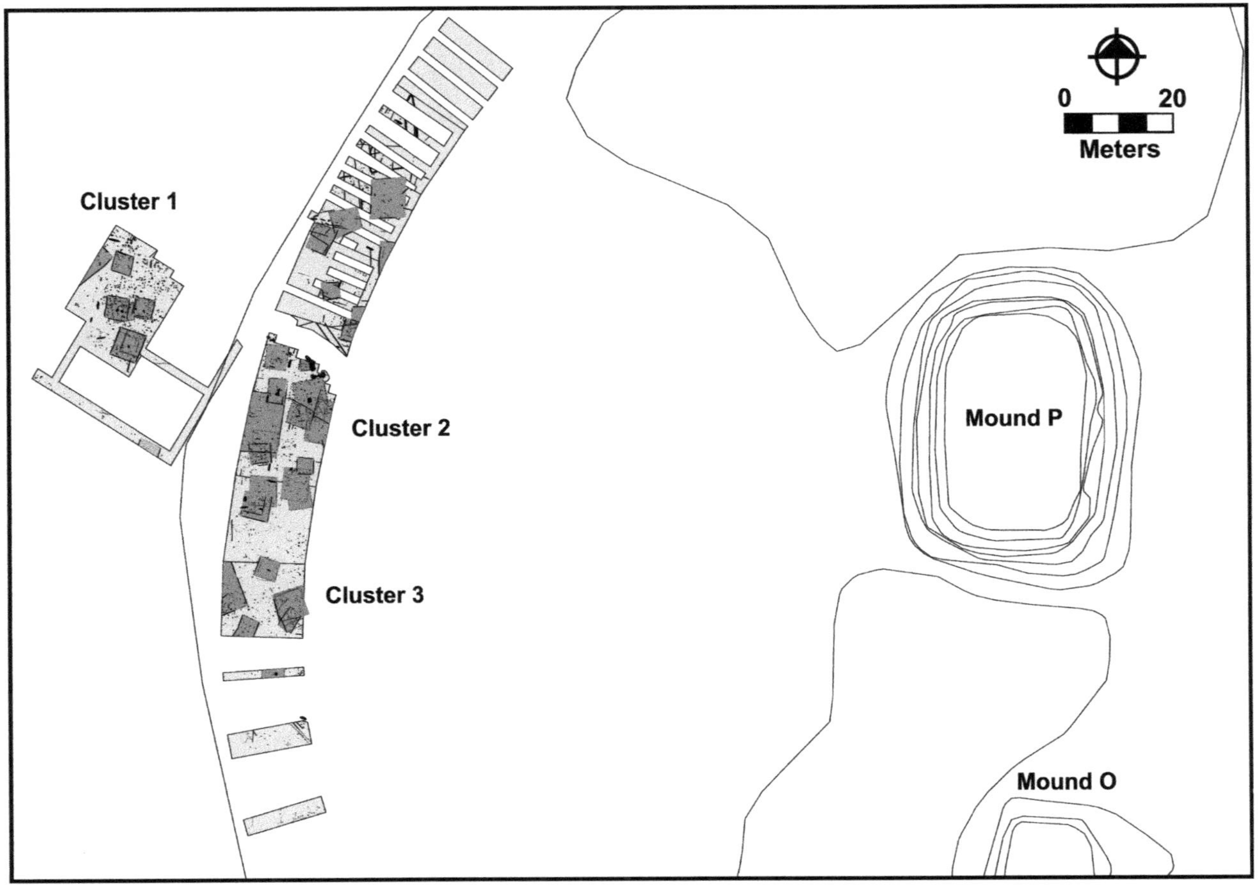

Figure 4.11. Residential Group 1 (2+50 to 7+50 and Museum Parking Area).

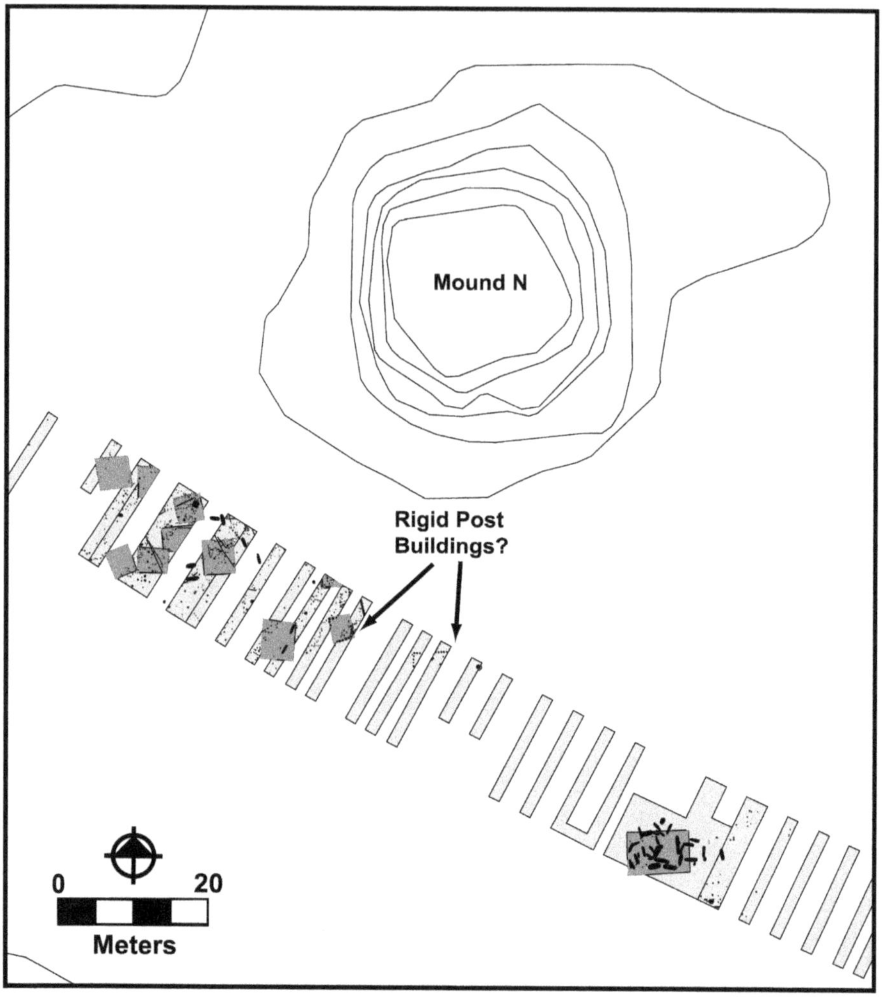

Figure 4.12. Residential Groups 2 (12+00 to 14+00) and 3 (15+00 to 15+50).

in this area is distinguishable by its large, closely spaced wall posts (McKenzie 1964b:236–239). These large posts suggest the building had a rigid-post construction, an architectural style that dates primarily to the late Mississippian period (see Lewis and Kneberg 1946; Polhemus 1987). Another two lines of large post molds immediately to the west of Structure 15 may represent a portion of another incompletely excavated and mapped rigid-post building.

Residential Group 3 consists of only one Class II structure located between Roadway blocks 15+00 and 15+50. Situated just 36 m north of Mound M, this structure may be associated with a larger residential group outside the limits of the

Roadway excavation. Both Residential Groups 2 and 3 include clusters of burials dating to the Moundville II and III phases.

Residential Group 4

Residential Group 4 includes Roadway blocks 17+50 to 24+50 and is situated immediately north of Mounds L and K. Like Residential Group 1, this is a large and densely occupied portion of the Moundville Roadway. However, the number and arrangement of buildings and other features in this area are impossible to determine as a result of the piecemeal fashion in which it was excavated (Figure 4.13).

One set of superimposed structures in this group requires additional discussion because of its contested interpretive history. The original excavation photograph for this area is presented in Figure 4.14. I have also included a GIS representation of this area in Figure 4.15. McKenzie (1964b:239–243) originally concluded that this set of features represented multiple structures rebuilt in the same location. Peebles (1971:83, 1979:857–858) later reinterpreted this palimpsest as a rebuilt structure with a central room and series of passageways or room partitions. On the basis of its unusual architectural style and the presence of a square hearth, Peebles (1971:83) argued that this building was a sweatlodge. However, my examination of the original maps and excavation photographs casts doubt on his complex interpretation. Both images clearly depict four superimposed structures, a pattern that corresponds with McKenzie's interpretation (Figures 4.14 and 4.15). Three of these, Structures 18, 19, and 108, are labeled on the GIS map in Figure 4.15. Structure 20 is the unlabeled structure in the upper left corner of Figure 4.15.

Some of the confusion over these buildings appears to have resulted from the way in which they were excavated. In attempting to identify different structure floors, portions of the floors from Structures 18 and 19 were excavated away, creating the illusion in the excavation photographs of a central room and a series of entranceways (Figure 4.14). In reality, such a complex architectural design would have been impractical considering the constraints of the flexed-pole technology associated with wall-trench buildings. On the basis of my simplified interpretation, all of the buildings in this palimpsest appear domestic in nature. While the rectangular hearth associated with Structure 18 is unusual for Moundville, Lewis and Kneberg (1946, 1995) identified numerous examples associated with early Mississippian structures in eastern Tennessee.

Residential Group 5

Residential Group 5 includes Roadway blocks 26+00 to 34+00 and is located immediately south of Mounds J and I. I identified a total of six Class I and two

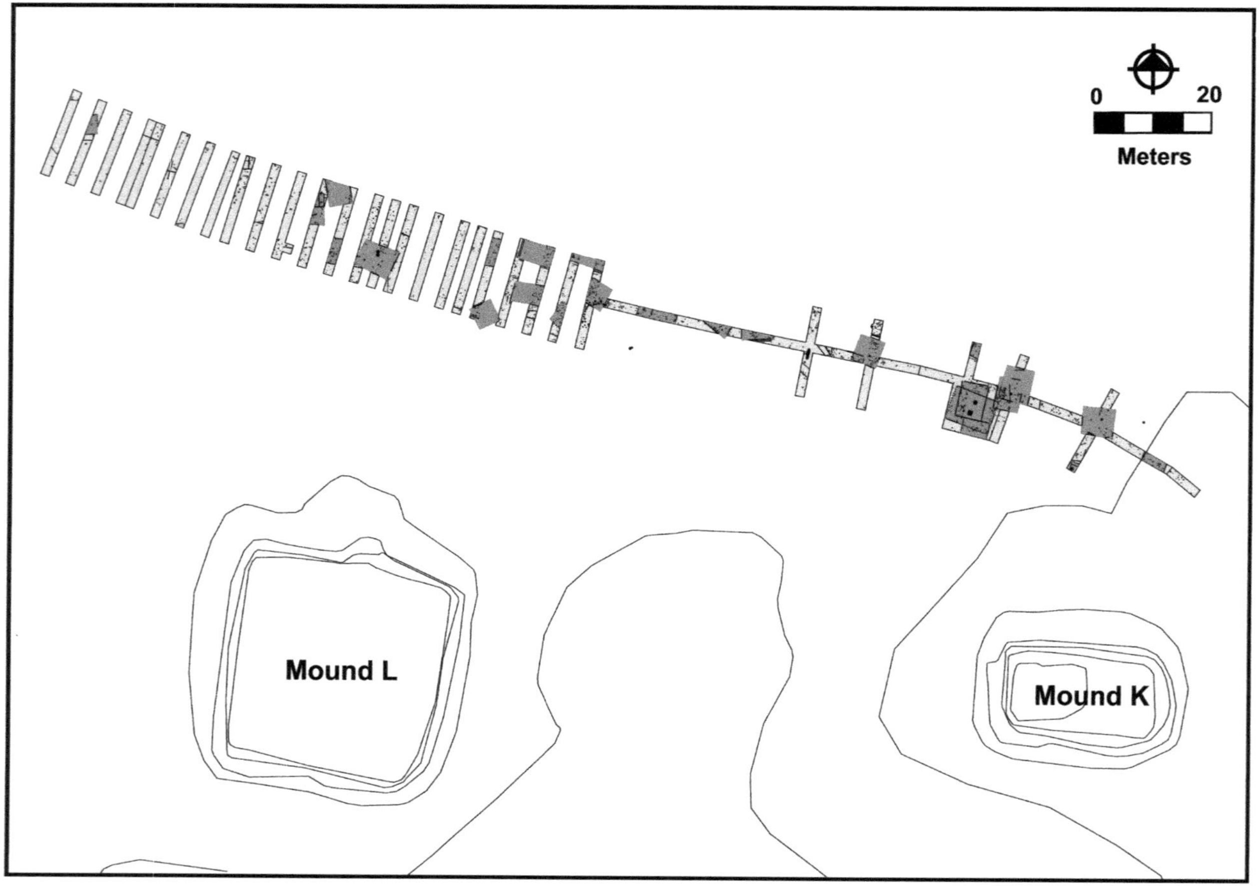

Figure 4.13. Residential Group 4 (17+50 to 24+50).

Figure 4.14. Superimposed structures located in Roadway blocks 17+50 to 24+50.

Class II structures in this area. These buildings are located in two separate clusters connected by a trench 56 × 2 m long with a number of postholes and unassigned wall-trench segments. Small Moundville II–III cemeteries superimpose each of these building clusters. It is possible that these two building clusters represent different social and residential groups (Figure 4.16). However, the narrow area of excavation between them limits a definitive interpretation.

Residential Group 6

Residential Group 6 includes Roadway blocks 35+50 to 37+60 and is situated approximately 40 m south of Mound H (Figure 4.17). Close examination of the residential features in this area is limited by the segmented fashion in which it was excavated. As a result, none of the structures in this group could be assigned to a discrete size class. However, on the basis of the density of architectural features and the location of several partially excavated buildings, this residential area appears to consist of one large or multiple smaller clusters of domestic structures. The two burials located in this area could not be assigned to a particular phase.

Residential Group 7

Residential Group 7 consists of a 15-×-18-m block excavation that was conducted prior to the construction of an administration building (ADM excavation). It is located 80 m southeast of Mound I. I identified three Class I structures in this area.

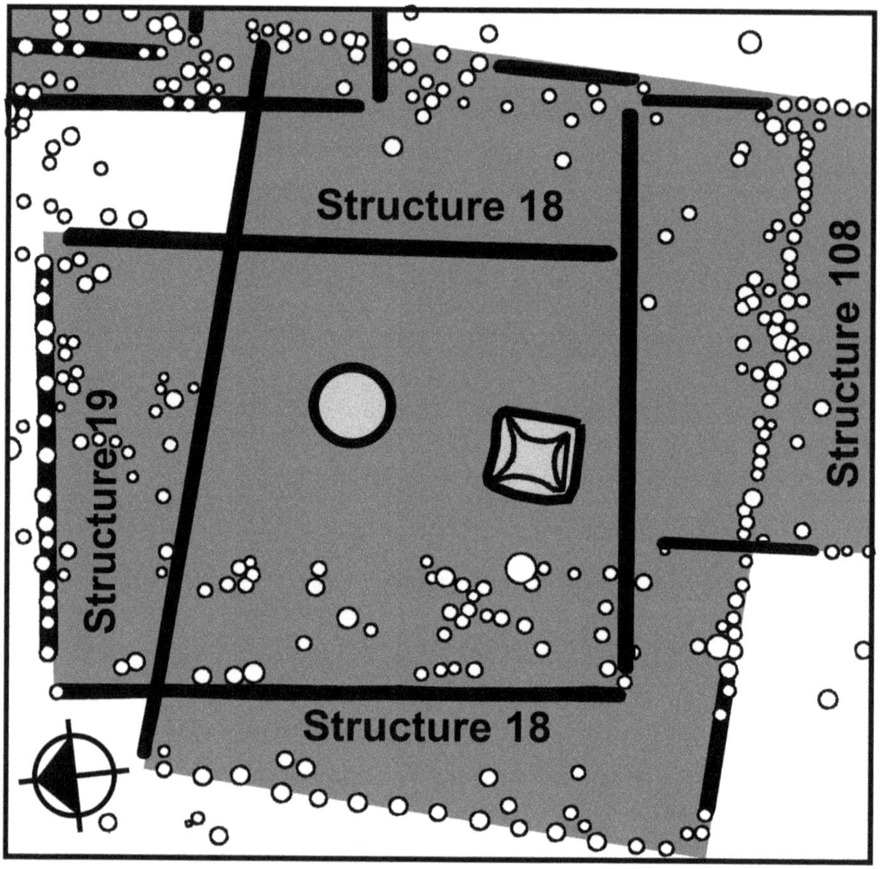

Figure 4.15. GIS representation of superimposed structures located in Roadway blocks 17+50 to 24+50.

Also present are several lines of posts and wall trenches that could not be associated with a discrete structure. Superimposed on these houses are a number of burials dating to the Moundville II and III phases (Figure 4.18).

Residential Group 8

Residential Group 8 includes Roadway blocks 43+50 to 46+50 and is situated immediately northeast of Mound G (Figure 4.19). The excavated portion of this residential area revealed seven structures, only two of which were completely excavated and mapped. Both of these are Class I domestic structures. In addition, several wall trenches, hearths, and lines of posts in this area could not be assigned to discrete structures. The buildings in this residential area appear to be situated in three closely spaced rows. During the Moundville II and III phases a number of burials were placed over the top of these abandoned buildings.

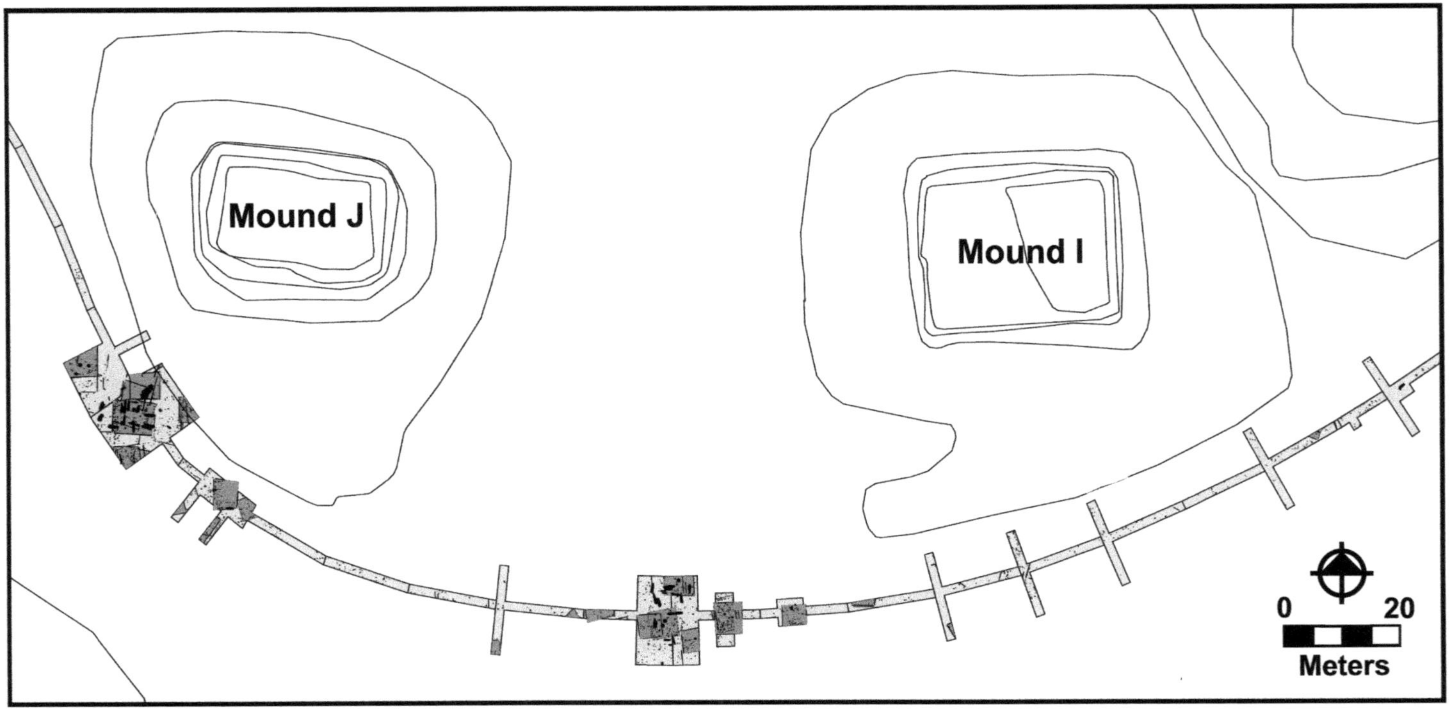

Figure 4.16. Residential Group 5 (26+00 to 34+00).

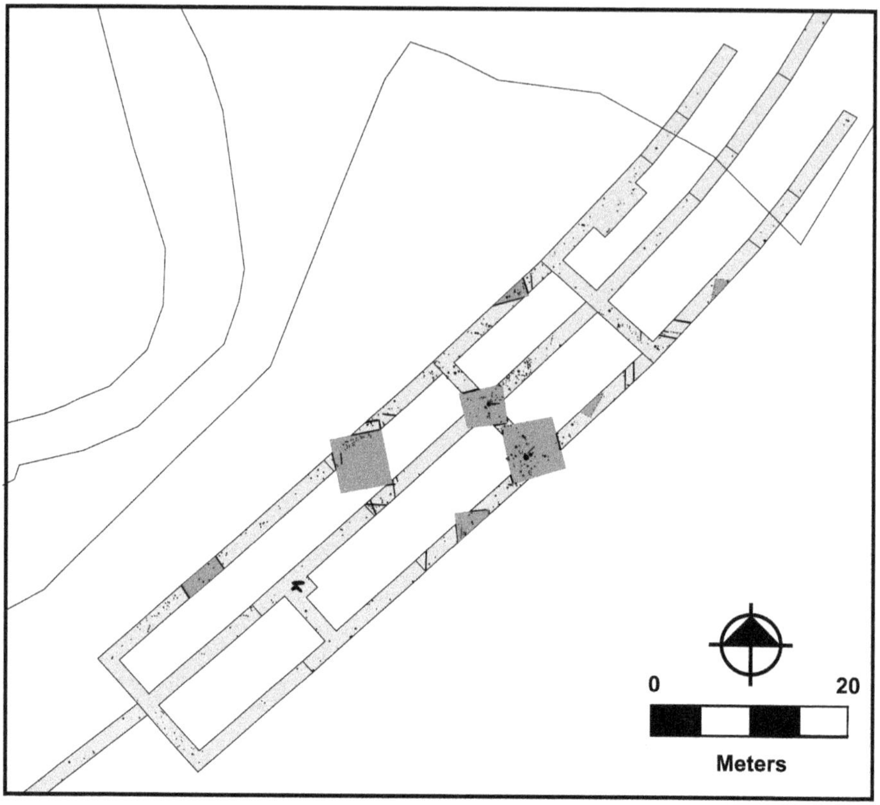

Figure 4.17. Residential Group 6 (35+50 to 37+60).

Residential Group 9

Residential Group 9 includes Roadway blocks 47+50 to 49+00 and is located 34 m southwest of Mound F. Architecture in this area consists of a nucleated cluster of eight Class I domestic structures arranged in a tight cluster around a 6-×-7-m central area that may have been a courtyard (Figure 4.20). In addition, there are numerous lines of posts and several hearths in this area that could not be assigned to discrete structures.

Immediately to the northeast of these domestic structures is a palimpsest of one Class III and three Class II structures. On the basis of their large size and unusual architectural features, these were probably public buildings used by the members of this local residential group. Several rectilinearly arranged burial clusters were placed in this area during the Moundville II and III phases.

Residential Group 10

Residential Group 10 includes Roadway blocks 66+00 to 72+00 and is located immediately north of Mound Q (Figure 4.21). The architecture in this area con-

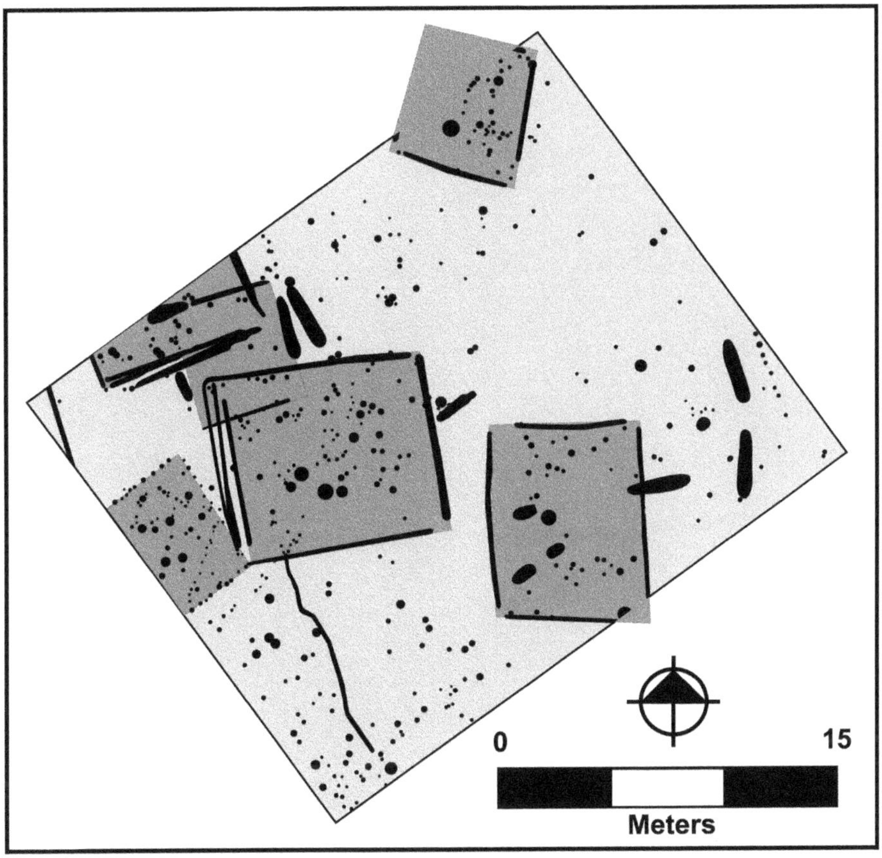

Figure 4.18. Residential Group 7 (Administration Building).

sists of three Class I, two Class II, and one Class III building. Also present in this area are a number of wall trenches and lines of posts that could not be assigned to a discrete building. These buildings and unassigned architectural features are distributed in two small clusters separated by a 31-m area of the Roadway devoid of features. The western cluster of buildings includes Structure 85, a square Class III structure with a floor area measuring 60 m^2. On the basis of its large size and close proximity to Mound Q, it was probably a public building. Several additional buildings and unassigned wall trenches are located immediately to the northeast and northwest of Structure 85, forming a central courtyard. Scattered throughout Residential Group 10 are small clusters of burials dating to Moundville II and III.

Residential Groups 11 and 12

Residential Groups 11 and 12 consist of the PA and ECB tracts, respectively (Figure 4.22). Both residential groups are located on the Moundville riverbank in the

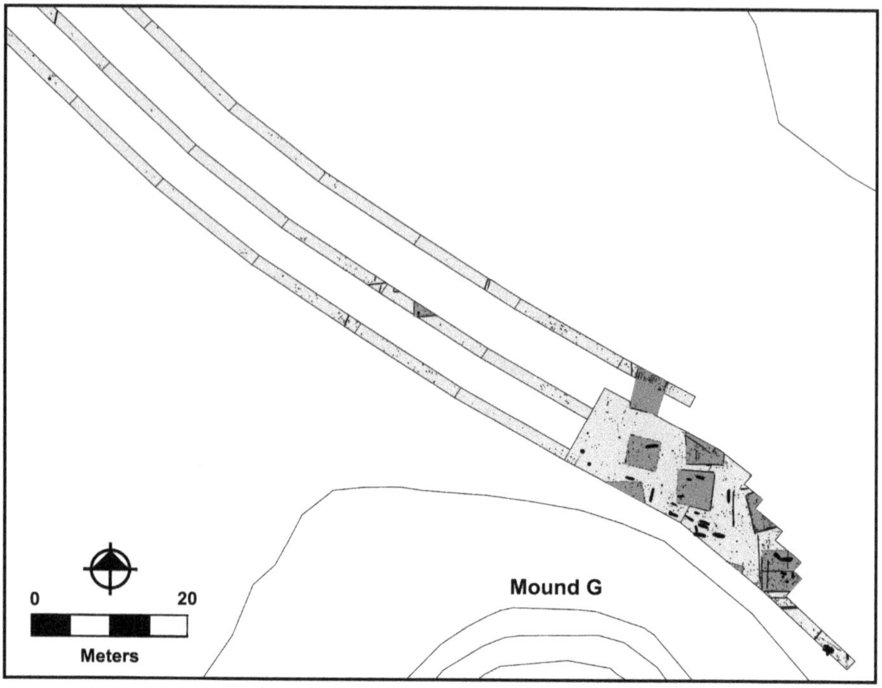

Figure 4.19. Residential Group 8 (43+50 to 46+50).

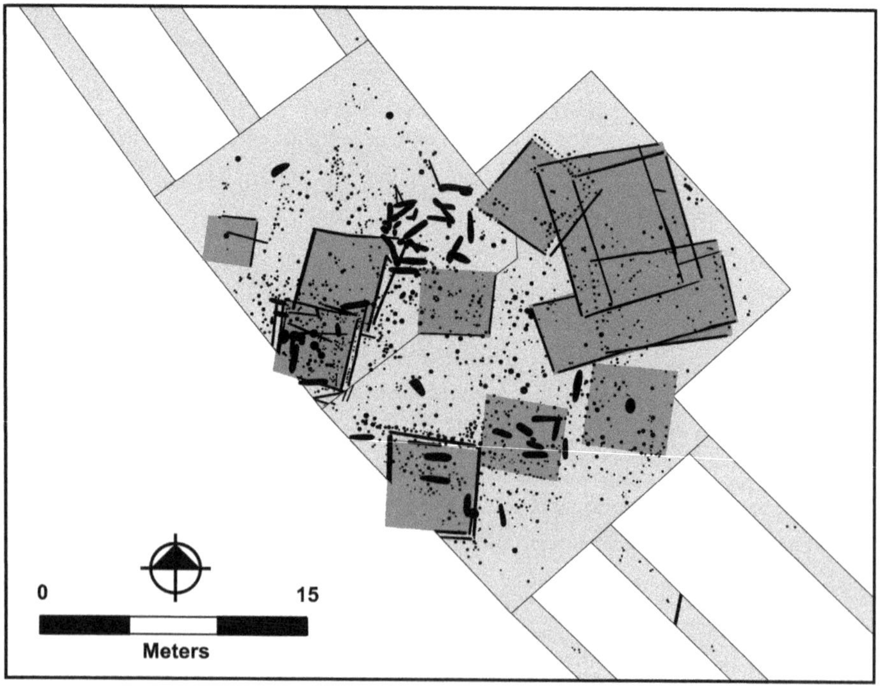

Figure 4.20. Residential Group 9 (47+50 to 49+00).

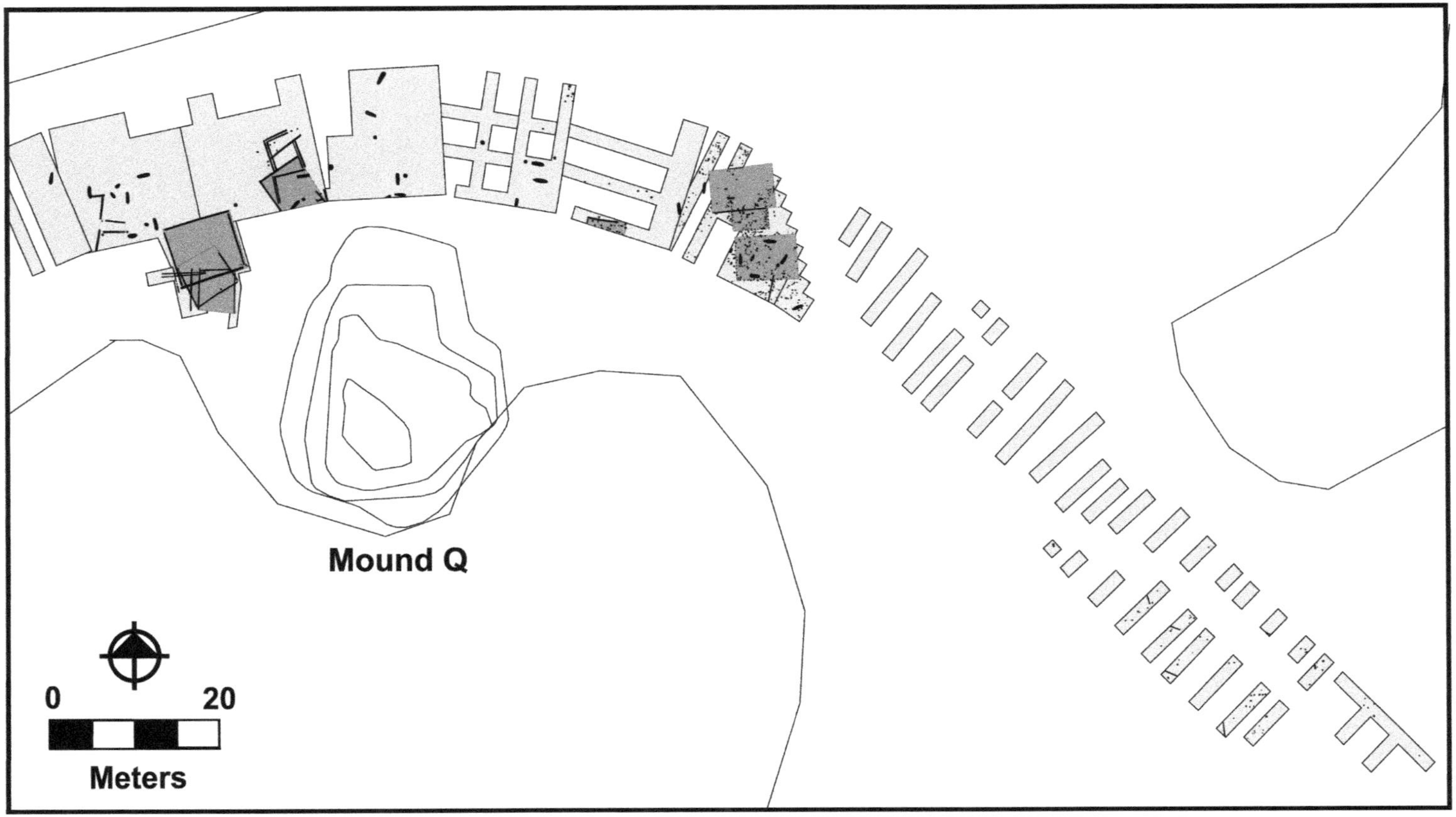

Figure 4.21. Residential Group 10 (66+00 to 72+00).

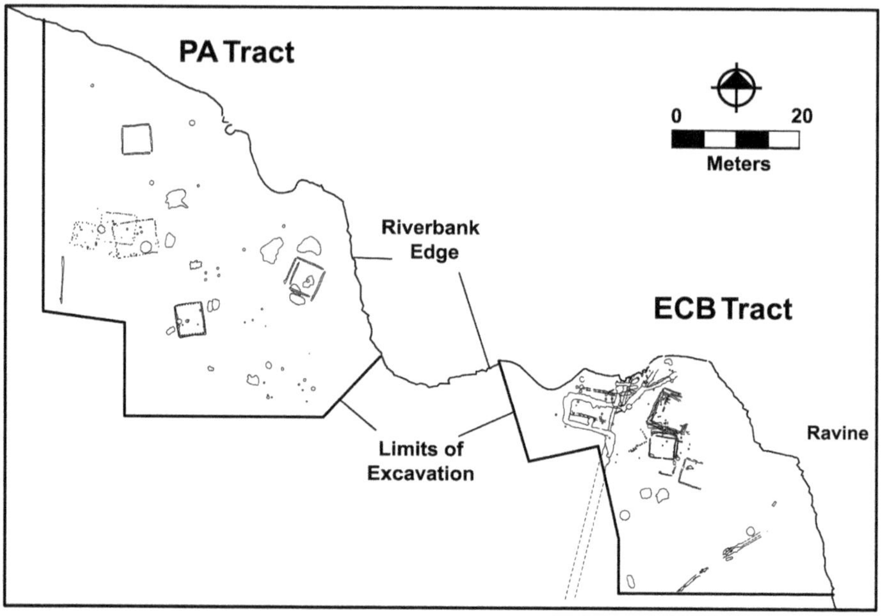

Figure 4.22. Residential Groups 11 (PA tract) and 12 (ECB tract).

northwestern portion of the Moundville site (Scarry 1995, 1998). The PA tract consists of six Class I structures. Three of these are superimposed single-post structures that likely represent a rebuilt dwelling associated with a single early Moundville I household (Scarry 1998). The three other structures in this area are widely spaced, a pattern that contrasts with the nucleated architectural arrangements throughout much of the Moundville Roadway.

The ECB tract contains a total of six structures. Two of these are Class II structures. The other four buildings were not completely mapped, making it impossible to assign them to a size class. Also present in this area is a portion of the palisade wall that surrounded the site during the Moundville I phase. Counting the number of palisade trenches visible in this area, Scarry (1998:82) was able to determine that this fortification wall was rebuilt a minimum of six times. The close proximity of late Moundville I structures in this area is a pattern that more closely corresponds with that of the nucleated residential organization throughout the Moundville Roadway.

Summary of Residential Group Patterns

There appear to be some consistencies in residential group organization. Most groups consist of a small, nucleated cluster of 10 to 20 domestic structures separated by areas with little or no evidence of subsurface features. The largest examples appear to consist of multiple smaller building clusters. Most of the buildings within residential groups are small Class I structures. However, large public structures are associated with four residential groups. Similar public buildings may have also been associated with other residential groups; however, the narrow boundaries of the Moundville Roadway often limit the complete identification of residential group size and composition.

Individual households are difficult to identify within residential groups, suggesting that multihousehold groups were the basal social and residential units at early Moundville. Houses within residential groups appear to be spatially arranged so as to provide space for both foot travel and small-group domestic tasks. For example, Residential Group 8 exhibits a linear arrangement of buildings consisting of three rows of at least six structures (Figure 4.19). Cleared pathways lie between these rows, perhaps to facilitate the movement of people to and from Mound G, located immediately to the south. This rowlike structure is also observable in Residential Group 5, where pathways between linearly aligned buildings would have enabled movement to and from Mound J, immediately to the north (Figure 4.16). Small, central yards are also observable in Residential Groups 5, 8, and 10. These cleared areas may have been the loci for a variety of domestic and ritual activities.

Changing Community Patterns

Analysis of the Roadway architecture allows for a detailed examination of Moundville's occupational history. In this section I consider how and when the nucleated early Mississippian community at Moundville was first settled and later abandoned. The principal evidence I use to examine this process consists of the number and location of chronologically sensitive architectural styles, methods of structure repair, and the date and location of burials.

Diachronic Changes in Household Distribution

I begin by comparing the number of early Moundville I buildings with those dating from late Moundville I to early Moundville II. The early Moundville I group includes single-post and hybrid single-post/wall-trench structures while the late Moundville I–early Moundville II group consists entirely of wall-trench structures. Table 4.2 presents the counts and percentages of different styles of Mississippian structures by residential group. The wall-trench structures (n = 100) represent 66.2 percent of all Mississippian structures uncovered in the Moundville Roadway and Riverbank excavations. The remaining 33.8 percent of Mississippian structures are represented by 24 single-post buildings, 11 hybrid buildings, and 16 buildings that could not be assigned to a particular style class. The unassigned buildings all have at least one wall-trench foundation and probably date to late Moundville I to early Moundville II. Because of their incomplete excavation, however, it is impossible to rule out the possibility that they are hybrid buildings.

Table 4.2. Counts of buildings by construction style

Residential Group	Area	Single Post		Hybrid		Wall Trench		Indeterminate		Total	
		N	%	N	%	N	%	N	%	N	%
1	2+50–7+50 and MPA	7	19.4	1	2.8	22	61.1	6	16.7	36	100.0
2	12+00–14+00	2	20.0	1	10.0	7	70.0			10	100.0
3	15+00–15+50					1	100.0			1	100.0
4	17+50–24+50	1	3.9	2	7.7	17	65.4	6	23.1	26	100.0
5	26+00–34+00	2	9.1	3	13.6	16	72.7	1	4.6	22	100.0
6	35+50–37+60	2	25.0	1	12.5	4	50.0	1	12.5	8	100.0
7	ADM	1	16.7			4	66.7	1	16.7	6	100.0
8	43+50–46+50	1	10.0	1	10.0	8	80.0			10	100.0
9	47+50–49+00	2	16.7	1	8.3	9	75.0			12	100.0
10	66+00–72+00	2	25.0			6	75.0			8	100.0
11	PA	3	50.0	1	16.7	2	33.3			6	100.0
12	ECB	1	16.7			4	66.7	1	16.7	6	100.0
Total		24	15.9	11	7.3	100	66.2	16	10.6	151	100.0

These data indicate a larger early Moundville I occupation of the Moundville site than previously expected. In addition, there appears to be a small early Moundville I occupation preceding a much larger late Moundville I occupation in nearly every residential group identified in the Moundville Roadway and Riverbank (Table 4.2). This evidence alters our understanding of how the Moundville community was initially settled. It now appears that aspects of Moundville's highly structured community organization, represented in the layout of monumental architecture, were already being negotiated during the early Moundville I phase.

Architectural Repair and Rebuilding

Patterns of architectural repair and rebuilding provide additional evidence regarding diachronic changes in household organization at Moundville. I have documented two techniques of architectural rebuilding at early Moundville that I argue relate to different kinds of residential organization (Wilson 2001). The first rebuilding technique consists of the complete rebuilding of a structure. Although salvageable construction materials from the previous structure may be recycled, the new structure is completely rebuilt, albeit usually in a different location. Insect infestation, soil depletion, and the accumulation of refuse would have provided strong motivation for people to choose new locations when rebuilding Mississippian flexed-pole structures. On the basis of the low number of in situ rebuilding episodes identified at Mississippian farmsteads throughout the Southeast it appears that when space was available, households opted to relocate rather than rebuild in the same location. Under such circumstances, domestic space would have also been less rigidly structured by public concerns regarding the placement of paths, storage facilities, and the location of specialized activity areas.

The second rebuilding technique involves in situ repair. In this scenario the use life of a structure is prolonged through the repair and replacement of key architectural components such as walls, roofs, and internal hearths. Under more nucleated conditions, households would have organized domestic space in direct relation to their neighbors. The incorporation of communal work areas and paths into the domestic sphere necessitates a more formalized spatial arrangement of houses and other residential facilities. As a consequence, households may not have had the luxury of relocating to new areas when structure rebuilding was necessary.

The archaeological signatures of a complete rebuilding strategy should be discernable from those of an in situ repair strategy, including the lack of a shared spatial alignment of nearby structures, an absence of paths between and around structures, and the presence of superimposed rebuilt structures whose walls have variable orientations. In contrast, an in situ repair strategy should exhibit a more formalized spatial arrangement of domestic structures in relation to shared work

Table 4.3. Counts of in situ building episodes by structure style

Number of Building Episodes	Single Post	Hybrid	Wall Trench	Indeterminate	Total
1	22	10	43	3	78
2	2		34	2	38
3			11		11
4			2		2
Total	24	10	90	5	129

spaces, storage facilities, and paths. There should also be multiple in situ building episodes, with later houses maintaining an alignment consistent with earlier building stages.

Table 4.3 lists the number of in situ building episodes for early Moundville I (single-post and hybrid) and late Moundville I–early Moundville II (wall-trench) structures from the Moundville Roadway and Riverbank excavations.[4] These data reveal a sharp contrast between the two architectural groups in terms of structure rebuilding techniques. Only 6 percent (n = 2) of the early Moundville I structures exhibit any evidence of in situ rebuilding. Moreover, these two structures were rebuilt only once (Table 4.3). In contrast, over half (52 percent) of the structures in the late Moundville I–early Moundville II group exhibit evidence of in situ rebuilding. Many of these buildings were rebuilt two and even three times (Table 4.3).

These contrasting strategies of architectural repair correlate with changes in the distribution of early Mississippian households at Moundville. During the early Moundville I phase, residential groups at Moundville consisted of only a few households occupying a small number of widely spaced domestic structures. Scarry (1995, 1998) first documented this household organizational pattern in her analysis of the Moundville Riverbank architecture. On the basis of the wide spacing of single-post and hybrid structures in the PA tract, she concluded that "there would have been room for gardens and, perhaps, some fields near the dwellings" (Scarry 1998:93). Indeed, my analysis of the Roadway architecture indicates that early Moundville I households took advantage of the space available to them, shifting their residences to new (though often adjacent) locations rather than repairing them in situ.

The expansion of residential groups during the late Moundville I phase entailed a reorganization of domestic space. Late Moundville I residential groups consisted of tightly arranged clusters of domestic structures, most of which shared a similar orientation. Domestic structures were sometimes built around shared activity spaces and other times aligned in rows to create pathways. In addition, large public structures were built that created well-defined ceremonial spaces within residential group areas. The shift to an in situ architectural repair strategy reveals the importance of maintaining a more formalized organization of domestic space. By repairing and rebuilding structures in place, structured domestic spatial arrangements could be maintained for several decades.

Although gardens could have been cultivated along the edges of these expanded residential groups, it is likely that most agricultural fields were located outside the palisaded boundaries of the nucleated late Moundville I community. Collectively, these agricultural changes and the expansion of residential groups may have entailed a reallocation of land use and reorganization of domestic labor during the late Moundville I phase. That is, the increasing size of residential groups may have promoted or even required closer socioeconomic ties just as the removal of agricultural fields from the domestic sphere may have entailed a more corporate system of land use and agricultural labor organization.

Estimating Occupation Span

The architectural palimpsests of the Moundville Roadway and Riverbank provide important information about the span of Moundville's early Mississippian occupation. The maximum number of sequential building episodes in a residential group can provide a reasonable estimate for how long it was occupied. Extracting this information, however, hinges on calculating reliable use-life estimates for Mississippian architecture.

Use-life estimates for Mississippian structures vary on the basis of whether one places more faith in ethnohistorical reports, archaeological analyses, or experimental studies (Le Page du Pratz 1972 [1758]; Milner 1998; Pauketat 1986, 1989; Swan 1855; Ward and Davis 1991). Ethnohistorical data from the southeastern United States cite longevity estimates ranging from two years for Creek structures (Swan 1855) to 20 years for Natchez structures (Le Page du Pratz 1972 [1758]; see also Davy 1982). These variable reports may result from differences in architectural construction techniques and types of building materials (Milner 1998; Pauketat 1986).

When combined with excavation data, experimental studies provide important insight into structure longevity. Warrick's (1988:37) study of Iroquoian village duration summarizes commercially gathered data on untreated wood-post longevity for northern portions of the Eastern Woodlands. Longevity figures for untreated wood posts varied from 4.5 to 26.9 years with respect to wood type. Surprisingly, soil type was not a major determinant in post longevity. Pretreatment techniques such as burning the butts of posts before setting them in the ground also made little difference in terms of extending use life. Warrick (1988) combined these commercial data with archaeological information on wall-post replacement to estimate the longevity of Iroquoian long houses from several sites in Ontario. The results of his application revealed that (with repair) the use lives of houses varied from 10 to 36 years.[5]

Warrick's study provides insight into how the selection of different wood types affected structure longevity in the Eastern Woodlands. Differences in construction and repair techniques, however, present potentially confounding factors in applying Warrick's method to the Mississippian case. As previously discussed, early Mississippian structures were commonly erected using a flexed-pole technique. In contrast, later Mississippian structures were more often constructed using a rigid-post technology. These two techniques would have produced different kinds of structures requiring different repair techniques and thus having potentially different use lives.

With flexed-pole structures, wall posts were simply bent over and interwoven to create a rounded roof. In this case, the structure's walls and roof were both constructed from the same poles, and the entire building's superstructure was held together through a kind of flexed tension (Lacquement 2004; Lewis and Kneberg 1946). As a result of this interwoven framework, it may have been difficult to conduct localized repairs. Thus, when individual posts began to rot it was probably necessary to replace entire linear wall/roof sections to repair the structure. This situation probably explains the pattern of frequent wall replacement commonly represented in the archaeological signatures of early Mississippian structures throughout the southeastern United States.

Pauketat (2003) has recently revised estimates for the longevity of early Mississippian flexed-pole structures in the American Bottom region of southwestern Illinois. These new estimates were derived from a tabulation of structure rebuilding and replacement episodes from the ICT-II and Tract 15A excavations at the Cahokia site. Superimposed structures and structures with rebuilt walls provided the principal evidence for his investigation. A highly consistent rate of structure rebuilding and replacement was evident for both residential areas at Cahokia. On the basis of a calculation of structure rebuilding per phase, Pauketat (2003) arrived at a minimum longevity estimate of 12 years for Mississippian structures in the American Bottom. Thus, Cahokian structures lasted for a minimum of 12 years before major rebuilding or replacement was necessary. However, minor forms of repair probably took place much earlier in a structure's use life.

On the basis of the technological similarities between Cahokian flexed-pole structures and those from the Moundville area, I adopt Pauketat's 12-year use-life estimate for the current study. The feasibility of this 12-year estimate depends on the availability of hardwoods for wall-post construction (Warrick 1988). In areas where hardwoods were scarce or in situations in which walls were built from a combination of wood types, structure use lives would have been more abbreviated.

Table 4.4. Residential group occupation estimates based on total building episodes

Residential Group	Area	EMI	LMI–EMII	Occupation Span (yr)[a]
1	2+50–7+50 and MPA	2 (24 yr)	5 (60 yr)	84
2	12+00–14+00	1 (12 yr)	4 (48 yr)	60
3	15+00–15+50	0	1 (12 yr)	12
4	17+50–24+50	1 (12 yr)	5 (60 yr)	72
5	26+00–34+00	1 (12 yr)	5 (60 yr)	72
6	35+50–37+60	1 (12 yr)	3 (36 yr)	48
7	ADM	1 (12 yr)	4 (48 yr)	60
8	43+50–46+50	1 (12 yr)	5 (60 yr)	72
9	47+50–49+00	1 (12 yr)	5 (60 yr)	72
10	66+00–72+00	1 (12 yr)	5 (60 yr)	72
11	PA	3 (36 yr)	2 (24 yr)	60
12	ECB	0	5 (60 yr)	60

[a](EMI + LMI–EMII) × 12.

A means of estimating the life span of rigid-post structures awaits further investigations of late Mississippian construction and repair techniques. Rigid-post structures had more substantial wall foundations than flexed-pole structures, in addition to separate roof components. Larger and more substantial wall posts would have positively contributed to structure longevity. Rigid-post structures may have also had a practical advantage over flexed-pole structures in terms of repair technology. With separate roof and wall components, it may have been possible to selectively replace individual components of a building's superstructure as they degraded. As a result of the more flexible repair strategies afforded by this architectural design, rigid-post structures probably had longer use lives than structures built using a flexed-pole method.

Occupation Estimates by Residential Group

Table 4.4 presents minimum estimates for the occupation spans of different early Mississippian residential groups at Moundville. These estimates were determined by summing the total number of in situ and superimposed building episodes in the most stratified palimpsest of each residential group. The total building episodes (TBE) were calculated separately for both the early Moundville I (EMI) and late Moundville I–early Moundville II (LMI–EMII) architectural groups. Finally, the TBE figures from both architectural groups were added and then multiplied by Pauketat's 12-year use-life estimate for Mississippian flexed-pole structures ([EMI + LMI–EMII] × 12 years) to calculate the minimum occupation span estimate for

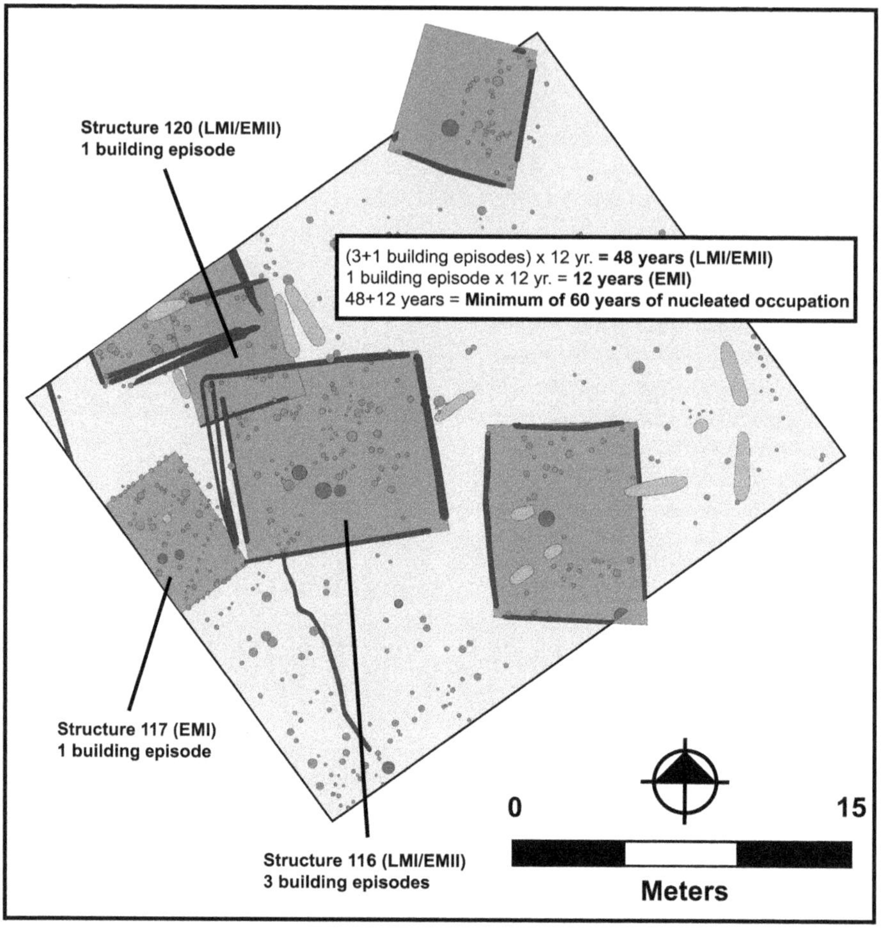

Figure 4.23. Use-life occupation estimate technique applied to Residential Group 7.

a residential group. This is a minimum estimate, as it is possible and probable that households built new structures that did not overlap with previous structures. This would have been the case particularly during the early Moundville I period when widely spaced households often rebuilt houses in new locations.

An example of this technique is presented in Figure 4.23, which illustrates a set of superimposed and in situ rebuilt structures from Residential Group 7. In this case, Structure 117 is a single-post structure with one building episode creating a TBE of 1 (12 years) for the early Moundville I architectural group. In addition, Structure 120 is a wall-trench building in this group with one building episode. It was superimposed by Structure 116, a wall-trench building with three building episodes creating a TBE of 4 (48 years) for the late Moundville I–early Moundville II group. Collectively, these two figures produce a minimum occupation estimate of 60 years for Residential Group 7.

Residential groups with larger excavation blocks and more numerous structures are better suited for this analysis than those with more segmented excavations and fewer structures. For example, the 12-year estimate for Residential Group 3 is based on only one structure and is not representative of most other areas. Likewise, the segmented excavation of Residential Group 6 hinders the accurate identification of structure building episodes.

Seven of the 12 residential groups in the study have a TBE of 5 for the late Moundville I phase. This building index correlates with a minimum occupation span of 60 years for the late Moundville I phase. The most complex set of superimposed structures during the early Moundville I phase is located in the PA tract. Here there are three superimposed single-post structures. This building index correlates with a minimum occupation span of 36 years. Collectively, the data on architectural rebuilding from the structure groups from both periods indicate about a century (96 years) of early Mississippian occupation.

Figure 4.24 compares the results of these occupation-span estimates to the 140-year Moundville I phase. The 60-year occupation-span estimate calculated for the late Moundville I–early Moundville II group fits nicely with the latter half of the Moundville I phase. This number also correlates well with estimates for the duration of Moundville's palisade (Scarry 1998:82). The 36-year occupation-span estimate for the early Moundville I phase is not as good a fit with the calibrated dates for this subphase. Taken at face value these data indicate that Moundville was occupied for only a portion of the early Moundville I phase. It is more likely, however, that the paucity of early Moundville I households, combined with their practice of rebuilding structures in new locations, generated far fewer palimpsests than did the more nucleated late Moundville I community.

Intracommunity Status Differences

The structured layout of mounds at Moundville has been interpreted as indicating the presence of a number of ranked social groups (Knight 1998). The incremental decrease in mound size from the northern to southern portion of the site is thought to mark a basic polarity of space and power (Knight 1998). However, it is unclear how pronounced this power asymmetry was. Were hierarchical relationships between groups primarily ceremonial in nature, or did they entail material inequalities in the day-to-day lives of community members?

Data on the size and style of domestic architecture from the Moundville Roadway provide one line of evidence by which to examine this issue. As discussed in

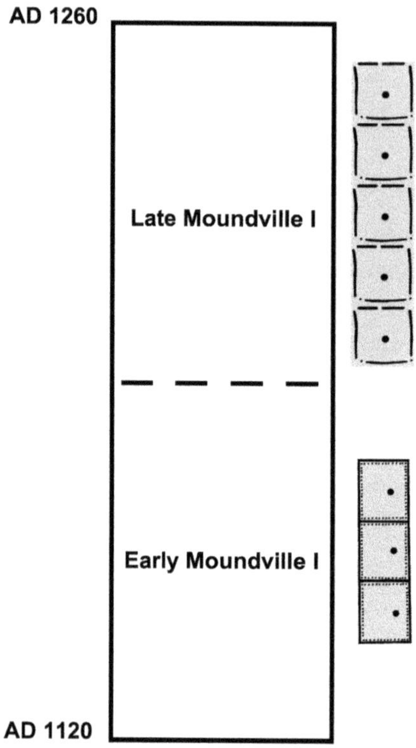

Figure 4.24. Calibrated Moundville I chronology with the total number of structure building episodes per subphase (each structure scaled to represent 12 years).

Chapter 2, house size is often correlated with household size. In turn, household size is correlated with status and wealth (Kramer 1982; Netting 1982; Wilk 1983). If hierarchical relationships produced material inequities between different social groups at Moundville, it should be observable in the distribution of house sizes.

Sample size differences make it difficult to directly compare the distribution of floor areas among individual residential groups. Thus, I combine structures into larger spatial groups for the purpose of comparison. Figure 4.25 compares the distribution of structure floor areas from the northern and southern portions of the Moundville Roadway; Figure 4.26 compares the distribution of floor areas from the eastern and western portions of the Moundville Roadway. Neither graph reveals any statistical differences between respective portions of the Moundville site with regard to structure size. Thus, while there do appear to be differences in household size within residential groups, there do not appear to have been dramatic differences between residential groups. This is an important point, as there are no detectable differences in household size that correspond with the ranked distribution and sizes of mounds at the site.

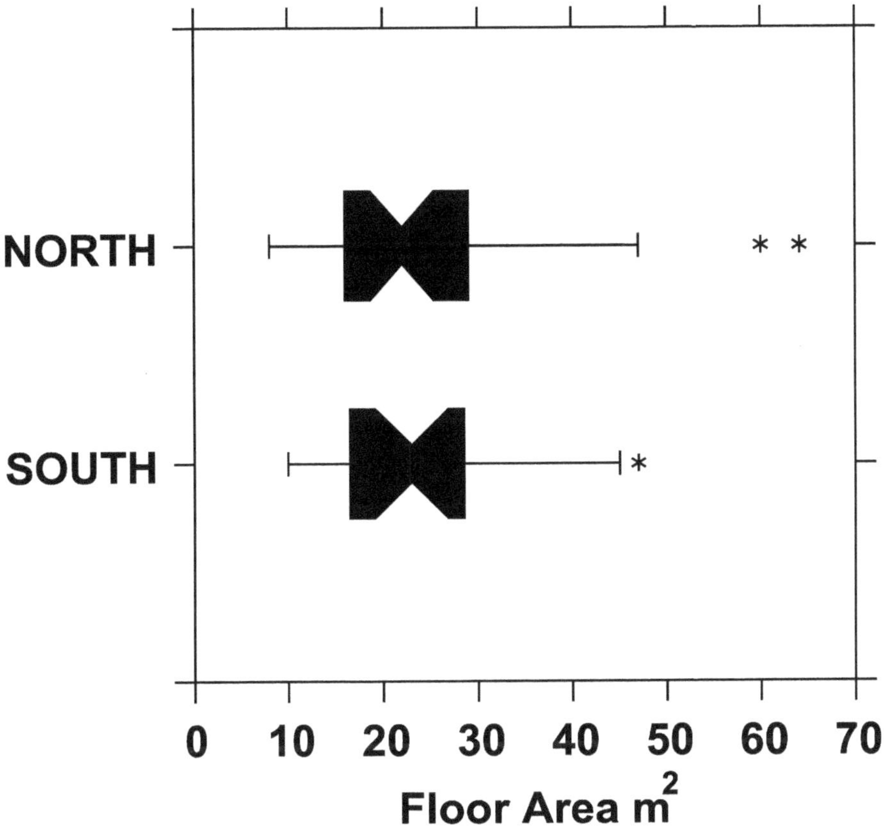

Figure 4.25. Structure floor areas from the southern and northern portions of the Moundville Roadway.

Mortuary Patterns

A total of 279 burials were identified in the Roadway excavations. Ten more were identified in the ECB tract Riverbank excavations (Scarry 1995). Most of these burials are distributed in small, rectilinear clusters with individual burials oriented generally in the cardinal directions (Figures 4.12 and 4.20). In terms of composition these cemeteries include men, women, and children of a variety of ages (Powell 1988). Moreover, while the dead were primarily buried in extended positions, there are also numerous examples of secondary mortuary treatments including bundles and individual cranium interments (Peebles 1979).

An examination of the original excavation maps reveals that these burials often superimpose the wall-trench and single-post foundations of early Mississippian structures (Figure 4.7). Indeed, not a single burial from the Roadway is super-

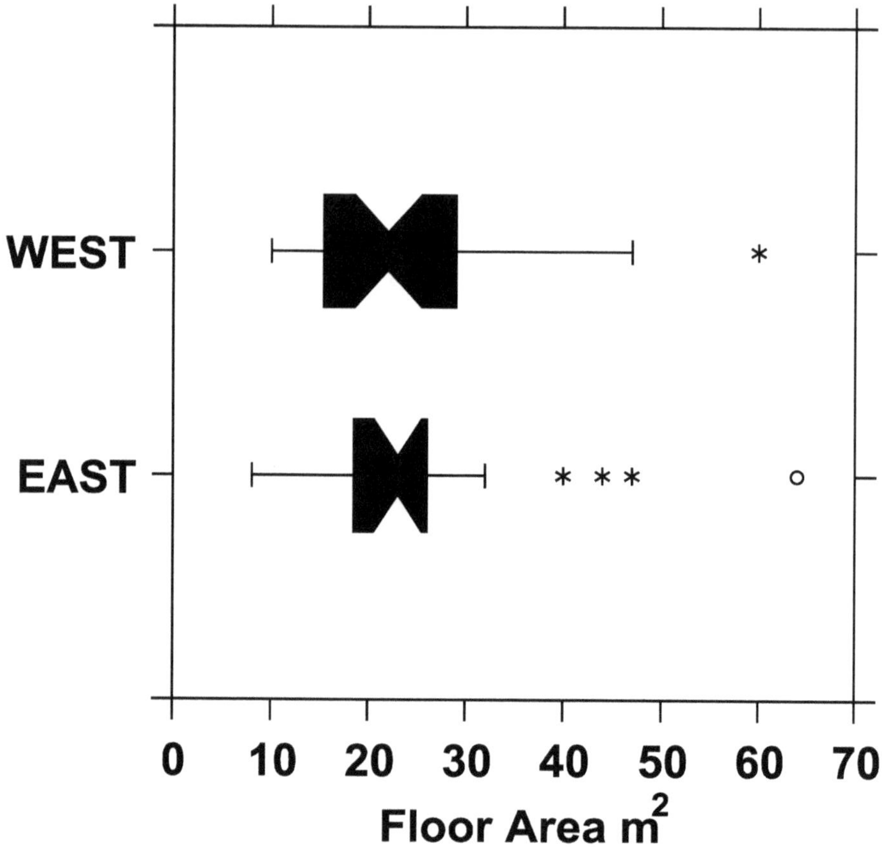

Figure 4.26. Structure floor areas from the eastern and western portions of the Moundville Roadway.

imposed by a wall-trench or single-post building foundation. Moreover, Steponaitis's (1983, 1998) analysis of mortuary vessels at Moundville has revealed that only one of the 34 datable Roadway burials (SK2884) positively dates to the Moundville I phase. In addition, Scarry (1995, 1998) has demonstrated that the 10 burials in the ECB tract postdate the Moundville I phase occupation of the area. These Roadway and Riverbank trends conform to a site-wide pattern identified by Steponaitis (1998:39) in which Moundville's residential population peaked during the Moundville I phase and declined considerably thereafter. During the Moundville II and III phases, Moundville was transformed into a necropolis in which the rural populace of the Black Warrior Valley interred their dead (Steponaitis 1998).

It is important to note that in nearly every case these small Moundville II and III cemeteries in the Moundville Roadway and Riverbank are placed in the same locations as earlier Moundville I residential groups. Very few burials are located outside of these earlier residential areas. Thus, it would appear that people maintained connections with very particular places at Moundville even after the nucleated population had dispersed.

Summary

This study of Mississippian architecture at Moundville has revealed a number of patterns relevant to understanding the span of Moundville's residential occupation and how it changed organizationally through time. I have created maps from five different residential groups to visually represent these organizational changes in the community (Figures 4.27–4.31). Each map reveals a similar pattern of occupation. The Mississippian occupation of every residential group was first established in the early Moundville I phase. During this time each residential group was composed of only a few households occupying a small number of single-post and hybrid buildings. Households took advantage of the space available to them and often shifted locations when they rebuilt their domestic structures.

During the subsequent late Moundville I phase Moundville's population increased dramatically. Each residential group expanded in size. In addition, larger houses and public structures were built, indicating an increasing diversification of household sizes. Though minor, this variation in house size suggests an increasing differentiation in household statuses at Moundville. Differences in house size, however, appear within every residential group and are not restricted to certain areas of the Moundville site. Thus, the ranking of clans at Moundville, represented in the distribution of volumes and sizes of mounds, does not appear to have correlated with differences in household size.

The late Moundville I expansion of residential groups entailed a more formalized use of domestic space. Residential group members adopted an in situ architectural rebuilding strategy to maintain a more structured layout and use of both domestic and ceremonial space. The size and corporate organization of these residential groups conform to ethnohistoric descriptions of Southeastern matrilineages (Hudson 1976:189; Speck 1907; Swanton 1922). Like matrilineages, early Mississippian residential groups functioned as social and economic groups, the members of which interacted on a daily basis. Moreover, the introduction of large public buildings linked with individual residential groups indicates some degree of corporate social and ceremonial autonomy. While the chiefly elite may have usurped important aspects of mound-and-plaza ceremonialism at Moundville, small-scale residential groups maintained their own ceremonial facilities and practices.

If these residential groups were organized like matrilineages, then their locations at Moundville may correspond with broader clan residential and ceremonial precincts at the site. Indeed, if Knight's (1998) interpretation of Moundville as a "planned community" is correct, the entire community was divided into a number

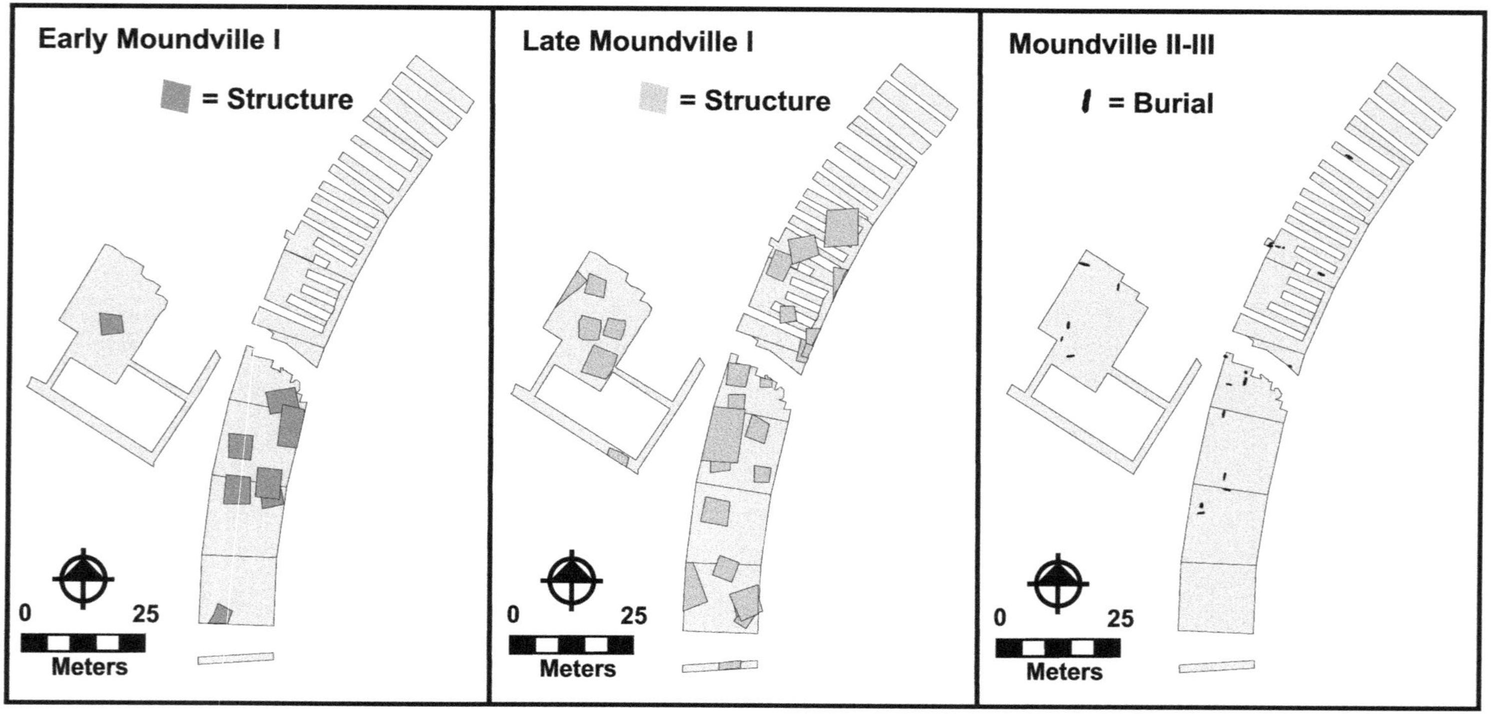

Figure 4.27. Model of diachronic occupational changes in Residential Group 1.

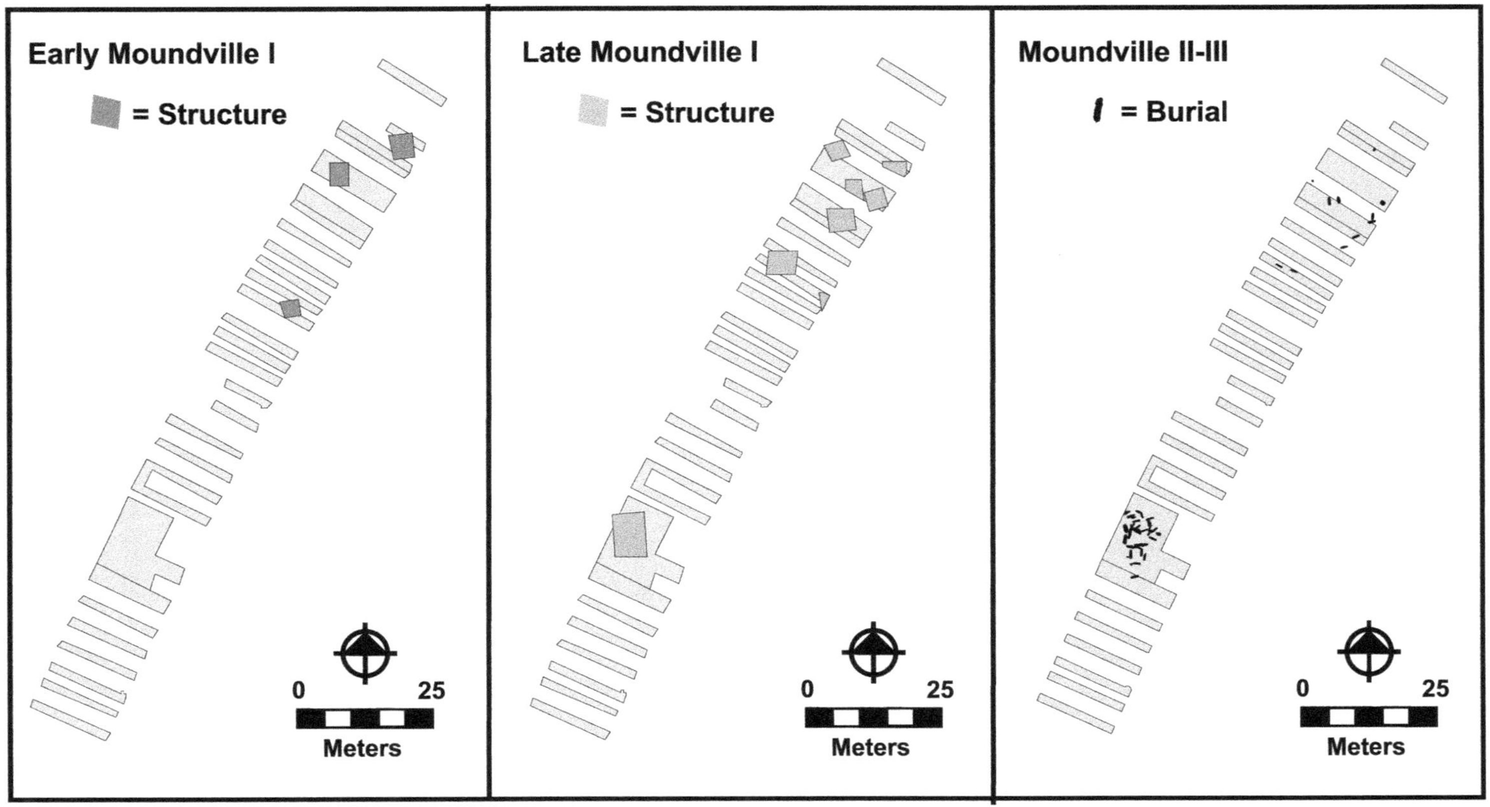

Figure 4.28. Model of diachronic occupational changes in Residential Groups 2 and 3.

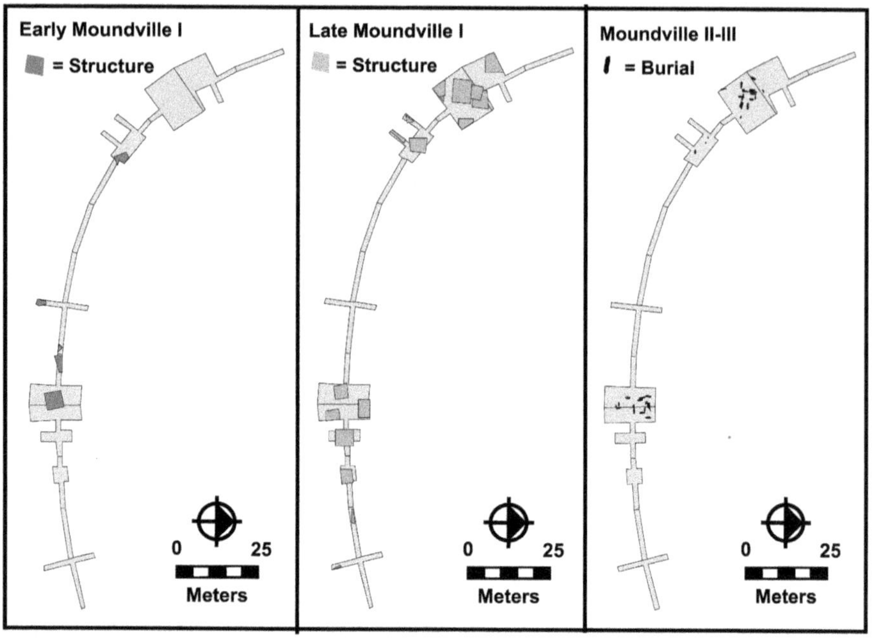

Figure 4.29. Model of diachronic occupational changes in Residential Group 5.

of corporate kin segments, each with its own platform and burial mounds and residential district. From this perspective, peoples' identities within the broader political and ceremonial order were physically mapped onto the Moundville community. Thus, it would have been important for kin groups to maintain a strong connection with their lineage/clan space at the Moundville site.

My analysis of architectural rebuilding episodes generated an estimate of 60 years for Moundville's late Moundville I occupation. After this period of nucleated occupation, most of Moundville's residents vacated the site. During the Moundville II phase residential group space was converted into mortuary space (see also Steponaitis 1998). Many small and compact cemeteries were placed directly on top of abandoned residential areas. Very few burials are located outside of these earlier residential group areas in the Moundville Roadway and Riverbank. Kin group ties to particular locations at Moundville may help explain this pattern—one of the most symbolic ways that group members can naturalize their connection and claim to a particular space is by burying their ancestors there (Charles and Buikstra 1983).

It appears that connections with particular places and spaces at Moundville were very important to community members. These social connections to community space were first initiated during the early Moundville I phase by a small number of Mississippian households. During the late Moundville I phase kin groups formal-

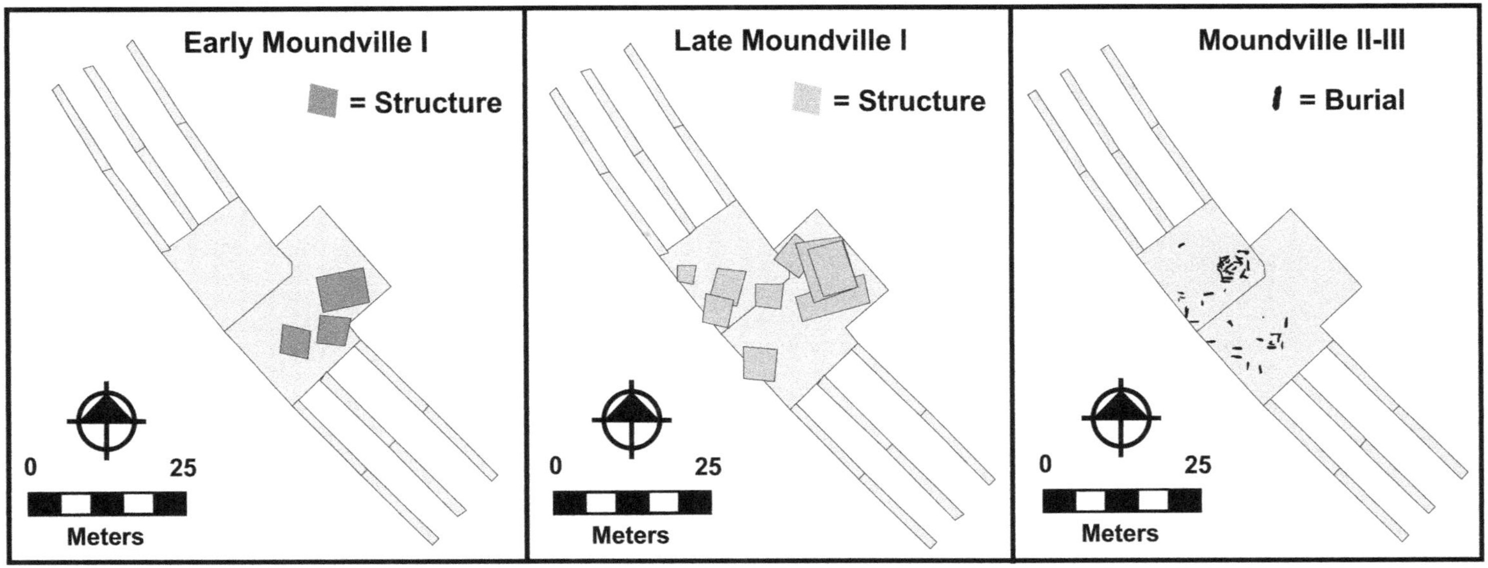

Figure 4.30. Model of diachronic occupational changes in Residential Group 9.

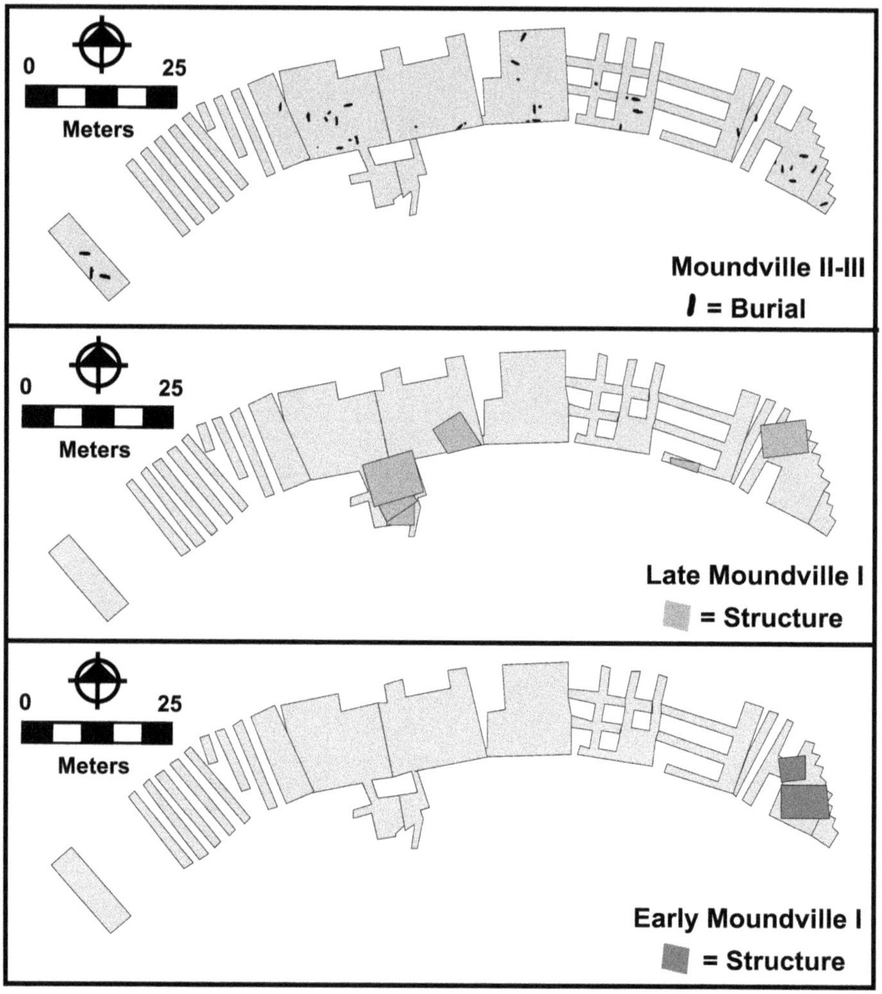

Figure 4.31. Model of diachronic occupational changes in Residential Group 10.

ized their connections to community space as they expanded in size and strengthened their corporate organization. During this period everyday domestic practices of house construction and rebuilding served to produce their space and place within the broader political and ceremonial order. These kin groups continued to claim these social and physical places by returning to bury their dead generations after their ancestors had moved away from Moundville.

5 Ceramics at Early Moundville

The analysis of archaeological ceramics in the southeastern United States has traditionally been directed toward building regional chronologies and defining areas of cultural interaction. In the past 20 years, however, there has been an expanding body of research aimed at linking archaeological ceramic assemblages to foodways (Blitz 1993a; Hally 1983a, 1984, 1986; Pauketat 1987, 1989; Steponaitis 1983, 1984; Wilson 1999; Wilson and Rodning 2002). Drawing from both technological and ethnohistorical studies, Southeastern archaeologists have devised an analytical framework by which to determine how pots were used and what the number, combination, and size of different pots in a domestic pottery assemblage indicate about past foodways. In many cases these functional studies have dovetailed with ceramic seriation efforts to provide more fine-grained understandings of socioeconomic organization in the prehistoric Southeast.

The goals of my analysis of the Moundville Roadway vessel assemblage are twofold. The first goal is to determine, on a general level, what the function and relative frequency of different Moundville I phase vessel classes indicate about food storage, preparation, and consumption at early Moundville. The second goal is to compare and contrast different vessel assemblages to determine how, when, and where Mississippian foodways varied at early Moundville. This chapter is devoted to achieving these goals. I begin with a summary of previous research on Mississippian ceramic technology in the Black Warrior Valley. Next, I examine the study assemblage as a whole and present a functional analysis of each vessel class within it. Then, I perform a number of comparisons among the five different ceramic assemblages that comprise the sample.

Methods of Analysis

To examine early Mississippian foodways at Moundville, I identify the full range of vessel types present in the study assemblage. Functional interpretations of individual vessel classes are based on frequency, shape, size, surface treatment, use wear, and paste composition. Below I present a brief discussion of how these different attributes relate to vessel function.

Minimum Number of Vessels

Determining the relative frequency of different vessel classes in a ceramic assemblage provides clues to the importance of various food preparation, storage, and serving activities. It is important to note that discard assemblages or midden assemblages differ in the relative frequency of different vessel classes from behavioral (or in-use) assemblages (Schiffer 1972, 1977, 1985). Variability in the rate of vessel breakage and replacement generates discard assemblages that differ from behavioral assemblages. Cooking vessels, for example, have higher breakage and replacement rates than serving vessels (David 1972; Foster 1960). Moreover, storage vessels that are infrequently moved about may have longer use lives than serving vessels that are frequently manipulated (DeBoer 1974; DeBoer and Lathrap 1979:128). Thus, the relative frequency of different vessel classes in domestic refuse assemblages can provide important insight into how vessels were used.

An accurate estimation of the minimum number of vessels (MNV) represented in domestic refuse assemblages is a necessary step to any assemblage-level functional analysis. Sherd counts in and of themselves are not a reliable means of estimating MNV (Chase 1985). Differences in vessel size, shape, paste composition, method of breakage, and postdepositional processes can alter the number of sherds that derive from whole vessels. To compensate for this problem it is necessary to tabulate the MNV from diagnostic vessel fragments. It is also necessary to ensure that vessel counts are not inflated by counting multiple sherds from the same vessel. I selected rim sherds for the purpose of estimating MNV because they are easily sorted into discrete vessel classes and provide a suite of other important information about vessel function.[1]

Shape and Size

On a fundamental level pots are tools designed to perform certain tasks. Shape-related factors such as access restriction and vessel stability provide insight into the intended function or functions of a particular vessel shape (Blitz 1993a; Braun 1980, 1983; DeBoer and Lathrap 1979; Hally 1984, 1986; Pauketat 1987; Turner and Lofgren 1966; Welch and Scarry 1995). Size is another important factor related to vessel function. Ethnoarchaeological studies have revealed that large cooking and serving vessels are often a sign that large groups of people gathered to share meals (Blitz 1993a; Turner and Lofgren 1966). In contrast, smaller vessels were often used by individuals or small groups (DeBoer and Lathrap 1979; Henrickson and McDonald 1983). Functional differences may also exist between different size modes with a discrete vessel shape class (Hally 1983b; Wilson and Rodning 2002).

To gather information on vessel shape I sorted each rim sherd in the study as-

Table 5.1. Moundville I vessel counts in the study assemblage by basic shape

Basic Shape	Count	Percent
Unburnished jar	1,278	63.20
Thickened-rim jar	49	2.42
Burnished jar	23	1.14
Bowl[a]	36	1.78
Simple bowl	220	10.88
Restricted bowl	55	2.72
Flaring-rim bowl	212	10.49
Carinated bowl	13	0.64
Cylindrical bowl	5	0.25
Terraced bowl	6	0.30
Peaked bowl	1	0.05
Bottles[b]	46	2.27
Indeterminate[c]	78	3.86
Total	2,022	100.00

[a]"Bowl" is not an actual basic shape category but refers to rims that could not be assigned to a specific bowl category.
[b]Bottles can be subdivided into slender ovoid bottle and cylindrical bottle basic shape classes.
[c]"Indeterminate"is not an actual basic shape category but refers to rims that could not be assigned to any of the other categories.

semblage into one of the 11 basic shape classes listed in Table 5.1. These basic shape classes were either adopted or adapted from previous ceramic research in the Black Warrior Valley and elsewhere in the Mississippian Southeast (see Steponaitis 1983). Vessel orifice diameter serves as a proxy for vessel size in this analysis. Orifice diameter was measured on all vessels with rims representing at least 5 percent of the total vessel orifice.

Paste Composition

Technological studies of archaeological ceramics have demonstrated that vessels with finer pastes exhibit a higher resistance to mechanical stress and a lower resistance to thermal stress than vessels with coarser pastes (Rice 1987; Shepard 1971:131; Steponaitis 1984). Mississippian potters typically used fine-shell and/or grog-tempered pastes to manufacture serving wares (such as bowls, bottles, and beakers) that were exposed repeatedly to mechanical stress (Million 1975; Steponaitis 1984). Coarser shell-tempered pastes typically were selected to manufacture cooking vessels such as jars and pans (Steponaitis 1983, 1984).

The temper of every sherd in the study assemblage was identified with the aid of a 10× hand lens. Temper types in the Moundville Roadway include shell, grog, shell and grog, and grit. A few sherds lacked tempering material. Atypical clays or fine tempers were also noted.

Surface Treatment

Surface treatment provides additional clues to vessel function. Mississippian archaeologists commonly interpret pots with burnished or slipped surfaces as serving containers (Steponaitis 1983). In contrast, pots with plain or unburnished surfaces are often interpreted as cooking or storage containers (Steponaitis 1983). These inferences are based on several lines of evidence. First, burnished or slipped surfaces strongly correlate with Mississippian vessel shapes like bowls and bottles that are conducive to food presentation and consumption. Jars, pans, and other utility wares have basic shapes more conducive to cooking and other preparation activities. Second, many burnished vessels from the Mississippian Southeast were intentionally fired in an oxygen-poor environment (reduced) to create a black, shiny surface. Some burnished vessels were further embellished with incised, excised, and/or engraved designs. Others were painted with mineral pigments to produce red, white, or yellow surface colors. Such decorative treatments are delicate and do not hold up well to prolonged exposure to a cooking fire (Steponaitis 1984). Considering the labor that was invested in decorating serving containers, it is not surprising that most lack sooting, oxidation, and other evidence of thermal alteration (Holmes 1886:272; Wilson 1999). Surface treatments identified in the study assemblage include plain, burnished, slipped, incised, excised, negative painted, and punctated.

Use Wear

Observations of use wear were made only for rim sherds. Three major types of use wear were identified in the study assemblage: sooting, oxidation, and abrasion. Sooting is a dark carbon deposit that accumulates on pots as a result of exposure to a wood fire (Hally 1983a). Oxidation is the result of the organic material in a clay pot being decomposed via exposure to a high-temperature (200°) open-air fire. The locations of sooting and oxidation on a vessel vary according to whether the vessel is placed directly on a fire or elevated above it (Hally 1983a:7). Pots placed directly on a cooking fire tend to accumulate soot in their upper portions and oxidation at their bases (Hally 1983a:10). If a pot is elevated above a cooking fire then sooting may accumulate on the vessel base and upper vessel portions, and there may be little evidence of oxidation.

Abrasion is the result of repeated physical contact with a vessel's surface. Such contact may consist of stirring a vessel's contents, scraping out or removing vessel contents, washing, and even repeated handling (Griffiths 1978). Use wear resulting from these activities includes surface pitting, scratches, and patches of erosion (Griffiths 1978; Hally 1983a, 1983b).

Previous Research on Vessel Function at Moundville

There has been considerable research directed at the issue of Mississippian ceramic technology in the Black Warrior Valley (Hardin 1981; Steponaitis 1983; Taft 1996; Welch 1991b). McKenzie (1964b, 1965) provided one of the first analyses of Mississippian vessel classes from Moundville. On the basis of an examination of whole vessels from mortuary contexts he defined three basic shape forms: jars, bowls, and bottles. McKenzie noted variation within these shape forms but did not define formal vessel subcategories.

Steponaitis (1983, 1984) provided the first functional analysis of Moundville ceramics. He defined two functional categories (service and utility wares) on the basis of a technological analysis of vessel paste recipes, surface treatments, and basic shapes (Steponaitis 1983:33–45). Service wares consist of vessels typically used for eating and storage. Utility wares, on the other hand, consist of vessels used to cook and otherwise prepare foods for consumption.

Steponaitis (1983) also defined 22 basic shape classes, variation among which was demonstrated to be both chronologically and functionally significant. Specific vessel shapes were found to correlate with certain paste recipes and surface treatments. For example, Moundville potters tended to use coarse shell-tempered pastes to make cooking jars and fine-shell and grog-tempered pastes to make serving bowls and bottles (Steponaitis 1983:23–29). Furthermore, Moundville potters typically left jar surfaces undecorated but applied burnished and incised/engraved decorations to the surfaces of bowls and bottles.

Most recently Taft (1996) identified functional differences among different vessel shapes present in Moundville II and III phase midden assemblages excavated from Mounds E, G, and Q at Moundville. Taft's (1996) functional inferences were based on an analysis of vessel shape, size (orifice diameter), and surface treatment. As a result she was able to define the full range of basic shapes present in each of the three assemblages and outline the food preparation, storage, and cooking activities that took place in each of these mound contexts.

Form and Function of Moundville I Vessel Classes

In this section I summarize functionally relevant data for each of the 11 basic shape classes identified in the study assemblage (Figure 5.1, Table 5.1). In so doing, I offer a functional analysis of Moundville I vessel assemblages that builds upon previous investigations. Interassemblage variability is then more fully addressed in the final portion of the chapter.

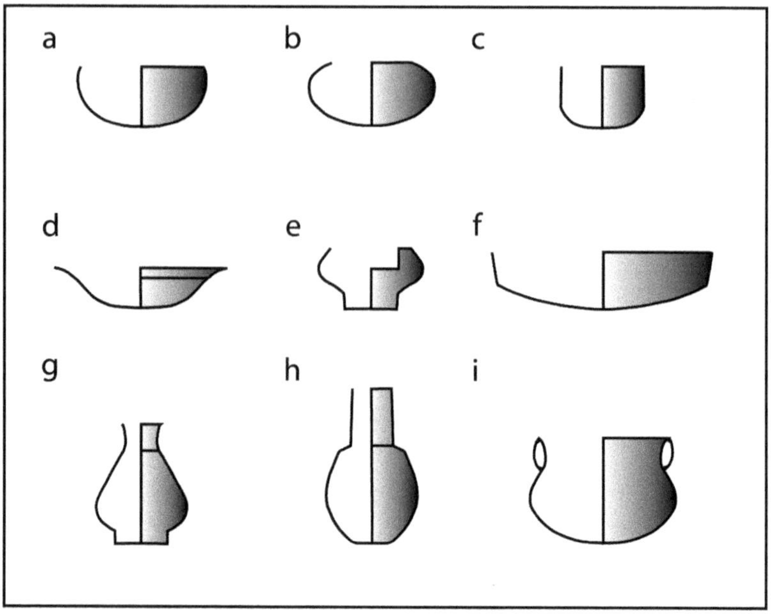

Figure 5.1. Selected Moundville I basic shapes: (a) simple bowl, (b) restricted bowl, (c) cylindrical bowl, (d) shallow flaring-rim bowl, (e) terraced bowl with a pedestaled base, (f) carinated bowl, (g) slender ovoid bottle, (h) cylindrical bottle, (i) unburnished jar (note: thickened-rim jars, burnished jars, and peaked bowls are excluded from this figure because of the fragmentary nature of the few representative vessels).

Unburnished Jars

A minimum number of 1,278 unburnished jars make up 63 percent of the total vessel assemblage. These are shouldered vessels with restricted orifices and subglobular bodies (Figure 5.2; Steponaitis 1983). Unburnished jars are the most common jar type as well as the most common basic shape class in Moundville I assemblages (Scarry 1995; Steponaitis 1983). It is noteworthy that most unburnished jars can be divided into two types on the basis of surface treatment: Mississippi Plain and Moundville Incised (Table 5.2). Mississippi Plain jars are more frequent, with rims representing an MNV of 915 vessels. Moundville Incised jars are less frequent, with rims representing an MNV of 353 vessels.[2] As discussed in Chapter 3, there are diachronic changes in the kinds of decorations (varieties) present on Moundville Incised jars, as well as a gradual decline in the overall popularity of Moundville Incised jars through time. Considering the study assemblage as a whole, Moundville Incised, *var. Moundville* is most common, followed by *varieties Carrollton, Oliver,* and *Snows Bend,* respectively (Table 5.2). The remaining 10 unburnished jars in the assemblage are represented by rims from possible nonlocal pots. These include one Evansville Punctated, one L'Eau Noire Incised, one Late Savannah

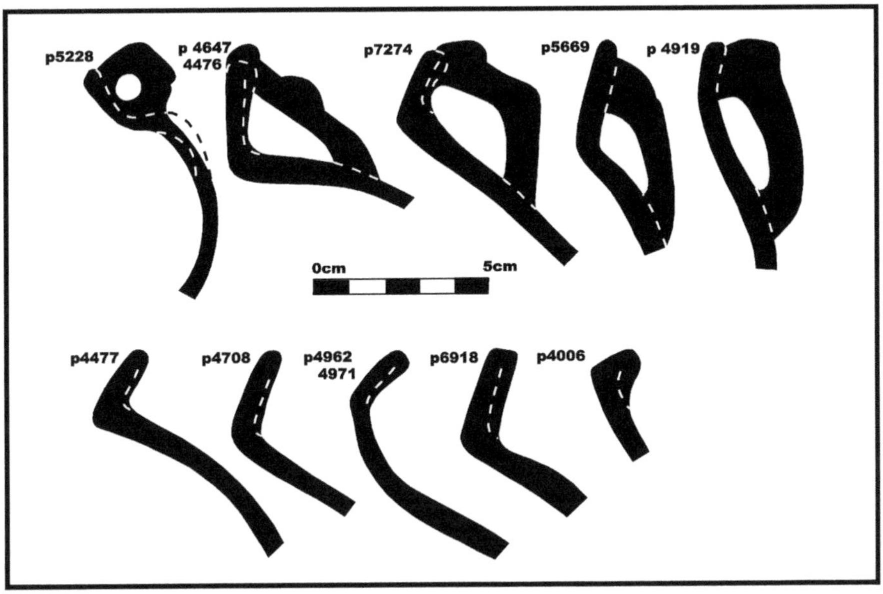

Figure 5.2. Unburnished jar rims.

Simple Stamped, one Mathews Incised, three Mazique Incised, and three Autauga Plain rims (Table 5.2).

There is a unimodal distribution of orifice diameters for unburnished jars that ranges from 9 cm to 52 cm with a median of 28 cm (Figure 5.3). Unburnished jars exhibit considerable evidence of thermal alteration. Traces of sooting were identified on rims from throughout the entire size range of this basic shape class. Moreover, oxidation was present on a number of basal fragments.

Given their shape, size, surface treatment, paste composition, and use-wear patterns, unburnished jars were primarily used for boiling foods like hominy and other dishes but may have also been used as storage containers (Hally 1986; Shapiro 1984; Taft 1996:49; Wright 1958). Hominy preparation requires a boiling period of three to four hours in which a mixture of shelled maize kernels and water is stirred repeatedly. The orifice constriction of unburnished jars would have increased containment security while decreasing rapid evaporation of water during boiling (Linton 1944:370). A pattern of neck abrasion found on several unburnished jars was likely a result of vessel contents being stirred with some kind of spoon or ladle during preparation. Steponaitis (1983) has also demonstrated that the coarse shell-tempered pastes used in the manufacture of most unburnished jars would have increased resistance to thermal shock. Likewise, the absence of burnishing and other delicate surface treatments indicates these vessels were intentionally designed for cooking tasks. Considering their obvious cooking

Table 5.2. Counts of unburnished jars by type and variety

	ADM	43+50–46+00	70+50–72+05	30+00–31+50	MPA	Total
Autauga Plain	2				1	3
Evansville Punctated		1				1
Late Savannah Simple Stamped					1	1
L'Eau Noire Incised					1	1
Mathews Incised		1				1
Mazique Incised		2	1			3
Mississippi Plain, *var. Hull Lake*	2	18	3		3	26
Mississippi Plain, *var. Warrior*	39	391	282	27	150	889
Moundville Incised, *var. Carrollton*	7	12	9		8	36
Moundville Incised, *var. Moundville*	35	104	65	11	43	258
Moundville Incised, *var. Oliver*	2	9	9	1	1	22
Moundville Incised, *var. Snows Bend*		1				1
Moundville Incised, *var. Unspecified*	6	18	5	5	2	36
Total	93	557	374	44	210	1,278

Key: ADM, Administration Building; MPA, Museum Parking Area.

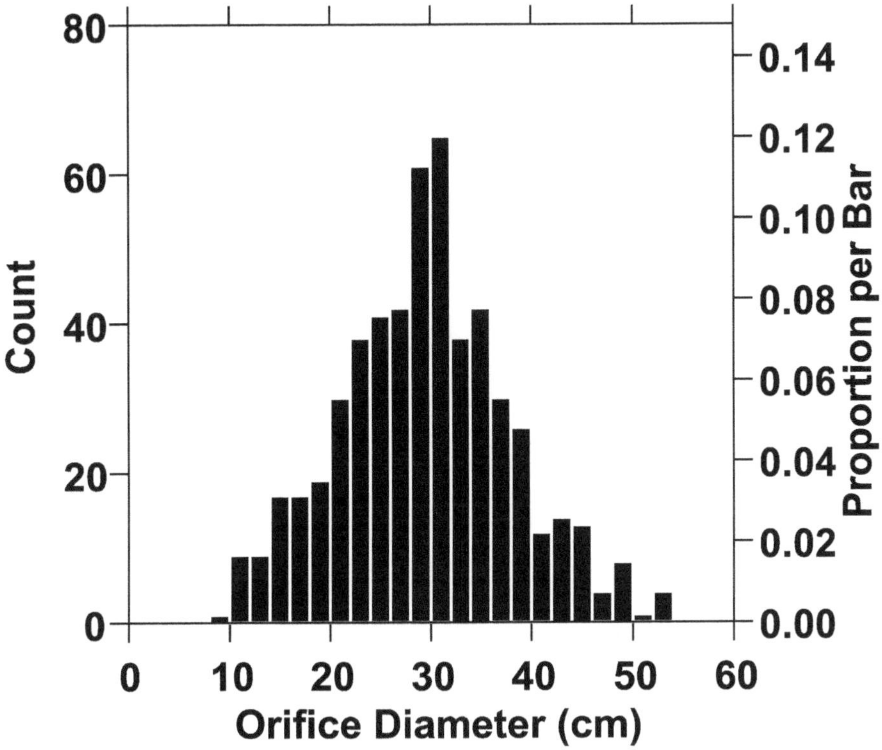

Figure 5.3. Unburnished jar orifice diameters.

function, it is no surprise that unburnished jars are the most frequent vessel class in Moundville I assemblages. Long-term exposure to cooking fires would have increased the breakage and replacement rates for these vessels (David 1972; Foster 1960; Pauketat 1989).

It is noteworthy that similar patterns of thermal use wear are present on both Mississippi Plain and Moundville Incised unburnished jars. In addition, Moundville Incised and Mississippi Plain jars are comparable in terms of orifice-diameter size distributions. Thus, both unburnished jar types appear to have been used for similar cooking and storage tasks.

Thickened-Rim Jars

Forty-nine thickened-rim jars were identified in the Moundville Roadway assemblage. As the name implies, these jars have rims that are reinforced by the application of a wide clay slab immediately below the vessel lip (Figure 5.4). On the basis of the identifiable rim sherds in the Roadway assemblages, it appears that thickened-rim jars differ from unburnished jars in overall shape. Thickened-rim jars generally have more vertical walls with less pronounced shoulders than un-

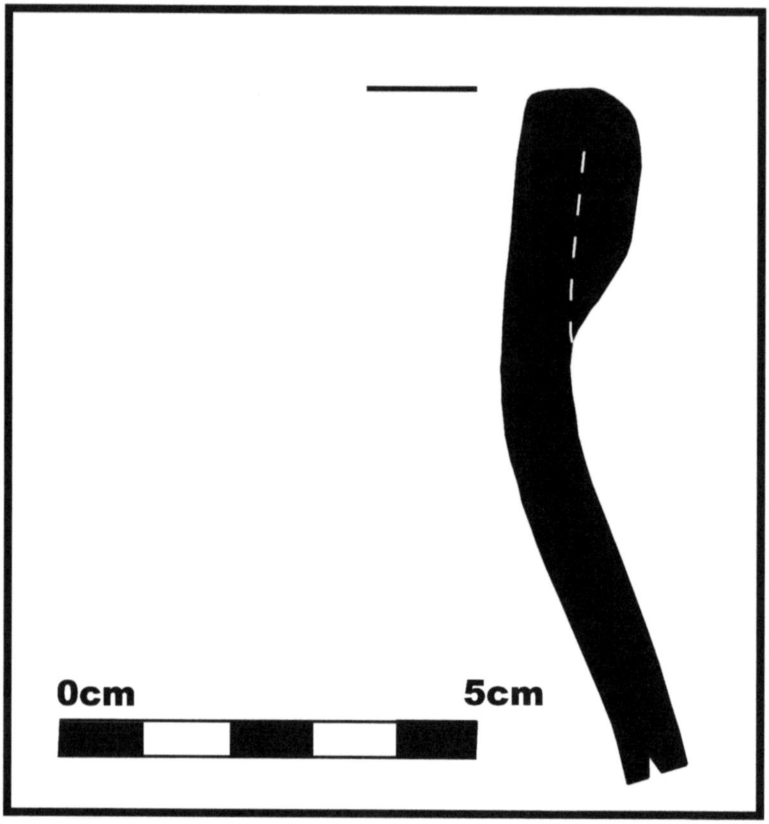

Figure 5.4. Thickened-rim jar profile.

burnished jars. Considering the shape of upper vessel portions, thickened-rim jars probably had deeper and more ovular bodies than unburnished jars. Clearly these pots were designed to contain bulk comestibles.

Thickened-rim jars tend to have considerably larger orifice diameters than other jar classes in Moundville I assemblages. In the past these vessels have been dubbed "oversized jars" because of examples with orifice diameters exceeding 60 and even 80 cm (Welch and Scarry 1995). Determining the size range of thickened-rim jars is complicated by the fact that many of these large vessels are represented by rim fragments too small to accurately calculate orifice diameter. Thus, the orifice diameter of only a small number of vessels from the study assemblage could be accurately determined. While a few thickened-rim jars have orifice diameters as low as 28 cm, the majority exceed 50 cm in size. On the basis of rough estimates some appear to have had orifice diameters exceeding 80 to 90 cm.

Determining the function or functions of thickened-rim jars is hindered by the fragmentary nature of the representative vessels. In the past it has been assumed that these pots were cooking vessels used to prepare mass quantities of foodstuffs.

From the available evidence, however, a tentative case can be made that thickened-rim jars were used domestically to store bulk foodstuffs. I base this inference on several lines of evidence. First, thickened-rim jars do not bear evidence of long-term exposure to cooking fires such as sooting and oxidation.[3] Moreover, although rare, thickened-rim jars are widely distributed. Examples of this distinctive vessel class have been identified in assemblages from the Picnic Area (PA) tract, East Conference Building (ECB) tract, North of Mound R, and throughout the Moundville Roadway (Scarry 1995). A more restricted pattern of distribution would be expected if these vessels had a ceremonial use (such as cooking large quantities of food for feasting). A domestic association for thickened-rim jars is also indicated by their co-occurrence with other domestic wares in midden assemblages.[4]

Considering their large size and the reasons discussed above, thickened-rim jars were probably designed to contain bulk comestibles. Once filled these vessels would have been too heavy to be manipulated or moved about frequently and were likely placed in the corners of houses and used for long-term storage purposes. Lack of mobility would have contributed to the long use lives of these vessels. Thus, the rarity of thickened-rim jars in the study assemblage may simply be a product of low breakage and replacement rates.

In addition to reinforcing the rims of these jars, the wide slabs placed on their exterior lips would have facilitated the use of skin covers to seal and preserve contents. Considering the scarcity of subterranean storage facilities at Moundville, bulk foodstuffs must have been stored above ground. Large storage jars along with corncribs or barbacoas could have served this purpose.

Burnished Jars

The term *burnished jar* is somewhat of a catch-all classification used here to describe jars in Moundville I assemblages with burnished or slipped surfaces (Steponaitis 1983). The 23 burnished jars in the Moundville Roadway assemblages include a couple of different types and varieties and a variety of basic shapes and secondary shape features (Table 5.3).

Two types of burnished jars can be identified on the basis of surface treatment: Bell Plain and Carthage Incised. In addition to surface treatment, Bell Plain and Carthage Incised jars differ in terms of basic shape and secondary surface attributes. Bell Plain jars in the assemblage are similar in shape and size (orifice-diameter distribution) to unburnished jars (Mississippi Plain and Moundville Incised) but often have more pronounced shoulders and upper rim sections that are more sharply in-slanting. Sixteen Bell Plain jars have reduced and burnished surfaces. One other is red slipped. In terms of secondary shape attributes one Bell Plain jar rim differs from the others in having evenly spaced nodes located immediately below its lip. Other Bell Plain jars in the assemblage lack distinctive secondary shape attributes.

Carthage Incised jars differ in a number of ways from other burnished jars in

Table 5.3. Counts of burnished jars by type and variety

	ADM	43+50–46+00	70+50–72+05	30+00–31+50	MPA	Total
Bell Plain, *var. Hale*	1	11	3		2	17
Carthage Incised, *var. Summerville*		3			3	6
Total	1	14	3		5	23

Key: ADM, Administration Building; MPA, Museum Parking Area.

the assemblage. I classified six burnished jars as Carthage Incised, *var. Summerville* on the basis of their burnished surfaces and the presence of incised arches on their upper vessel portions. These are well-made vessels with thin walls and fine, compact pastes. In terms of basic shape Carthage Incised jars have lower height-to-width ratios than other burnished and unburnished jars, making them shorter and squatter than other jar classes.[5] Carthage Incised jars are also embellished with four shoulder nodes executed by pushing out the vessel's shoulders from the interior. Thin and deeply incised arcs are located directly above these shoulder modifications. In addition, Carthage Incised jars often possess two strap handles on opposite sides of the vessel mouth. The tops of these handles often include flattened appendages (Figure 5.5).

Given their burnished and reduced surfaces, it is unlikely that burnished jars were used for cooking activities. An absence of sooting and oxidation supports this inference. Considering the effort that went into decorating these vessels, in particular the Carthage Incised examples, a serving function is probable. The general shape characteristics of burnished jars would have facilitated the serving of a variety of foodstuffs. The short, restricted necks of these vessels would have provided some degree of containment security without hindering access to contents (Taft 1996:49). Indeed, burnished jars have fine and compact pastes that would have increased resistance to mechanical shock. This is particularly the case with the Carthage Incised examples in the assemblage.

Carthage Incised burnished jars are smaller, shallower, and more elaborately decorated than other burnished jars. Considering their small size and unrestricted shapes these vessels were individual serving containers. Bell Plain burnished jars have a wider range of orifice diameters and may include both individual and small-group serving containers.

Simple and Restricted Bowls

In total, 220 simple bowls and 55 restricted bowls were identified in the study assemblage. Thirty-six additional bowls were assigned to a general bowl category, as

Figure 5.5. Carthage Incised, *var. Summerville* burnished jars.

they were too fragmentary to confidently classify as either simple or restricted. Because of general similarities in shape, size, and surface treatment, I discuss these three vessel classes collectively.

As defined by Steponaitis, Moundville simple bowls "have an approximately hemispherical profile, without inflection or corner points. The lip diameter must be greater than three fourths of the maximum diameter; on simple bowls that lack a point of vertical tangency, the lip is equivalent to the maximum diameter" (Steponaitis 1983:68). For the current study, I widen the simple bowl classification to include a number of large, panlike bowls with out-slanting rims.

Restricted bowls are similar to simple bowls in overall shape but have in-curving rims that result in an orifice diameter "less than three fourths of the maximum diameter of the body" (Steponaitis 1983:68). Another way to describe restricted bowls is that they are essentially bottles without the restricted, vertical neck.

Rims representing 118 simple and restricted bowls were complete enough to determine orifice diameter. Three histograms plotting these orifice diameters reveal a bimodal distribution of bowl sizes (Figures 5.6–5.8). The smaller size mode consists of 111 rims with orifice diameters ranging from 8 to 34 cm. Both simple and restricted bowls are represented in this small size mode. The larger size mode is represented by seven simple-bowl rims with orifice diameters ranging from 40 to 50 cm.

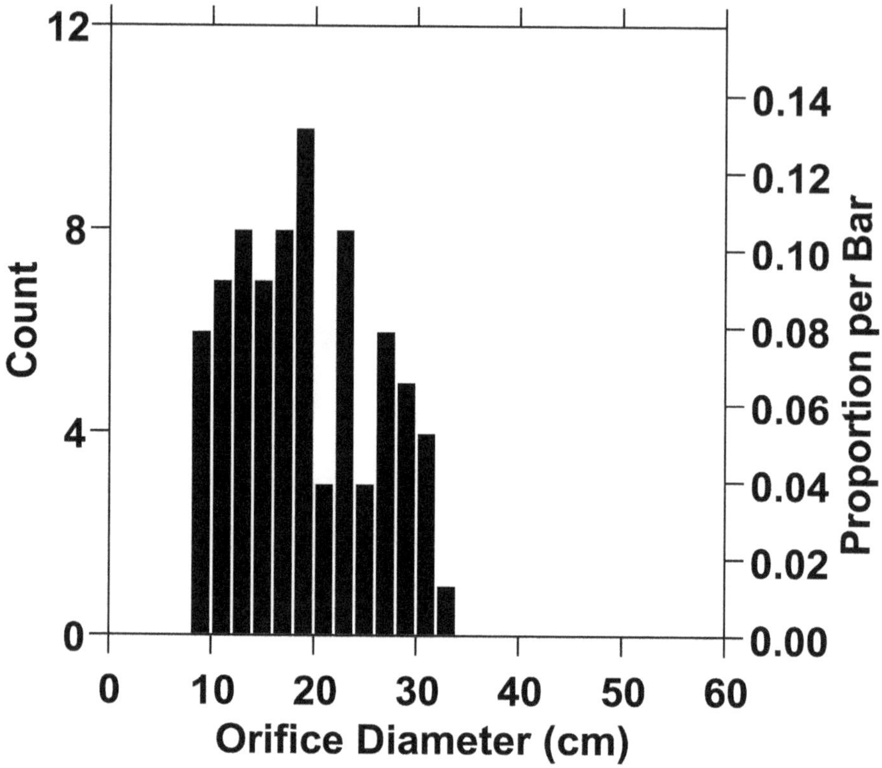

Figure 5.6. Orifice diameters for Bell Plain bowls.

A total of 300 rims from both vessel classes can be sorted into one of three type categories on the basis of surface treatment: Bell Plain, Mississippi Plain, and Carthage Incised (Table 5.4). The 10 remaining bowls are represented by one Addis Plain rim, two Bell Plain, *var. Goldsmith,* one D'Olive Incised, one unclassified shell-and-grog-tempered vessel, three Moundville Engraved, *var. Elliot's Creek,* one Mazique Incised, and one unclassified engraved rim. Figures 5.6, 5.7, and 5.8 plot the distribution of the orifice-diameter measurements for simple and restricted bowls by surface treatment. All three major surface-treatment categories possess the small size range discussed earlier. Moreover, each of these surface-treatment categories displays a similar range of vessel sizes within this small size mode. Plain surface vessels, however, represent the only category that includes the larger size mode of bowls (Figure 5.8). Moreover, all six of the vessels comprising this large size mode are simple bowls.

The large size mode of Mississippi Plain simple bowls represents a previously undefined Mississippian vessel subclass in Moundville I assemblages (Figure 5.9). Two of these vessels have a wide and shallow basic shape that is similar to pans, as defined elsewhere in the Mississippian Southeast (Milner 1984). The other large

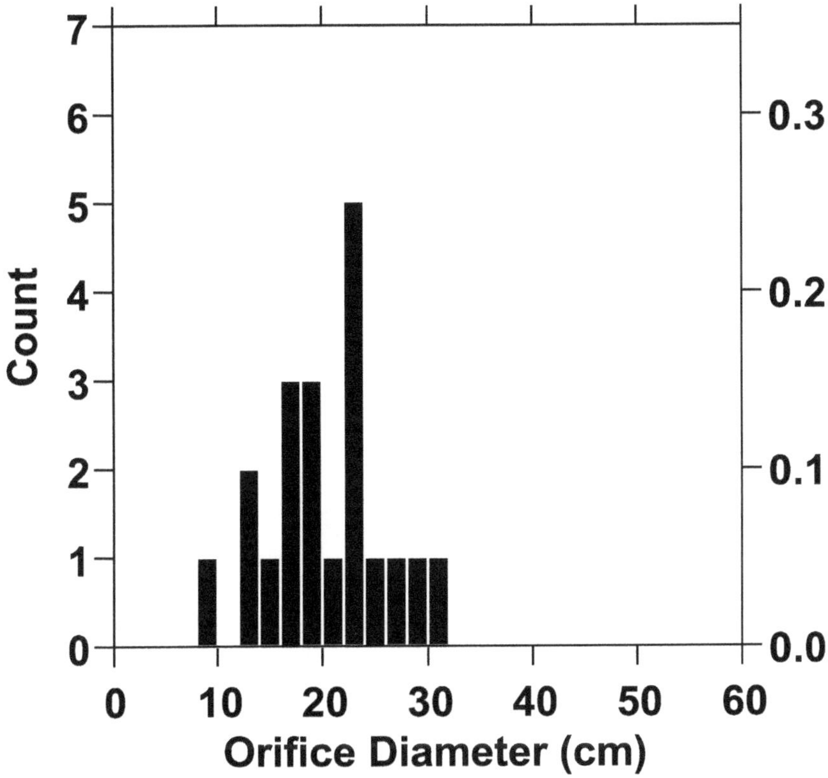

Figure 5.7. Orifice diameters for Carthage Incised and other decorated bowls.

simple bowls have deeper bodies and out-slanting rims. Sooting and oxidation were identified on two vessels. On the basis of the lack of decorative surface treatment, large size, and evidence of thermal shock, these large bowls were probably used for cooking and possibly mixing tasks. Their coarse shell tempering also indicates a cooking function as this paste composition would have provided increased resistance to thermal shock (Steponaitis 1984).

The small size mode of simple and restricted bowls consists primarily of burnished and/or incised vessels with fine-shell or shell-and-grog paste. It is important to note that many of the Mississippi Plain bowl rims in this category are eroded vessels that may have been originally burnished. Considering that Mississippi Plain, Carthage Incised, and Bell Plain bowls in this small size mode share comparable orifice-diameter distributions and are consistent in vessel morphology, I contend that they were probably used for similar serving tasks. Restricted bowls, however, clearly provided a higher level of containment security with more access restriction than simple bowls and may have been used more frequently for the serving and short-term storage of liquid foodstuffs.

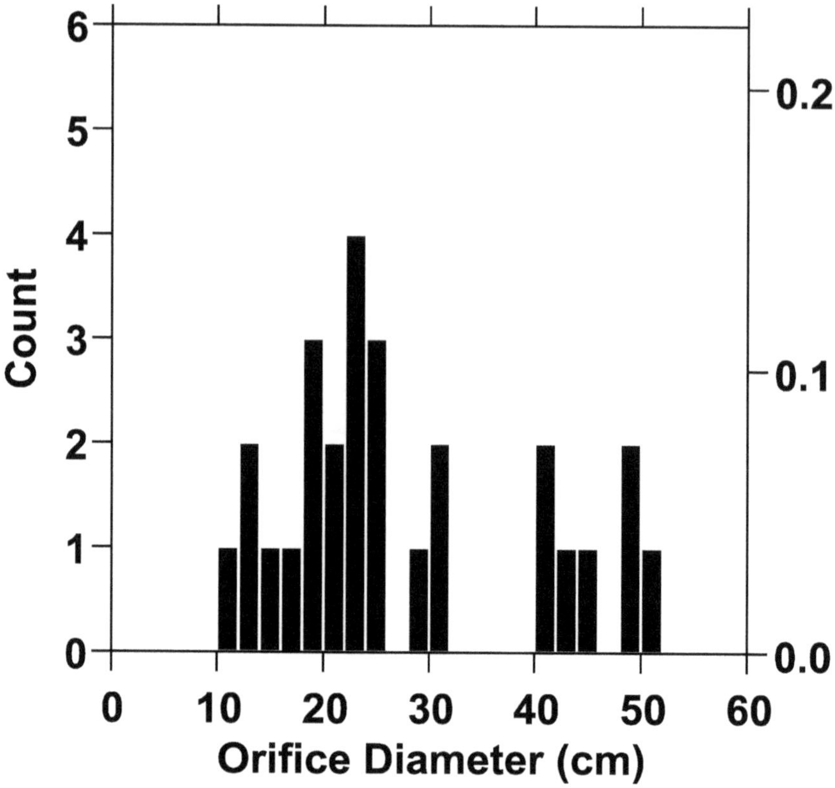

Figure 5.8. Orifice diameters for Mississippi Plain bowls.

Small simple and restricted bowls lack sooting, oxidation, and other evidence of thermal alteration. The small size of these vessels, their fine-shell and/or grog-tempered pastes, and their burnished and otherwise decorated surfaces suggest they were primarily used as individual serving containers (Taft 1996:51). The rounded bases found on most of these bowls would have decreased overall stability, suggesting that they were frequently carried or held rather than used communally. That being said, some of the larger simple and restricted bowls may have been used for serving meals to household members and other small groups.

Taft (1996:51) has demonstrated that simple bowls were sometimes used for nonfood-related activities. A simple bowl recovered from Mound Q was encrusted with glauconite, a green pigment. Another bowl recovered from the Moundville site contained hematite, a red pigment. From this evidence, Taft (1996) argues that these pots were sometimes used to store paints for a variety of craft activities.

Flaring-Rim Bowls

Rims representing a minimum number of 212 flaring-rim bowls were identified in the study assemblage. These vessels generally have hemispherical bodies with

Table 5.4. Counts of simple and restricted bowls by type and variety

	ADM	43+50–46+00	70+50–72+05	30+00–31+50	MPA	Total
Addis Plain					1	1
Bell Plain, *var. Goldsmith*		2				2
Bell Plain, var. Hale	27	75	24	9	39	174
Carthage Incised, *var. Akron*	6	15	5		12	38
Carthage Incised, *var. Moon Lake*		1				1
Carthage Incised, *var. Summerville*	2	4	2		1	9
Carthage Incised, *var. Unspecified*	5		2		2	9
D'Olive Incised		1				1
Indeterminate plain shell/grog		1				1
Mazique Incised		1				1
Mississippi Plain, *var. Hull Lake*		2				2
Mississippi Plain, *var. Warrior*	6	30	15	3	13	67
Moundville Engraved, *var. Elliot's Creek*	1		2			3
Unclassified engraved	1					1
Total	48	132	50	12	68	310

Key: ADM, Administration Building; MPA, Museum Parking Area.

sharply out-flaring rims (Figure 5.10; Steponaitis 1983:68). Steponaitis (1983) distinguishes between deep and shallow flaring-rim bowls. Deep flaring-rim bowls have upper vessel portions that have a point of vertical tangency. Shallow flaring-rim bowls have out-slanting upper vessel portions that do not reach a point of vertical tangency. This distinction is important as deep bowls do not appear in the Black Warrior Valley until the Moundville III phase. Only shallow flaring-rim bowls were identified in the study assemblage. That being said, many of the rims representing flaring-rim bowls were too fragmentary to confidently assign to one of these subcategories.

Nearly half of the flaring-rim bowls (n = 88) in the study assemblage can be classified as Bell Plain, *var. Hale* on the basis of their burnished but otherwise undecorated surfaces (Table 5.5). The remaining vessels are represented by a total of

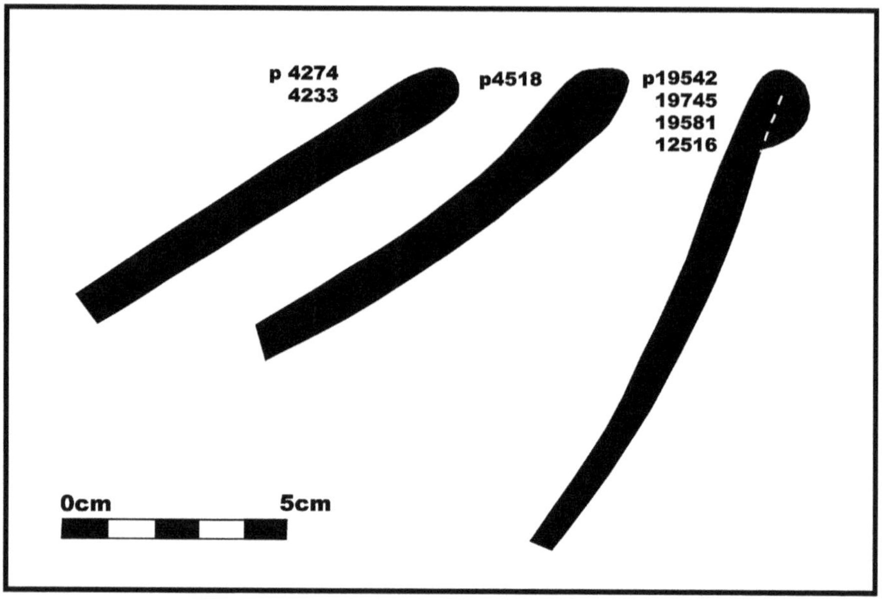

Figure 5.9. Large simple bowl or pan rims.

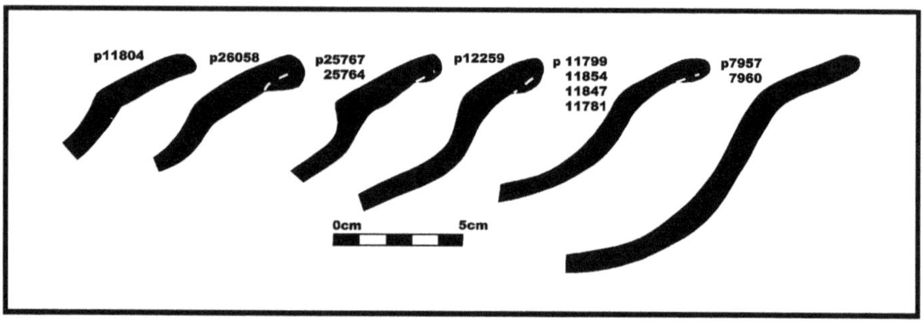

Figure 5.10. Flaring-rim bowl rims.

39 Carthage Incised, 27 Mississippi Plain, 5 Moundville Engraved, 3 unclassified engraved, and 1 D'Olive Incised rim (Table 5.5).

Flaring-rim bowls clearly were used for food serving on the basis of their shape, surface treatment, and lack of thermal alteration (Taft 1996:50; Welch and Scarry 1995:412). The flaring rims provided a practical means of carrying these vessels as well as a highly visible area to place incised and/or engraved decorations. These vessels have a shallow shape that would have provided less containment security for liquid foods than simple or restricted bowls. Thus, flaring-rim bowls may have been used for serving and eating solid foods or thick gruels rather than soups or stews. Considering their small size, most flaring-rim bowls probably were used as

Table 5.5. Counts of flaring-rim bowls by type and variety

	ADM	43+50–46+00	70+50–72+05	30+00–31+50	MPA	Total
Addis Incised		48			1	49
Bell Plain, *var. Hale*	12		51	6	19	88
Carthage Incised, *var. Akron*		2				2
Carthage Incised, *var. Carthage*	1					1
Carthage Incised, *var. Fosters*		1				1
Carthage Incised, *var. Moon Lake*	1	6	7		4	18
Carthage Incised, *var. Summerville*	2	1				3
Carthage Incised, *var. Unspecified*		6	2		6	14
D'Olive Incised		1				1
Mississippi Plain, *var. Hull Lake*		1		1		2
Mississippi Plain, *var. Warrior*	1	10	5		9	25
Moundville Engraved, *var. Elliot's Creek*	2					2
Moundville Engraved, *var. Unspecified*		1			2	3
Unclassified engraved	1	1			1	3
Total	20	78	65	7	42	212

Key: ADM, Administration Building; MPA, Museum Parking Area.

individual serving containers (Taft 1996:50). The largest examples could have been used by small groups.

Carinated Bowls

A minimum number of 13 carinated bowls were identified in the Moundville Roadway assemblage. They are wide and shallow vessels with a vertical or slightly in-slanting rim that joins a relatively flat base at a corner point (Figure 5.11). Their unrestricted shape would have provided ready access to contents. In addition, their low height-to-width ratios and flat bases would have contributed to overall vessel stability. These bowls are essentially serving platters and are among the rarest and most elaborate vessels in Moundville I assemblages. The base portion of one cari-

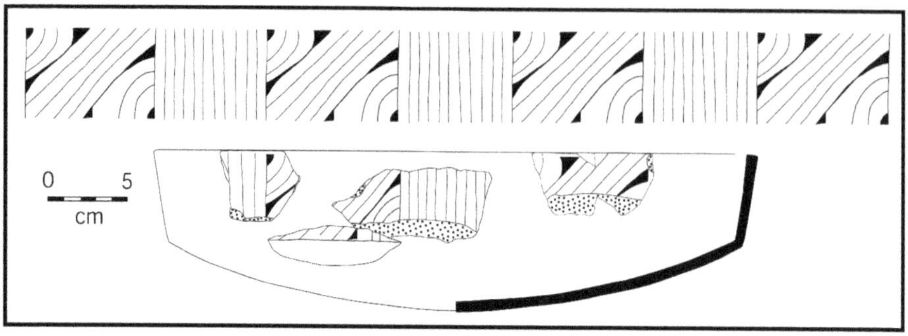

Figure 5.11. Moundville Engraved, *var. Chapman* carinated bowl.

nated bowl exhibits a pattern of pitting that was likely the result of the bowl's contents being scooped out with a ladle (Hally 1983a; Shapiro 1984).

In terms of type-variety classifications, seven carinated bowls can be classified as Moundville Engraved, *var. Chapman* on the basis of their incised and excised design fields, which consist of quarter circles bordered by vertical parallel lines (Figure 5.11). The outer surfaces of these bowls are reduced and burnished. In addition, engraved and excised areas are sometimes embellished with a red slip. Two other carinated bowls are classified as Bell Plain, *var. Goldsmith.* Both are made from a pinkish-brown shell-and-grog-tempered paste that is virtually identical to that of the *Chapman* vessels, but they have undecorated surfaces. The remaining four carinated bowls are represented by two unclassified engraved, one Moundville Engraved, *var. Elliot's Creek,* and one Bell Plain, *var. Hale* rim (Table 5.6).

Cylindrical Bowls

Five cylindrical bowls represent less than 1 percent (0.25 percent) of the study assemblage. These vessels have approximately vertical walls and a rounded or flattened base. Three of these pots are classified as Bell Plain, *var. Hale* on the basis of their burnished but otherwise undecorated surfaces. Two others are labeled unclassified engraved (Table 5.7).

Because of their basic shape characteristics, cylindrical bowls were probably used as liquid serving and drinking containers. The large height-to-width ratio of this vessel shape would have created a high degree of access restriction, making it difficult to remove solid foods. Their fine pastes and burnished and decorated surfaces also suggest a serving function. Considering their small size, most cylindrical bowls were likely used as individual drinking containers. Larger examples could have been used by small groups.

Terraced Bowls

Six terraced bowls make up less than 1 percent (0.3 percent) of the study assemblage. The defining feature of this vessel class is a terraced or scalloped lip wherein

Table 5.6. Counts of carinated bowls by type and variety

	43+50–46+00	70+50–72+05	Total
Bell Plain, *var. Goldsmith*	1	1	2
Bell Plain, *var. Hale*		1	1
Moundville Engraved, *var. Chapman*	6	1	7
Moundville Engraved, *var. Elliot's Creek*	1		1
Unclassified engraved	2		2
Total	10	3	13

Table 5.7. Counts of cylindrical bowls by type and variety

	ADM	43+50–46+00	70+50–72+05	Total
Bell Plain, *var. Hale*	1	1	1	3
Unclassified engraved		2		2
Total	1	3	1	5

Key: ADM, Administration Building.

the rim in one portion of the vessel is lower than the rest (Steponaitis 1983:69). Most terraced bowls are square to rectangular in shape with a flat base. Others have rounded, ovoid bodies with pedestaled bases.

Four of the terraced bowls in the study assemblage were classified as Moundville Engraved, *var. Chapman* on the basis of their pinkish-brown shell-and-grog-tempered pastes and incised and excised design fields (Figure 5.12). One terraced bowl was classified as Bell Plain, *var. Goldsmith.* This vessel was made from a paste virtually identical to that of the Moundville Engraved, *var. Chapman* vessels but had undecorated surfaces. The final terraced bowl was classified as Moundville Engraved but was too fragmentary to assign to a variety designation (Table 5.8).

Terraced bowls are rare and elaborate vessels that required considerable labor investment to manufacture. A service function for these pots is indicated by their unconventional shapes, elaborate surface treatments, and fine pastes. The open-sided shape of these vessels would have been well suited to display a vessel's contents. While terraced bowls may have been used for the presentation of foods, it is also possible they were used to present or display nonfood items.

Peaked-Rim Bowls

One peaked (or square) bowl rim was identified in the Moundville Roadway assemblage. Because of the fragmentary nature of this rim sherd, it is difficult to determine the overall shape of the vessel. However, more complete square-rimmed vessels have been recovered from the Stirling phase (A.D. 1100–1200) American

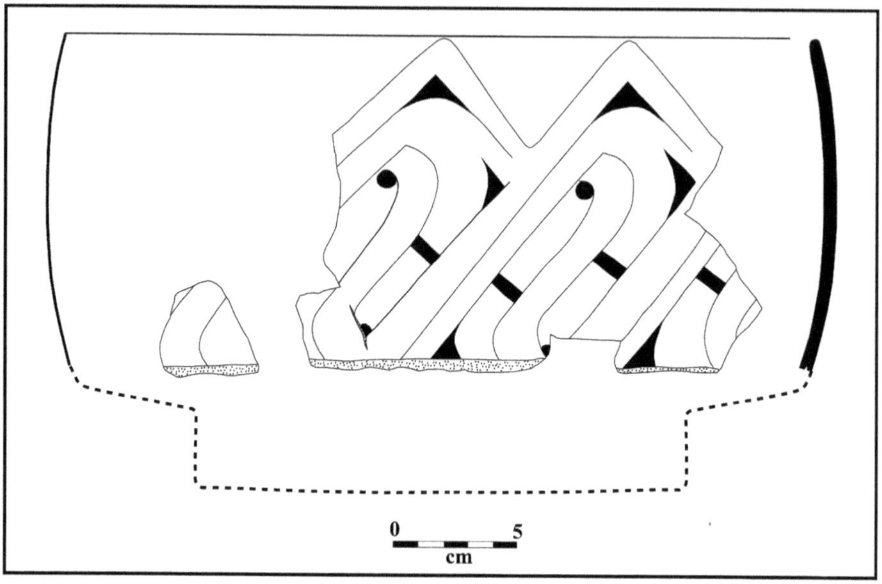

Figure 5.12. Moundville Engraved, *var. Chapman* terraced bowl.

Table 5.8. Counts of terraced bowls by type and variety

Type and Variety	43+50–46+00	Total
Bell Plain, *var. Goldsmith*	1	1
Moundville Engraved, *var. Chapman*	4	4
Moundville Engraved, *var. Unspecified*	1	1
Total	6	6

Bottom in southwestern Illinois (Milner 1983:135–136; O'Brien 1972:Figure 60a). These Cahokia examples were wide and shallow four-sided vessels with rounded bases.

This vessel's fine paste and burnished surfaces (Bell Plain, *var. Hale*) indicate a serving function. However, the fragmentary nature of this vessel limits functional interpretations. If this Moundville example is similar in overall shape to the Cahokia examples, then it was likely used as a serving platter for food presentation.

Bottles

Rim sherds representing a minimum number of 46 bottles were identified in this analysis. In general, bottles are vessels with more or less vertical, restricted necks attached to distinct bodies (Steponaitis 1983:66). Steponaitis (1983:66–68) has defined a variety of different bottle shape classes at Moundville. Moundville I bottles typically have elongated or ovoid bodies with pedestaled bases. Cylindrical bottles are another bottle form in Moundville I assemblages. As their name implies, these bottles have cylindrical (barrel-shaped) bodies and wide necks (Steponaitis 1983:66). Toward the end of the Moundville I phase ovoid bottles began to be replaced with subglobular bottles. By the latter portion of the Moundville II phase potters began making subglobular bottles without pedestaled bases.

The fragmentary nature of most bottle rims recovered from domestic refuse contexts makes it difficult to distinguish among different bottle shape classes. Indeed, most of the bottles in the study assemblage are represented by rim sherds broken at the point where the neck meets the body. That being said, several pedestaled bases were identified in the analysis. Moreover, it was possible to tentatively identify a number of cylindrical bottles on the basis of paste and surface-treatment attributes unique to this particular bottle class.

Thirty-five bottles were classified as Bell Plain, *var. Hale* on the basis of their burnished surfaces. Three of these are red slipped. Six other bottle rims were classified as Mississippi Plain, *var. Warrior.* Several of these rims may have originally had burnished or slipped surfaces that have eroded. A minimum number of two rims was assigned to the type Moundville Engraved, *var. Chapman.* Both of these rims were manufactured from a very similar pinkish-brown, fine shell-and-grog-tempered paste. Finally, one burnished and incised bottle rim was classified as type Carthage Incised (Table 5.9). Because of its fragmentary nature, however, it could not be assigned to a particular variety.

As I will discuss in greater detail later, the two Moundville Engraved, *var. Chapman* bottles are part of a distinct suite of elaborate serving wares found in Moundville I assemblages. On the basis of the one complete vessel and the few larger body fragments recovered from Moundville, these bottles have cylindrical bodies with long and wide necks. Moreover, they all appear to share similar surface treatments and designs. Vessel bodies are decorated with a bull's-eye motif executed through an elaborate set of incised curves and excised triangles and circles. These incised and excised areas are usually filled with a red, hematite-based slip. Outer surfaces are burnished and reduced to a dark brown to black color. However, because of the soft and easily erodable pastes from which these bottles were manufactured, sometimes only traces of this burnishing and red slipping are detectable. In some cases vessel necks are also decorated with three horizontally incised parallel lines.

Orifice diameters for most bottles in the Moundville Roadway assemblage range from 4 cm to 12 cm. However, two bottle rims with orifice diameters measuring 18 and 22 cm, respectively, may represent a larger size class of these vessels (Figure 5.13). Given their small size and restricted necks most bottles were used as individual and small-group liquid serving containers. Indeed, several bottle rims have patches of neck and lip abrasion that were likely created from repeated handling with wet hands. Bottles are typically made from finer and more compact pastes

Table 5.9. Counts of bottles by type and variety

	ADM	43+50–46+00	70+50–72+05	MPA	Total
Bell Plain, *var. Goldsmith*		2			2
Bell Plain, *var. Hale*	12	9	7	7	35
Carthage Incised, *var. Unspecified*			1		1
Mississippi Plain, *var. Warrior*			5	1	6
Moundville Engraved, *var. Chapman*		2			2
Total	12	13	13	8	46

Key: ADM, Administration Building; MPA, Museum Parking Area.

than most other vessels in the study assemblage. This paste composition would have increased resistance to mechanical shock and breakage, an important quality as bottles would have been frequently handled and passed around.

Interassemblage Comparison

In this section I perform a number of interassemblage comparisons to evaluate organizational similarities and differences in foodways between different residential groups at early Moundville. In addition to the Moundville Roadway assemblages I also examine assemblages from the North of Mound R excavations (Steponaitis 1983) and the ECB and PA tract assemblages from the Moundville Riverbank (Scarry 1995). I begin by comparing the relative frequencies of different vessel classes in each assemblage. Data generated from this comparison highlight general patterns of food preparation, storage, and serving activities. In addition, this comparison provides information on how everyday foodways differed from special occasions such as feasts and other ceremonial events. I also consider interassemblage diversity in type and variety frequencies. This comparison highlights spatial patterning in pottery distributions that crosscut different vessel types.

In the next set of analyses I compare the size (orifice diameter) distributions of individual vessel classes from different portions of the Moundville site. As discussed at the beginning of this chapter, vessel size provides insight into differences and similarities in the size and composition of groups sharing meals. In turn, this information provides insight into a variety of factors ranging from household social status to the domestic cycle.

Basic Shape Frequencies

For the purposes of this interassemblage comparison I collapsed all vessels into four broad shape classes: jars, bowls, flaring-rim bowls, and bottles. Table 5.10 pre-

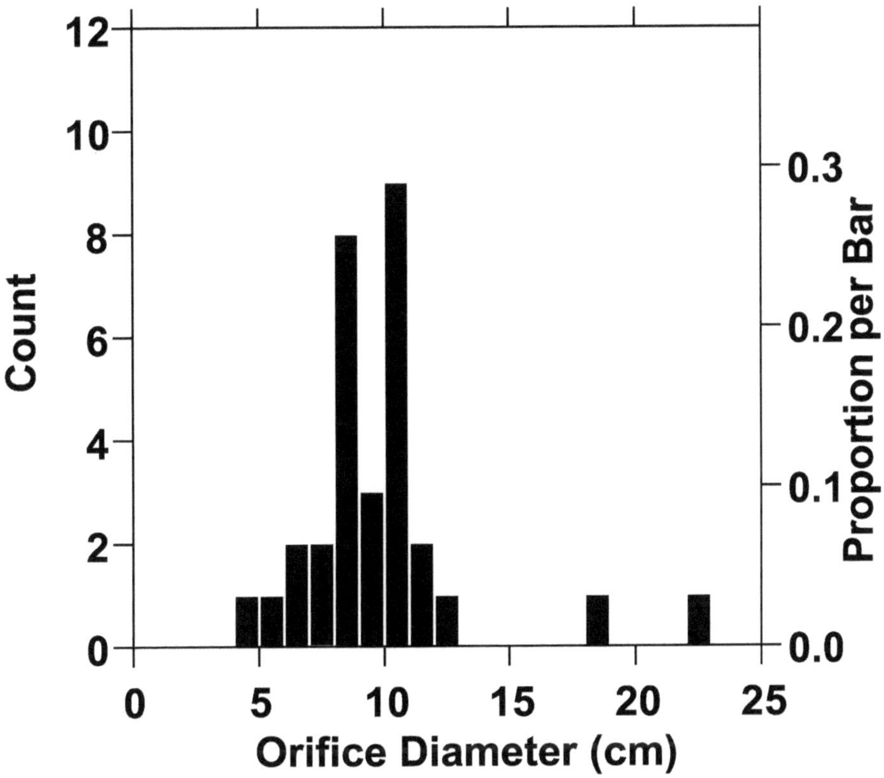

Figure 5.13. Orifice diameters for bottles in the study assemblage.

sents counts and percentages for these four vessel classes by context. Assemblages examined for this comparison include the Moundville I assemblage from North of Mound R (MI NR), the Moundville II–III assemblage from North of Mound R (MII–III NR), assemblages from Roadway blocks 30+00 to 31+50, 43+50 to 46+00, and 70+50 to 72+05, and assemblages from the Administration Building (ADM) and Museum Parking Area (MPA).[6]

An examination of these data reveals that assemblages vary in terms of the relative frequencies of jars, bowls, and bottles. Flaring-rim bowl frequency, however, remains roughly consistent in each assemblage relative to other vessel classes (Table 5.10). As a general trend, assemblages with higher relative frequencies of bowls and bottles have lower relative frequencies of jars. This trend does not necessarily mean that jars are less ubiquitous in these assemblages. Most likely, jar ubiquity remained fairly constant, and bowls and bottles are more ubiquitous in some assemblages than others.

What factors are responsible for these interassemblage differences? In an oft-cited study on Mississippian foodways at Moundville, Welch and Scarry (1995)

Table 5.10. Counts and frequencies of general vessel classes by assemblage

	Jars		Bowls		Flaring-Rim Bowls		Bottles		Total vessels
	N	%	N	%	N	%	N	%	
MII–III NR	132	54.10	62	25.41	35	14.34	15	6.15	244
MI NR	75	52.82	38	26.76	16	11.27	13	9.15	142
30+00–31+50	44	69.84	12	19.05	7	11.11	0	0	63
MPA	228	65.71	70	20.17	42	12.10	7	2.02	347
ADM	94	53.41	49	27.84	21	11.93	12	6.82	176
43+50–46+00	587	70.64	152	18.29	79	9.51	13	1.56	831
70+50–72+05	396	75.00	54	10.23	65	12.31	13	2.46	528
Total	1,556		437		265		73		2,331

Key: MII–III, Moundville II–III; NR, North of Mound R; MI, Moundville I; MPA, Museum Parking Area; ADM, Administration Building.

argue that interassemblage variation in Mississippian serving-ware frequencies at Moundville is a product of status-based differences in foodways. In this scenario, high-status households at Moundville hosted a variety of ceremonial events such as feasts that generated discard assemblages with elevated serving-ware frequencies. Because of the different method by which I calculated the minimum number of vessels for the Roadway assemblages I cannot directly engage with Welch and Scarry's data. However, I will consider the relevance of a status-based explanation for the pattern of variation noted in Figure 5.14 for the Moundville Roadway and North of Mound R assemblages. A status-based difference in foodways is not the only possible explanation for these ceramic trends. Another possible explanation for this interassemblage variation may be chronology. Previous ceramic studies have revealed diachronic changes in both the types and frequencies of Mississippian serving wares at Moundville (Knight 2002; Steponaitis 1983).

To examine this second possibility, I ordered the study assemblages from earliest to latest, as determined by the seriation presented in Chapter 3 (Figure 5.14). The seriation diagram in Figure 5.14 reveals trends in the percentages of jars, bowls, and bottles. With few exceptions, the latest Moundville I and Moundville II–III assemblages from North of Mound R have the highest percentages of bowls and bottles. In contrast the earliest Moundville I assemblages from Roadway blocks 70+50 to 72+05 and 43+50 to 46+00 have the lowest percentages of bowls and bottles.[7]

On the basis of the results of this analysis, I suggest that most of the interassemblage variation in serving-ware frequencies identified in Table 5.10 is the product of diachronic changes rather than synchronic differences in foodways at Mound-

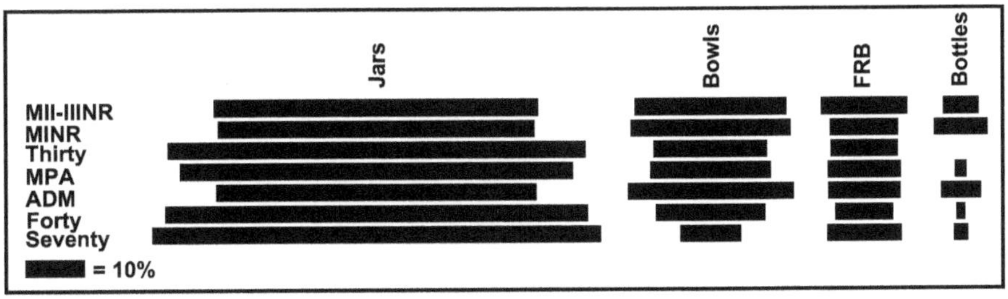

Figure 5.14. Ford's method seriation of MNV percentages by context.

ville. The Administration Building assemblage is an exception to this trend. Although it is the third-earliest assemblage in the seriation, it contains a higher relative frequency of bowls than any other assemblage. One possible explanation for this pattern is that the Administration Building ceramic assemblage consists of a mixture of domestic and ceremonial refuse deposits. Another possibility is that the Administration Building assemblage may date later in the Moundville I phase than indicated by the ceramic seriation. Indeed, the architectural evidence presented in Chapter 4 contrasts with the ceramic seriation in that it indicates the Administration Building context dates late in the sequence. In any case, the Administration Building assemblage represents only a minor exception to the broader trend represented in Figure 5.14.

The upshot of this analysis then is that there appears to be little status-based variation between different residential areas at early Moundville, at least in terms of the frequencies of vessels used to prepare and serve food. However, if this interpretation is correct there was a relatively sharp increase in the production and use of bowls and bottles during the Moundville I phase. Exactly when these serving containers peak in popularity is unclear. However, there is a decrease in the relative frequency of bowls and bottles from the Moundville I to the Moundville II–III assemblages from North of Mound R (Table 5.10). Knight (2002:94–95) reports a similar decrease in serving wares (particularly bottles) relative to jars during the transition from Moundville II to III in assemblages from Mound Q.

Type-Variety Distribution

In this section I examine the distribution of different serving-ware types and varieties (Appendix 2). By highlighting types and varieties I hope to identify spatial patterning in pottery distributions that cross-cut different vessel types. Specifically, I examine the distribution of local serving-ware types including Bell Plain, *vars. Hale* and *Goldsmith,* Carthage Incised (all varieties), and Moundville Engraved, *vars. Elliot's Creek* and *Chapman.* Probable nonlocal serving-ware types are not considered here.

Sherds representing Bell Plain, *var. Hale* vessels make up a total of 17 percent of all the Moundville I assemblages listed in Table 5.11 and these are by far the most common serving containers during the Moundville I phase (Figure 5.15). Bell Plain, *var. Hale* sherds are also widely distributed at Moundville. As listed in Table 5.11, Bell Plain, *var. Hale* sherds make up at least 11 percent of every Moundville I assemblage considered in my analysis. On the basis of their frequency and ubiquitous distribution, I believe that Bell Plain, *var. Hale* pots were domestic serving containers used on a daily basis throughout the early Moundville community.

I hesitate to draw any conclusions from interassemblage differences in Bell Plain frequencies (see Table 5.11). There are several reasons for my caution. First, as I discussed above, chronology affected serving-ware frequencies at Moundville. Later Moundville I assemblages are more likely to have higher relative frequencies of burnished sherds than earlier Moundville I assemblages. Moreover, there is interanalyst variation in the criteria used to distinguish burnished (Bell Plain) and plain (Mississippi Plain) sherds. No two analysts appear to draw the line between Bell Plain and Mississippi Plain in exactly the same place. In addition, diversity in both feature formation processes and preservation factors also affects the identification of burnished sherds. Pottery assemblages that have endured greater exposure to the elements possess fewer sherds with intact burnished surfaces than more pristine assemblages.[8]

Carthage Incised sherds are considerably less common than Bell Plain sherds, representing 1 percent of all Moundville I assemblages. Though rare, Carthage Incised sherds are widely distributed at Moundville. In addition, there are minimal differences between different Moundville I assemblages in terms of the frequency of Carthage Incised sherds (Table 5.11). There is only a 1.33 percent difference between the assemblages with the highest (Administration Building) and the lowest (30+00–31+50) frequencies of Carthage Incised (see Table 5.11). The interassemblage diversity that does exist is difficult to evaluate, as Carthage Incised sherds make up such a small amount of the total variation in any Moundville I assemblage. Just a few Carthage Incised sherds added to or subtracted from any assemblage could alter relative percentages dramatically. Considering their wide distribution, Carthage Incised pots were probably used similarly to Bell Plain, *var. Hale* vessels. Though less common, Carthage Incised pots are essentially Bell Plain vessels with incised decorations. Both serving-ware types share the same suite of basic shape forms and sizes.

Other important local serving-ware types in Moundville I assemblages include Moundville Engraved, *vars. Elliot's Creek* and *Chapman,* Bell Plain, *var. Goldsmith,* and unclassified engraved. These are by far the most rare and elaborate serving containers found at early Moundville. Considerable labor was invested in the manufacture and decoration of these pots. Figure 5.16 plots the presence of these four varieties in the Moundville Riverbank, North of Mound R, Administration Build-

Table 5.11. Sherd counts and percentages for early Mississippian serving-ware type varieties by context

	Total Sherds	Bell Plain, *var. Hale*		Carthage Incised (all varieties)		Moundville Engraved, *var. Elliot's Creek*		Moundville Engraved, *var. Chapman*		Bell Plain, *var. Goldsmith*		Unclassified Engraved	
	N	N	%	N	%	N	%	N	%	N	%	N	%
ADM	2,182	435	19.94	36	1.70	10	0.46					3	0.14
43+50–46+00	5,928	754	12.71	66	1.08	9	0.15	60	1.01	44	0.74	13	0.22
70+50–72+05	2,649	386	14.57	31	1.01	12	0.45	3	0.11	1	0.04	1	0.04
30+00–31+50	552	64	11.59	2	0.37								
MPA	3,009	419	13.92	47	1.46	1	0.03	1	0.03			1	0.03
PA tract	2,345	279	11.90	12	0.51	3	0.13						
ECB tract	3,833	678	17.69	43	1.12	4	0.10						
NR	2,813	973	34.59	15	0.53	8	0.28						
Total	23,311	3,988	17.11	252	1.08	47	0.20	64	0.27	45	0.19	18	0.08

Key: ADM, Administration Building; MPA, Museum Parking Area; NR, North of Mound R.

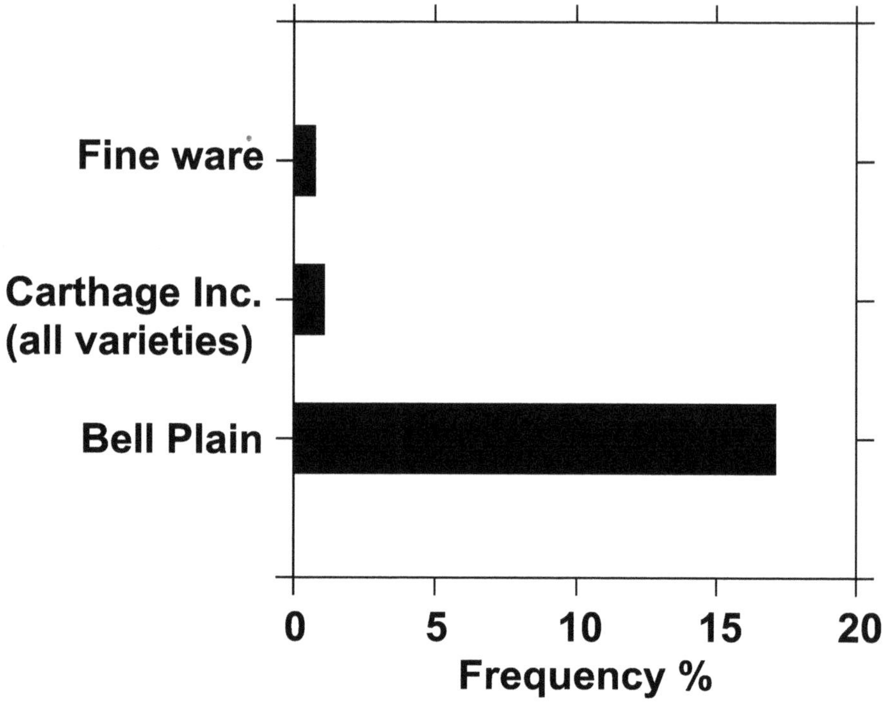

Figure 5.15. Sherd percentages by serving-ware type for combined Moundville I assemblages (note: the fine-ware category includes Bell Plain, *var. Goldsmith,* Moundville Engraved, *var. Chapman,* Moundville Engraved, *var. Elliot's Creek,* and unclassified engraved).

ing, Museum Parking Area, and the three Moundville Roadway assemblages considered here. Also plotted are the locations of individual sherds identified from preliminary analyses of other portions of the Moundville Roadway.

As represented in Figure 5.16, these elaborate serving wares are widely distributed at Moundville. Indeed, representative sherds have been identified in almost every sizable Moundville I ceramic assemblage that has been systematically analyzed to date (Scarry 1995; Steponaitis 1983). However, despite their wide distribution, these elaborate vessels are exceedingly rare when compared with other pottery types at Moundville. Sherds classified as Moundville Engraved, *vars. Elliot's Creek* and *Chapman,* Bell Plain, *var. Goldsmith,* and unclassified engraved collectively represent less than 0.75 percent of all Moundville I assemblages (Figure 5.15, Table 5.11). It is important to note that interassemblage differences in these serving-ware frequencies are minor and appear to relate primarily to variation in sample size. This is a significant discovery, as a more restricted or uneven distribution would be expected if the use and exchange of these vessels were tightly controlled by the Moundville elite.

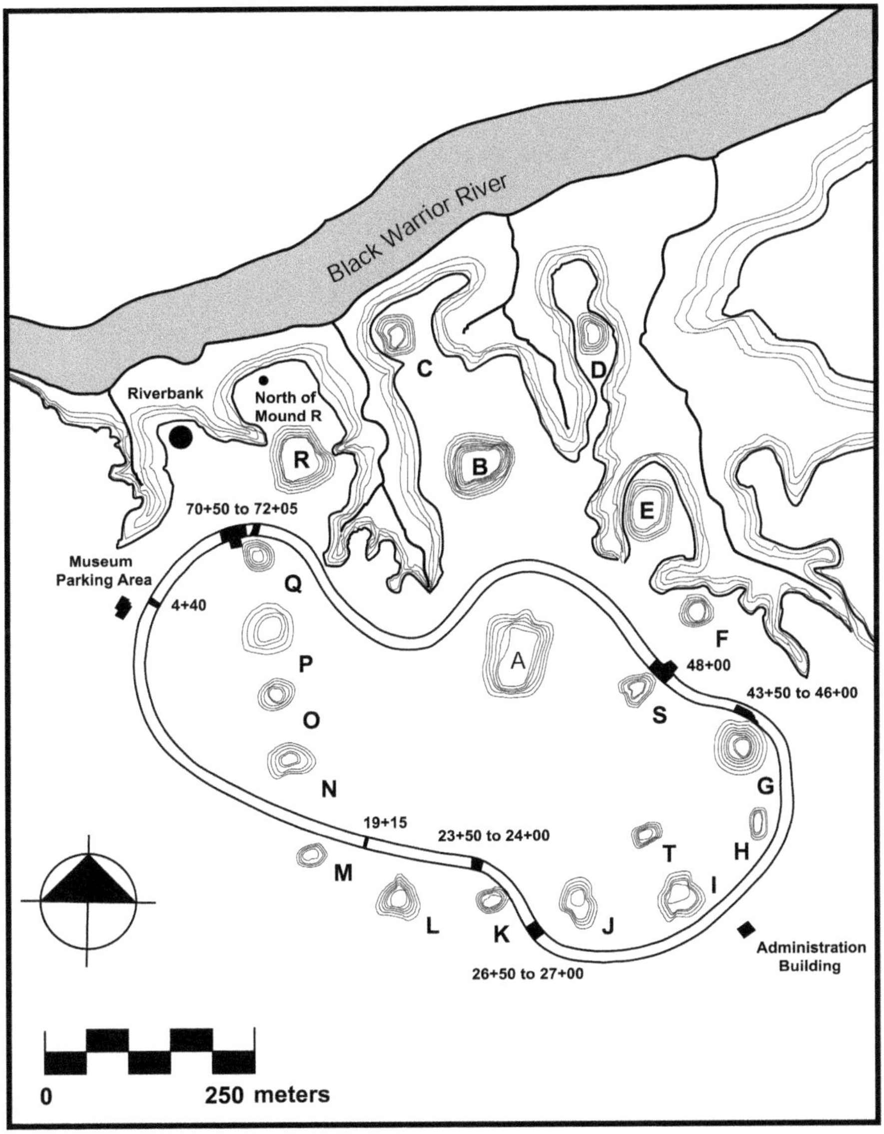

Figure 5.16. Assemblages that include Moundville Engraved, *var. Chapman,* Moundville Engraved, *var. Elliot's Creek,* Bell Plain, *var. Goldsmith,* or unclassified engraved sherds.

Vessel Size Comparisons

In this section I evaluate interassemblage differences and similarities in the sizes of jars and bowls. For the purpose of this analysis the jar category refers to unburnished jars and the bowl category consists of all bowl classes except flaring-rim bowls. Collapsing different bowl classes into one category substantially increases the sample sizes for each assemblage. Importantly, a size comparison of individual bowl classes from each assemblage generated a trend comparable to that obtained in this interassemblage comparison. Other basic shape classes were excluded because of small sample size. Orifice-diameter measurements provide the data on vessel sizes. I use boxplots to compare the distribution of orifice diameters in each Moundville I assemblage. Because of sample sizes, the ECB and PA tract jar assemblages from the Moundville Riverbank were combined. Small sample size also necessitated the exclusion of both the ECB and PA tract bowl assemblages from this comparison.

Figures 5.17 and 5.18 display the distribution of jar and bowl orifice diameters for each assemblage. An examination of Figure 5.17 reveals that the jar orifice distributions for each assemblage are generally comparable. The whiskers (representing the range of assemblage values) of each boxplot overlap. Likewise, the hinges (which represent 50 percent of the variation in each assemblage) of each boxplot overlap. That being said, there are differences worth noting. Closer inspection of the data reveals that the assemblages from North of Mound R and the Administration Building are different from several of the other assemblages. Specifically, the notched confidence intervals of the Administration Building jar assemblage boxplot do not overlap with those for assemblages from Roadway blocks 70+50 to 72+05 and 43+50 to 46+00 and the Museum Parking Area. In addition, the notched confidence intervals of the North of Mound R boxplot do not overlap with assemblages from the Museum Parking Area and Roadway blocks 70+50 to 72+05. These results reveal statistically significant differences between these assemblages at the .05 level.

The bowl assemblage comparison in Figure 5.18 reveals a similar though less pronounced pattern. Although no two bowl assemblages are significantly different, both the Administration Building and the North of Mound R assemblages have smaller orifice-diameter distributions than the other assemblages. As discussed earlier in this chapter vessel size distributions often correspond with the size of social groups that come together to prepare and consume meals. Thus, the smaller orifice-diameter distributions identified for the Administration Building and North of Mound R assemblages may indicate the presence of somewhat smaller residential groups in these two areas than in the other areas.

Though relatively minor, these differences are nonetheless important, as they may correspond with different stages in a residential group's domestic cycle. As re-

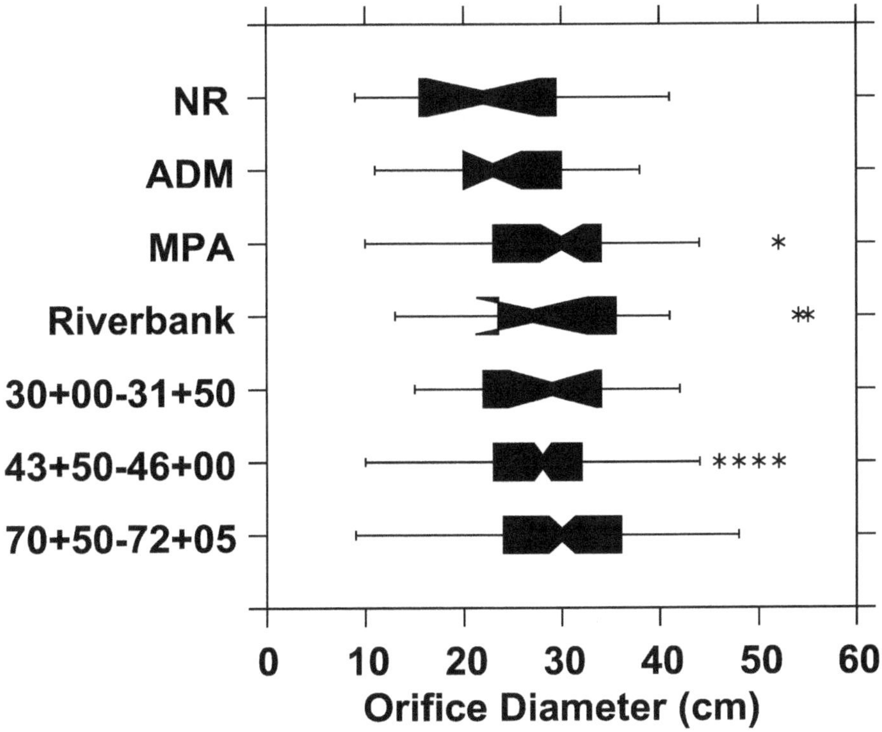

Figure 5.17. Jar orifice diameter distributions by assemblage.

vealed by the architectural analyses presented in Chapter 4, the Administration Building exhibits the lowest late Moundville I occupation span estimate (48 years) of all the contexts from which ceramic assemblages were analyzed. Unfortunately, comparable architectural data from the North of Mound R excavations are not available. Nevertheless, the presence of smaller jars and bowls in the Administration Building assemblage may relate to particular stages of this residential group's development when it consisted of a small number of residents. As a result of the processes of biological reproduction, older and more established residential groups may have included more residents relative to younger groups that came together to prepare and consume meals.

Discussion

One way of discussing early Mississippian pottery assemblages at Moundville is to divide them into vessel sets. Broadly speaking, there is the Mississippi Plain set, the Bell Plain, *var. Hale* set, and the Carthage Incised set. There is also what I would classify as a fine-ware set, consisting of Moundville Engraved, *vars. Elliot's Creek* and *Chapman,* Bell Plain, *var. Goldsmith,* and unclassified engraved, the latter con-

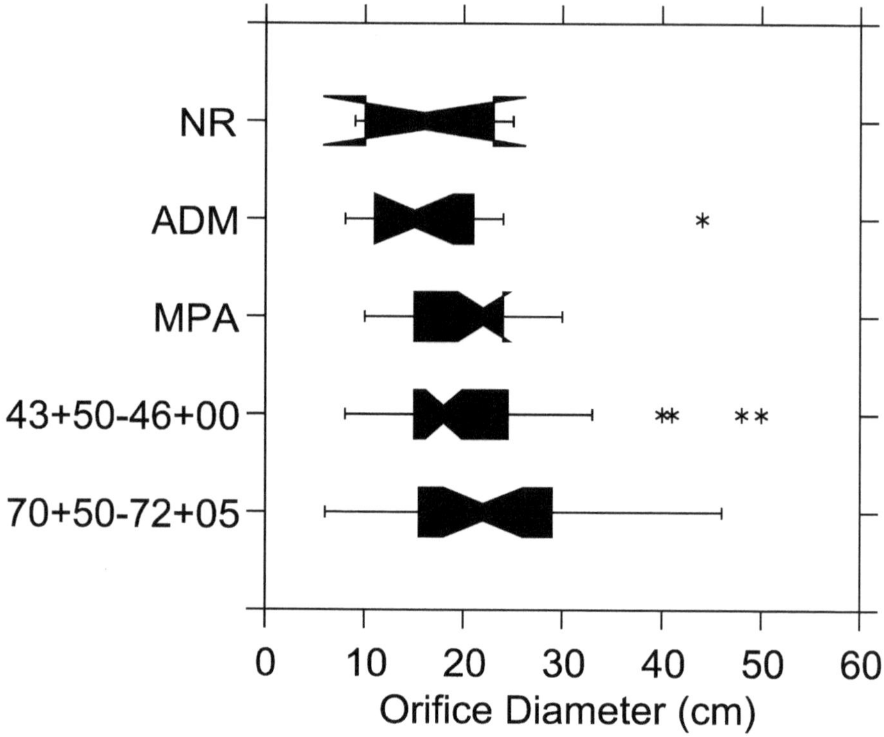

Figure 5.18. Bowl orifice diameter distributions by assemblage.

sisting of a small number of eccentrically decorated sherds that do not fit into any of the other categories. The pots that make up each of these sets share certain similarities in paste composition, surface treatment, and general function.

The Mississippi Plain set consists entirely of utilitarian pots, most of which are cooking jars, but also includes a smaller number of storage jars, pans, and unburnished serving vessels (bowls and bottles).[9] These are by far the most common and widely distributed vessels in Moundville I assemblages. This is not surprising, as they were used primarily for everyday cooking tasks and to store household foodstuffs. My analysis revealed that most households living in different portions of early Moundville used a similar range of cooking jar sizes. This pattern suggests certain consistencies in the sizes of residential groups at Moundville that gathered to prepare and share meals (see Turner and Lofgren 1966).[10] If households or other coresidential groups were considerably larger in one area of the Moundville community than another, then this should be represented in the larger sizes of the vessels that were used to prepare their food. The variation that does exist is minor and likely relates to the different stages of a residential group's domestic cycle. One of the two assemblages with the smallest jar and bowl size distributions had the shortest occupation span estimates as determined in the architectural analyses presented in Chapter 4.

Bell Plain, *var. Hale* and Carthage Incised are related serving-ware sets that include the same series of vessel shapes and sizes. Both sets consist primarily of small restricted and simple bowls, flaring-rim bowls, and bottles, most of which were probably individual-serving containers. While vessels in the Bell Plain, *var. Hale* set were more common than Carthage Incised pots, both were probably consistently used as everyday domestic serving wares. These serving-ware sets increased in popularity throughout the Moundville I phase, suggesting that organizational changes took place in domestic foodways in the decades following Moundville's regional consolidation.

The fine-ware set at early Moundville is perhaps the most difficult to interpret. These are the rarest and most elaborate vessels in Moundville I assemblages. They exhibit considerable standardization in form, decoration, and paste composition. On the basis of the labor invested in their manufacture and elaborate decoration, it is tempting to interpret these serving containers as wealth or prestige goods. However, interassemblage differences in fine-ware sherd frequencies are minor. A more restricted or uneven distribution would be expected if these vessels were tightly controlled by the Moundville elite. That being said, fine-ware sherds are far too rare for these vessels to have been manufactured and used by every household at early Moundville.

Is there an alternative to interpreting fine ware as either prestige goods or utilitarian items? Insight into this issue can be achieved through an examination of Moundville's community organization. As discussed in Chapter 6, Moundville's early Mississippian population was divided into a number of multihousehold groups similar to ethnohistorically described matrilineages. Ceremonial events conducted by these different social groups may have entailed the use of fine-ware pots as well as other ritual items. While not part of every household's domestic inventory, ceremonial items like fine-ware pots would have been used, broken, and discarded by numerous residential groups throughout early Moundville. In this scenario, fine-ware pots were important ceremonial items but not prestige goods in the traditional sense. They were too widely circulated to have been tightly controlled by the Moundville elite. Moreover, they were not produced in sufficient quantity to have functioned as wealth items.

6 Discussion and Conclusions

Moundville was among the largest Mississippian polities, and thus it was clearly more complex than most other settlements in the late prehistoric Southeast. However, this observation raises the question, how complex was Moundville and in what ways was it complex? These are important issues, as Moundville has become an oft-cited example of how Mississippian polities were organized and how they compare to other so-called middle-range societies around the world (Cobb 2003; Earle 1987; Price and Feinman 2001; Scarry and Fish 1999).

Knight (1998) argues that the paramount center of Moundville was designed as a sociogram. On the basis of a comparison with ethnographic case studies of Southeastern and Plains tribes, Knight contends that hierarchical relationships among clans were mapped onto the Moundville community through the structured arrangement of monumental architecture. The ranked position of each clan was represented in the size and arrangement of paired earthen mounds around a large, central plaza. Larger earthen mounds on the northern portion of the plaza are thought to have been associated with higher-ranking clans and smaller mounds to the south with lower-ranking clans (Figure 1.1). One of the central issues I have struggled with here is, what kind of hierarchy was this? Did the ranking of clans at Moundville entail notable material differences between different social groups at the site? If so, what were these material inequalities and how did they correspond with the spatial arrangement of ranked clans at the site?

Over the past 20 years scholars have made a strong case that Moundville was highly differentiated politically, socially, and economically (Peebles 1983, 1987a; Peebles and Kus 1977; Welch 1981; Welch and Scarry 1995). This perspective situates Moundville as the administrative node in a highly centralized regional political and economic network. The basis of elite power at Moundville hinged upon controlling the production of prestige goods used in a variety of social transactions and the production of utilitarian items necessary for agricultural food production (Peebles and Kus 1977; Welch 1981, 1996). It has been argued that these centralized control strategies contributed to Moundville's long-term political stability (Welch 1996:91).

These studies contributed a great deal to our understanding of Moundville as a regional polity. Moreover, they injected into Southeastern archaeology much-needed concepts about chiefly control and social inequality that helped overturn managerial explanations for the origins of ascribed political hierarchies (Peebles and Kus 1977). That being said, important aspects of these previous models of Moundville's political economy have not been supported by my research. For example, I have found few organizational differences between residential areas at the Moundville site that can be related to variability in status or wealth. There are a few possible exceptions to this pattern. I briefly summarize the evidence below.

Domestic architecture and pottery assemblages provided the data for this investigation. From my architectural analysis it appears that early Mississippian households built domestic structures of similar sizes, shapes, and styles throughout the Moundville community. An expansion in structure floor areas from the early to late Moundville I phase, however, does suggest an increasing variability in household sizes and statuses that should not be ignored. These larger households were few in number and widely distributed such that a comparison between any two residential groups would produce a similar distribution of structure sizes (Chapter 4).

My analysis of early Mississippian pottery assemblages at Moundville generated similar results. Assemblages from different residential groups consist of a similar range of vessel shapes, styles, and sizes. While there are minor intra-assemblage differences in the relative frequencies of serving bowls and bottles, these differences appear to be primarily chronological in nature. Specifically, those assemblages resulting from the mixing of early and late Moundville I middens produced lower relative serving-ware frequencies than assemblages from more discrete late Moundville I contexts. The Administration Building was an exception to this trend in that it possesses more bowls relative to other assemblages relative to its place in the ceramic seriation. However, overall there were important consistencies in the ways households stored, prepared, and consumed food throughout much of the early Moundville community (Chapter 5).

Generally, early Moundville appears to have been a community in which differences in status and wealth were downplayed in everyday life. A strong ethos of equality apparently structured the socioeconomic relationships among most residential groups during this era. I am not suggesting there were no socioeconomic differences at Moundville. The large-scale construction of earthen mounds around the perimeter of Moundville's central plaza is strong evidence that a political elite established itself during the late Moundville I phase (Knight and Steponaitis 1998). Knight's (1998) mound excavations and analyses have revealed that the elite used these monuments as temples, homes, and mortuaries during the Moundville II and III phases (see also Markin 1994, 1997; Ryba 1995; Taft 1996). The use and occupation of these mounds during Moundville I is less understood because of a lack of excavations on mound living surfaces dating to this period. Nevertheless, it is reasonable to assume that during the late Moundville I phase, small elite groups occupied and used these monuments in ways that were analogous to their use in the late Mississippian period.

It is intriguing that most early Mississippian households at Moundville acted to level inequalities among one another while they simultaneously acted to promote the political interests of small elite groups. Answers to this conundrum likely relate to the number of ranked political groups making up the Moundville community. When kin groups acted to increase the prestige of their leaders relative to other clan leaders they may have conceived of it as promoting their collective corporate interests. Given the data presented in this study, there appear to have been restricted contexts in which inequalities could be materially expressed at early Moundville—mound ceremonialism and mortuary ritual perhaps being the key examples (Knight 1998; Peebles and Kus 1977). Promoting strong leaders in life and death may have been the primary mechanism through which clans could elevate their corporate status in a social order in which material expressions of inequality were downplayed on the level of the household or residential group. From this perspective, the basis of chiefly power at Moundville was the language of kinship and ritual. Indeed, considering the natural productivity of the Black Warrior Valley combined with its relatively low population density during the early Mississippian period, it would have been very difficult for the elite to have exerted direct control over the economic means of production in the region.

Moundville's complexity was in some respects a product of the sheer number of different kin groups that linked themselves together to form this polity. Factional competition among clans created a political arena in which inequities in status and wealth could be manifested in specific contexts and groups. Meanwhile, everyday practices and interactions among much of the populace structured and were structured by egalitarian processes and strong leveling mechanisms.

Community and Everyday Practices

If this chapter were to end here this investigation would have contributed to a better understanding of Moundville's political economy during the early Mississippian period. It would have contributed very little, however, to an understanding of how Moundville's political and ceremonial order was embedded within and generated by the everyday practices of most of its populace. This is an important point, as there are diverging explanatory trends in the contemporary archaeology of political complexity. At one end of the scholarly continuum, there are those who would categorize polities on the basis of the character of their leadership strategies with little regard for what the masses were doing. It is probably no surprise to the reader that I place myself on the opposite end of the continuum, which emphasizes the role of everyday domestic practices and small-scale domestic groups in shaping community- and polity-scale organization.

The site of Moundville was not always a sociogram just as it was not always the political capital of a large Mississippian polity. At some point changes in the everyday social practices and negotiations among early Mississippian households made it possible for a hereditary elite to emerge and for a complex, kin-based political and ceremonial hierarchy to be established. My goal in this investigation has been to document these everyday domestic practices and the social groups that performed them in order to better understand the emergence of the Moundville polity. In the remainder of this chapter I summarize diachronic trends in Moundville's residential organization. Changes in the use of space by small-scale kin groups provide insight into how broader political and ceremonial relationships were negotiated at Moundville.

Early Moundville I

There is much we do not understand about the early Moundville I occupation of the Black Warrior Valley. The only two mounds in the region at this time were both located on the Moundville terrace, indicating that Moundville was already a place of emerging political and ceremonial importance (Knight and Steponaitis 1998; Steponaitis 1992). It is unclear how expansive the residential occupation was in the immediate vicinity of these two mounds. However, my analyses of the Roadway architecture and ceramic assemblages have demonstrated that the early Moundville I occupation of the Moundville site was more widespread than previously believed. There was a small early Moundville I occupation in nearly every area that later became a larger and more formally organized residential group during the late Moundville I phase.

This pattern suggests that households were not casually dispersed across the Moundville terrace but were already staking claims to specific portions of the landscape. By settling into certain areas of the Moundville terrace and carrying out the everyday tasks of building houses and planting small fields and gardens, these households were initiating a process of routinized domestic behaviors that served to define relationships among different kin groups and the physical landscape. This process ultimately culminated in the construction of the Moundville sociogram during the late Moundville I phase.

Late Moundville I

Kin groups formally defined their corporate identities and connection to community space during the late Moundville I phase. The initiation of large-scale mound construction at this time indicates that Moundville community members had a vested interest in inscribing their clan-based social identities on the landscape. My analysis has revealed strong parallels on the domestic level to these community-level behaviors that defined the corporate group.

An abrupt expansion in residential group size took place during the late Moundville I phase as an estimated 10 to 20 structures per group were built in areas previously occupied by only a few households during the early Moundville I phase. As shown in the analysis of associated midden deposits, it appears that these residential groups engaged in a wide variety of domestic activities such as woodworking, hide processing, pottery manufacture, flint knapping, food preparation, eating, and sleeping (Peebles and Kus 1977; Scarry 1995, 1998; Steponaitis 1983; Welch 1996; Wilson 2001). There are also clues to the kinds of ritual activities these kin groups organized and participated in. Residential group members built large public buildings that provided them the means of exerting some degree of ritual autonomy within Moundville's broader political and ceremonial order (Chapter 4). Moreover, fragments of decorated fine-ware pots, clay pipes, ground pigments, turtle-shell rattles, and small pottery gaming disks hint at a well-developed ceremonial life that took place within the spatial domain of these residential groups (Scarry 1995; Wilson 2001).

As residential groups increased in size, they adopted a more formalized organization of domestic space. Houses were arranged in ways that created shared work spaces, paths, and ritual areas. They were also repeatedly rebuilt in situ to maintain particular domestic spatial schemes (Figure 6.1). These numerous in situ architectural rebuilding events demonstrate the importance that kin groups placed on creating and maintaining connections with particular spaces in the Moundville community. Although Moundville's occupation during this period was nucleated, there were sizable unoccupied areas between residential groups. Rather than spread out or relocate when houses required repair or replacement, however, households opted to rebuild in place, reproducing particular architectural arrangements in particular places.

These well-maintained architectural arrangements would have structured the ways residential group members routinely used and moved through space and interacted with one another. The habitual performance of everyday routines in specific spatial contexts has been argued to be a mechanism by which people internalize social norms and other information about their positions in society (Bourdieu 1977, 1984). Meanings, identities, and rules for social action become embodied in everyday practices as well as in the artifacts, architecture, and physical locations that structure how and where they are carried out (Gillespie 2000; Hodder and Cessford 2004). By carefully creating and maintaining particular architectural spatial arrangements, residential groups were actively producing their space and place in the Moundville sociogram and the network of relationships it referenced.

It is noteworthy that recent settlement-pattern studies in the Black Warrior Valley have documented the presence of dispersed clusters of Mississippian farmsteads that may represent the rural equivalents of nucleated residential groups at the Moundville site (Hammerstedt 2000; Maxham 2004; Myer 2002). Maxham's (2000, 2004) research at the Grady Bobo site (1TU66) indicates that these rural farming communities included sites used for community gatherings in which a variety of ceremonial activities took place. Additional research is needed to refine our

Figure 6.1. Close-up of numerous superimposed hearths (Roadway block 43+95) associated with in situ rebuilt domestic structures in Residential Group 8.

understanding of Moundville's rural settlement organization. Nevertheless, a pattern of multihousehold residential groups appears to have characterized both rural and centralized settlements in the Mississippian Black Warrior Valley.

Moundville II–III

Sometime around A.D. 1260 most residential groups vacated the Moundville site and settled into dispersed farming villages in the rural countryside of the Black Warrior Valley (Knight and Steponaitis 1998; Maxham 2004; Steponaitis 1998). The motivation for this out-migration is not well understood. Knight and Steponaitis (1998:18) have raised the possibility that this settlement shift was part of an elite aggrandizing strategy to create social and physical distance between themselves and the nonelite. Moundville's remaining population is thought to have consisted of small groups of elite and ritual specialists.

This out-migration marked a new era in the way community space and social relationships were defined at Moundville. Rurally relocated kin groups converted their former residential areas at Moundville into small corporate cemeteries. Most Moundville II and III burials were interred in small rectilinear clusters that superimpose the wall foundations of earlier domestic structures (Figure 6.2). Very few burials in the Moundville Roadway and Riverbank are located outside of these former residential spaces. By burying their dead in traditional kin spaces, the rural in-

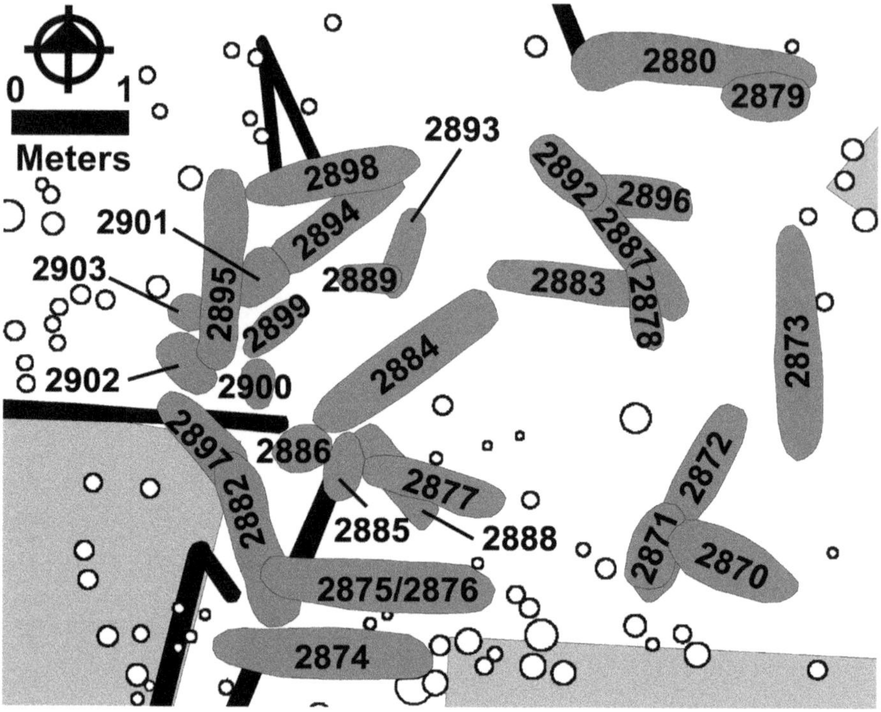

Figure 6.2. Small cemetery in Residential Group 9 dating to Moundville II–III.

habitants of the Black Warrior Valley continued to assert their place in the Moundville sociogram and the network of relationships it referenced. Indeed, there are few more overt ways that groups can naturalize their connection to a place than by burying their ancestors there (Charles and Buikstra 1983).

There is some evidence for elaborate mortuary rituals involving these kin-group cemeteries. Although the dead were often interred in extended positions (Figure 6.3), there are numerous examples of secondary burials such as disarticulated bundles (Figure 6.4) and even individual cranium interments (Peebles 1979). As recently discussed by Hutchinson and Aragon (2002), these variable mortuary treatments likely represent different "snapshots" in a complex, multistage mortuary sequence in which the living exerted claims about their corporate identity and status (see also Kuijt 2000). Indeed, the variety of different mortuary treatments present in any one of these kin-group cemeteries indicates that the dead were often subject to different ritual steps of inhumation, exhumation, and reburial. In this way these cemeteries served as a kind of social resource in which kin groups could promote their corporate status through the ritualized manipulation and processing of ancestral skeletal materials.

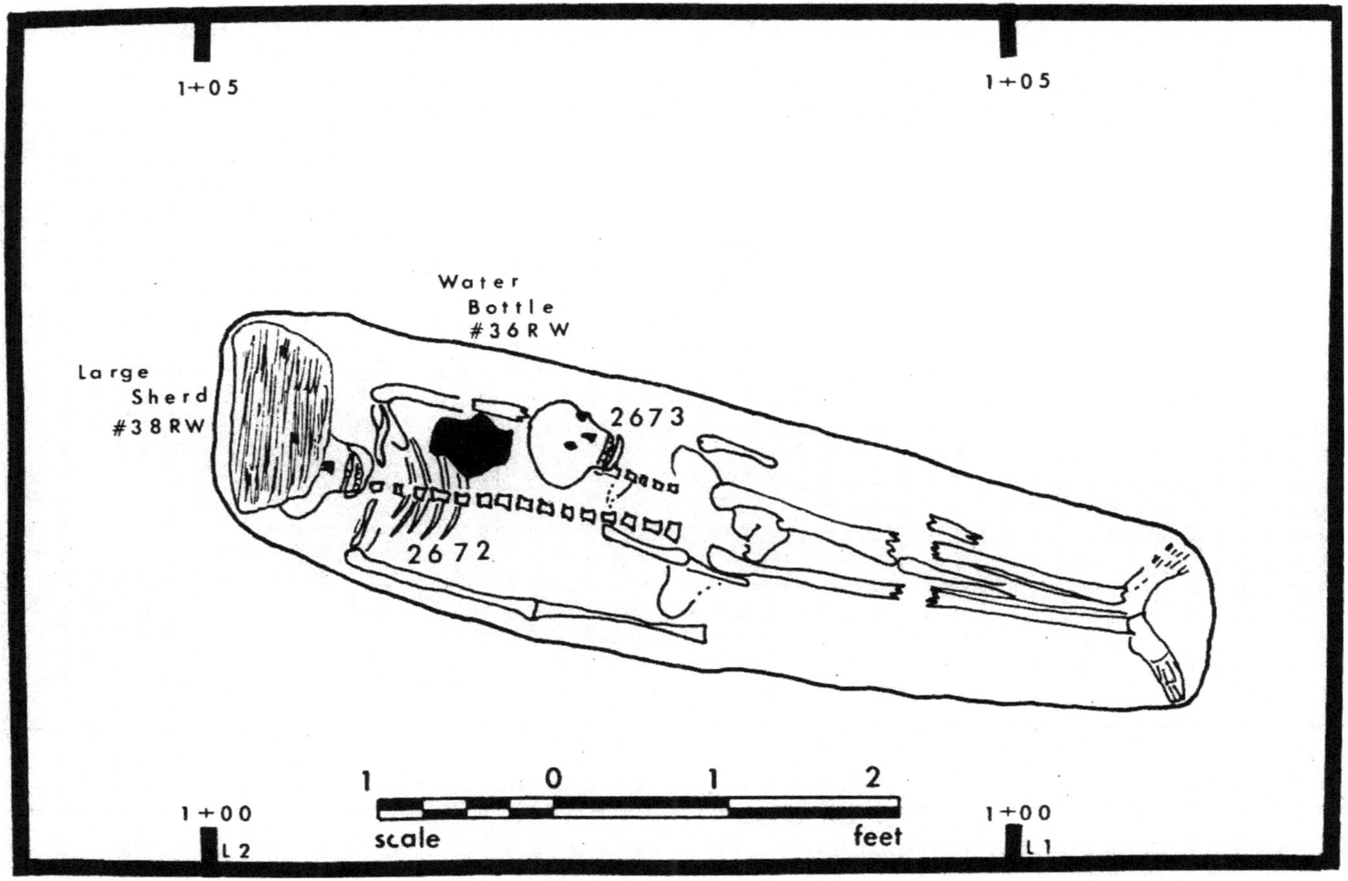

Figure 6.3. Extended burials in Residential Group 1.

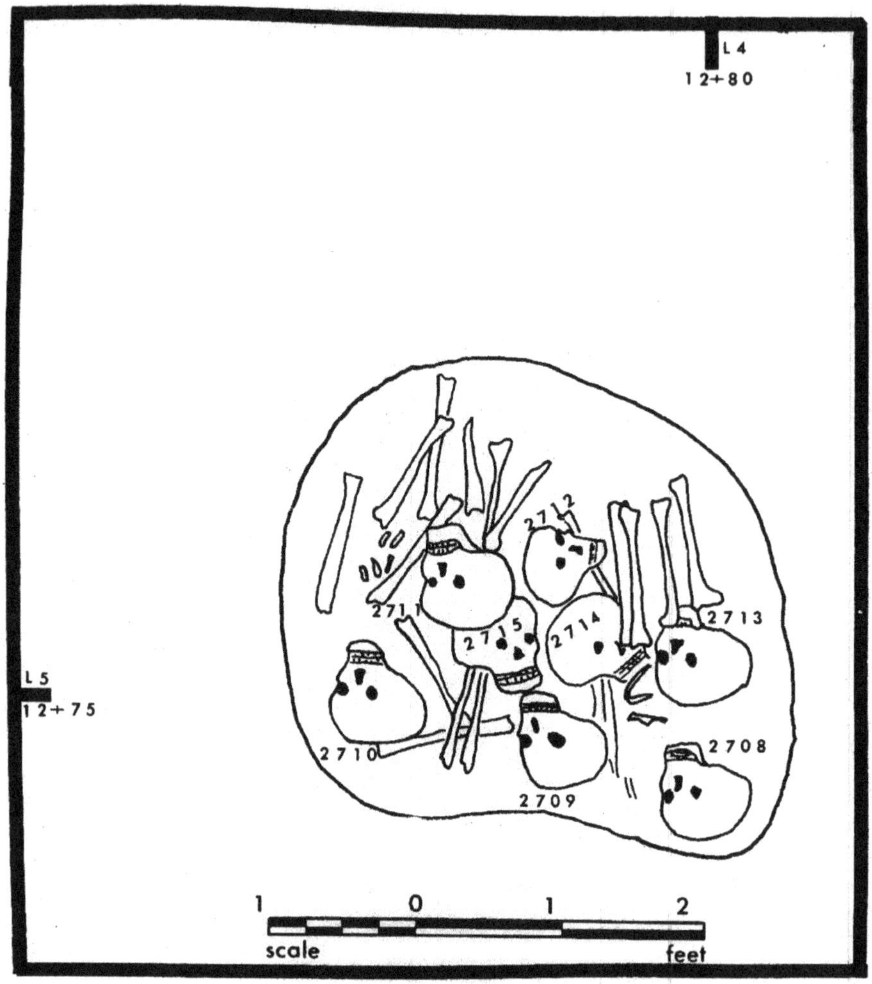

Figure 6.4. Secondary burials in Residential Group 2.

Conclusion

I have offered a history of Moundville's early Mississippian occupation by examining the daily practices of a broad cross section of the community's populace. I began by documenting and describing different residential groups at Moundville and the kinds of routine activities that made up everyday domestic life. I found that early Moundville was occupied by numerous small-scale social groups. These groups organized themselves in ways that are comparable to descriptions of matrilineages from the early historic southeastern United States (Hudson 1976; Knight 1990; Speck 1907; Swanton 1922). All evidence indicates these residential groups were at once social, economic, and ritual units that consisted of multiple households occupying different domestic structures.

The organizational changes in Moundville's residential occupation highlight the different ways in which kin groups defined and redefined their corporate status and identities over the long term. During their initial, sparse settlement of the Moundville terrace in the early Moundville I phase, households began to establish strong ties to particular parts of the physical landscape and to one another. The abrupt and large-scale transformation of this landscape during the late Moundville I phase is a chronicle of the intensified corporate-building and corporate-defining activities carried out by these groups. Because Moundville was organized as a sociogram, the physical spaces occupied by different groups coincided with their positions in the broader network of social relationships. This was a generative process. Neither the Moundville sociogram nor the regional political hierarchy existed outside of the various competitive and corporate activities in which these early Mississippian kin groups engaged.

This explanation highlights the role of small social groups in the emergence of social and political complexity during the early Mississippian Black Warrior Valley of west-central Alabama. Rather than ask how aspiring elites imposed a ranked hierarchy on Moundville society, I have considered how changes in the everyday practices and relationships among small social groups made it possible for an elite to emerge. I conclude that Mississippian organizational complexity in the Black Warrior Valley was the outcome of the social negotiations among corporate kin groups and their connections to and modification of the physical landscape.

Appendix 1

Architectural Data

Structure	Area	Length	Width	Floor Area	Class[a]	Building Episodes	Status[b]	Type[c]
1	2+50–7+50	4.00	4.00	17.00	I	2	C	I
2	2+50–7+50	4.00	4.00	14.00	I	2	C	WT
3	2+50–7+50	3.00	3.00	10.00	I	1	C	WT
4	2+50–7+50	5.00	5.00	25.00	I	2	C	WT
5	2+50–7+50	4.00	4.00	16.00	I	2	C	I
6	2+50–7+50	4.00	3.00	11.00	I	1	C	I
7	2+50–7+50					1	I	H
8	2+50–7+50						I	I
9	12+00–14+00	4.00	4.00	19.00	I	1	I	SP
10	12+00–14+00	4.00	3.00	12.00	I	1	I	WT
11	12+00–14+00	3.00	3.00	13.00	I	1	C	WT
12	12+00–14+00	4.00	4.00	14.00	I	1	C	H
13	12+00–14+00					1	I	WT
14	12+00–14+00					1	I	WT
15	12+00–14+00	3.00	3.00	10.00	I	1	I	SP
16	15+00–15+50	8.00	6.00	47.00	II	1	C	WT
17	17+50–24+50						I	WT
18	17+50–24+50	8.00	6.00	45.00	II	1	I	WT
19	17+50–24+50	6.00	5.00	28.00	I	1	C	WT
20	17+50–24+50	5.00	4.00	23.00	I	3	I	WT
21	17+50–24+50	6.00	5.00	29.00	I		I	WT
22	17+50–24+50	6.00	5.00	26.00	I	1	I	WT

Structure	Area	Length	Width	Floor Area	Class[a]	Building Episodes	Status[b]	Type[c]
23	26+00–34+00	5.00	4.00	23.00	I	1	C	WT
24	26+00–34+00	5.00	4.00	20.00	I	2	C	WT
25	26+00–34+00	7.00	6.00	40.00	II	2	C	WT
26	26+00–34+00	5.00	4.00	21.00	I	2	I	WT
27	26+00–34+00	4.00	4.00	17.00	I	1	C	WT
28	43+50–46+50	5.00	5.00	22.00	I	1	C	WT
29	47+50–49+00	5.00	5.00	24.00	I	2	I	WT
30	43+50–46+50	4.00	4.00	16.00	I	1	C	WT
31	43+50–46+50					1	I	SP
32	43+50–46+50					2	I	WT
33	43+50–46+50					1	I	WT
34	43+50–46+50					1	I	H
35	43+50–46+50					3	I	WT
36	35+50–37+60					1	I	SP
37	35+50–37+60						I	H
38	35+50–37+60					1	I	SP
39	35+50–37+60					1	I	WT
40	35+50–37+60					2	I	WT
41	35+50–37+60						I	
42	None					1	I	H
43	26+00–34+00					1	I	WT
44	26+00–34+00					2	I	WT
45	26+00–34+00					1	I	H
46	26+00–34+00					1	I	H
47	26+00–34+00					1	I	H

48	26+00–34+00					2	I	WT
49	26+00–34+00					1	I	SP
50	26+00–34+00					1	I	WT
51	26+00–34+00						I	WT
52	26+00–34+00					2	I	WT
53	26+00–34+00					2	I	WT
54	17+50–24+50						I	I
55	17+50–24+50						I	WT
56	17+50–24+50					2	I	WT
57	17+50–24+50					2	I	WT
58	17+50–24+50						I	I
59	17+50–24+50					2	I	WT
60	17+50–24+50					1	I	SP
61	17+50–24+50						I	I
62	17+50–24+50					3	I	WT
63	17+50–24+50						I	I
64	17+50–24+50					2	I	WT
65	17+50–24+50						I	I
66	17+50–24+50	6.00	5.00	30.00	I	2	C	WT
67	17+50–24+50					1	I	WT
68	17+50–24+50					1	I	H
69	17+50–24+50					1	I	WT
70	17+50–24+50						I	H
71	12+00–14+00					2	I	WT
72	12+00–14+00					2	I	WT
73	12+00–14+00					1	I	WT
74	2+50–7+50						C	WT

Structure	Area	Length	Width	Floor Area	Class[a]	Building Episodes	Status[b]	Type[c]
75	2+50–7+50	6.00	5.00	27.00	I	3	I	WT
76	2+50–7+50					1	I	SP
77	2+50–7+50	5.00	4.00	22.00	I	1	C	WT
78	2+50–7+50	5.00	5.00	25.00	I	1	I	WT
79	2+50–7+50					2	I	WT
80	2+50–7+50	5.00	4.00	17.00	I	2	C	WT
81	2+50–7+50	3.00	3.00	11.00	I	1	I	WT
82	2+50–7+50					2	I	WT
83	68+36–70+00	5.00	4.00	22.00	I	2	I	WT
84	68+36–70+00	6.00	5.00	30.00	I		C	WT
85	71+00–72+00	8.00	7.00	60.00	III	1	I	WT
86	68+36–70+00					3	I	WT
87	66+00–67+00					1	I	WT
88	66+00–67+00	4.00	4.00	18.00	I	2	C	SP
89	66+00–67+00	7.00	5.00	39.00	II	1	C	SP
90	66+00–67+00	8.00	5.00	40.00	II	1	I	WT
91	47+50–49+00	5.00	5.00	24.00	I	2	C	WT
92	47+50–49+00	4.00	4.00	18.00	I	3	C	WT
93	47+50–49+00	11.00	4.00	47.00	II	2	C	WT
94	47+50–49+00	8.00	5.00	44.00	II	3	C	WT
95	47+50–49+00	9.00	7.00	64.00	III		C	WT
96	47+50–49+00					1	C	H
97	47+50–49+00	5.00	5.00	22.00	I	2	C	WT
98	17+50–24+50						I	I
99	26+00–34+00					3	I	WT

100	26+00–34+00					1	I	WT
101	26+00–34+00	6.00	5.00	27.00	I	3	I	WT
102	43+50–46+50					4	I	WT
103	43+50–46+50					2	I	WT
104	43+50–46+50					1	I	WT
105	2+50–7+50					1	I	WT
106	2+50–7+50					2	I	WT
107	2+50–7+50					1	I	WT
108	17+50–24+50					1	I	WT
109	17+50–24+50					2	I	WT
110	26+00–34+00						I	WT
111	26+00–34+00						I	I
112	35+50–37+60						I	WT
113	35+50–37+60					1	I	WT
114	47+50–49+00	5.00	5.00	23.00	I	1	C	SP
115	ADM	4.00	4.00	14.00	I	1	I	WT
116	ADM	6.00	5.00	32.00	I	3	C	WT
117	ADM					1	I	SP
118	ADM					3	I	WT
119	ADM	6.00	4.00	25.00	I	1	C	WT
120	ADM						I	I
121	26+00–34+00	5.00	5.00	23.00	I		C	SP
122	47+50–49+00	4.00	4.00	16.00	I		C	WT
123	47+50–49+00	5.00	4.00	19.00	I	2	C	SP
124	47+50–49+00	3.00	3.00	8.00	I	1	C	WT
125	2+50–7+50					1	I	WT
126	2+50–7+50					1	I	I

Structure	Area	Length	Width	Floor Area	Class[a]	Building Episodes	Status[b]	Type[c]
127	2+50–7+50	5.00	4.00	21.00	I	1	C	SP
128	2+50–7+50	5.00	4.00	19.00	I	1	C	I
129	2+50–7+50	6.00	5.00	29.00	I	1	C	SP
130	2+50–7+50					1	I	SP
131	2+50–7+50					1	I	WT
132	2+50–7+50	5.00	5.00	23.00	I	1	C	SP
133	2+50–7+50	6.00	5.00	29.00	I	1	C	SP
134	MPA	3.76	3.68	14.06	I	1	C	WT
135	MPA					1	I	WT
136	MPA	4.41	4.34	18.85	I	2	C	WT
137	MPA	3.82	3.82	14.84	I	2	C	WT
138	MPA	5.71	5.40	30.01	I	2	C	WT
139	MPA					1	I	WT
140	MPA	4.15	3.78	15.88	I	1	C	SP
PA-1[d]	PA	6.50	5.00	32.50	I	1	C	SP
PA-2	PA	5.00	4.50	22.50	I	1	C	SP
PA-3	PA	4.50	4.00	18.00	I	1	C	H
PA-4	PA	4.25	4.00	17.00	I	1	C	WT
PA-5	PA	5.00	4.50	22.50	I	2	C	WT
PA-6	PA	4.00	3.50	14.00	I	1	C	SP
ECB-1	ECB					1	I	SP
ECB-2	ECB					1	I	WT
ECB-3	ECB					1	I	WT

ECB-4	ECB							I	I
ECB-5	ECB		3.80	3.60	13.70	I	2	C	WT
ECB-6	ECB		4.50	4.50	20.25	I	4	I	WT

Key: ADM, Administration Building; MPA, Museum Parking Area; ECB, East Conference Building; PA, Picnic Area.

[a]Class: I, average floor area 21 m^2; II, average floor area 43 m^2; III, average floor area 62 m^2.

[b]Status: C = complete; I = incomplete.

[c]Type: I = indeterminate; WT = wall trench; H, hybrid; SP = single post.

[d]Picnic Area and East Conference Building data from Scarry (1995).

Appendix 2

Counts and Frequencies of All Sherds by Context

Type/Variety	ADM		43+50–46+00	
	N	%	N	%
Anna Incised				
Autauga Plain	13	0.60	2	0.03
Avoyelle Incised				
Baytown Plain	1	0.05	7	0.12
Bell Plain, *var. Goldsmith*			44	0.74
Bell Plain, *var. Hale*	435	19.94	754	12.71
Carters Engraved			1	0.02
Carthage Incised, *var. Akron*	13	0.60	30	0.51
Carthage Incised, *var. Carthage*	1	0.05		
Carthage Incised, *var. Fosters*			1	0.02
Carthage Incised, *var. Moon Lake*	2	0.09	8	0.13
Carthage Incised, *var. Summerville*	6	0.27	8	0.13
Carthage Incised, *var. Unspecified*	14	0.64	19	0.32
D'Olive Incised			2	0.03
Evansville Punctated			4	0.07
Langston Fabric Impressed			1	0.02
Late Savannah Simple Stamped				
L'Eau Noire Incised				
Mathews Incised			1	0.02
Mazique Incised			5	0.08
Mississippi Plain, *var. Hull Lake*	2	0.09	28	0.47
Mississippi Plain, *var. Warrior*	1,506	69.02	4,623	77.99
Moundville Engraved, *var. Chapman*			60	1.01
Moundville Engraved, *var. Elliot's Creek*	10	0.46	9	0.15
Moundville Engraved, *var. Hemphill*				
Moundville Engraved, *var. Maxwells Crossing*				
Moundville Engraved, *var. Northport*				
Moundville Engraved, *var. Prince Plantation*				
Moundville Engraved, *var. Tuscaloosa*				
Moundville Engraved, *var. Unspecified*	9	0.41	9	0.15
Moundville Engraved, *var. Wiggens*	1	0.05	1	0.02
Moundville Incised, *var. Carrollton*	28	1.28	34	0.57
Moundville Incised, *var. Moundville*	107	4.90	208	3.51
Moundville Incised, *var. Oliver*	2	0.09	18	0.30
Moundville Incised, *var. Snows Bend*	1	0.05	1	0.02
Moundville Incised, *var. Unspecified*	26	1.19	37	0.62
Nashville Negative Painted				
Owens Punctated	2	0.09		
Unclassified engraved	3	0.14	13	0.22
Total	2,182	100.00	5,928	100.00

Key: ADM, Administration Building; MPA, Museum Parking Area.

70+50–72+05		30+00–31+50		MPA		Total	
N	%	N	%	N	%	N	%
				6	0.20	6	0.04
1	0.04	1	0.18	3	0.10	20	0.14
1	0.04				0.00	1	0.01
12	0.45	3	0.54	18	0.60	41	0.29
1	0.04					45	0.31
386	14.57	64	11.59	419	13.92	2,058	14.37
						1	0.01
12	0.45	1	0.18	19	0.63	75	0.52
						1	0.01
						1	0.01
9	0.34			5	0.17	24	0.17
2	0.08			3	0.10	19	0.13
8	0.30	1	0.18	20	0.66	62	0.43
						2	0.01
						4	0.03
						1	0.01
				2	0.07	2	0.01
				1	0.03	1	0.01
						1	0.01
1	0.04					6	0.04
5	0.19	4	0.72	41	1.36	80	0.56
2,028	76.56	436	78.99	2,282	75.84	10,875	75.94
3	0.11			1	0.03	64	0.45
12	0.45			1	0.03	32	0.22
				4	0.13	4	0.03
				1	0.03	1	0.01
				1	0.03	1	0.01
1	0.04			1	0.03	2	0.01
				1	0.03	1	0.01
				18	0.60	36	0.25
				2	0.07	4	0.03
15	0.57	1	0.18	26	0.86	104	0.73
120	4.53	22	3.99	120	3.99	577	4.03
13	0.49			1	0.03	34	0.24
1	0.04			3	0.10	6	0.04
16	0.60	18	3.26	9	0.30	106	0.74
1	0.04	1	0.18			2	0.01
						2	0.01
1	0.04			1	0.03	18	0.13
2,649	100.00	552	100.00	3,009	100.00	14,320	100.00

Notes

Chapter 2

1. These excavations were conducted in 1991 and 1992 prior to efforts by the United States Army Corps of Engineers to protect this portion of the site from further erosion. Knight directed these excavations (Scarry 1995).

2. Early Mississippian architecture is discussed more thoroughly in Chapter 4.

3. It is unclear whether this feature was of intentional design or merely a disturbance.

4. A small concentration of unworked mica was also identified in a single context at the northwest fringes of the Moundville site. No direct evidence, however, for the manufacture of mica items, in the form of partially manufactured artifacts, has been found.

Chapter 3

1. Because of their spatially restricted nature the North of Mound R contexts were excluded from this analysis.

Chapter 4

1. Twenty-four Class I structures possess hearths while 37 do not.

2. In one case the wall-trench foundation of a structure is superimposed by a burial dating to the early Moundville II phase.

3. All wall trenches were measured and their lengths were summed by excavation block. This sum was then multiplied by the average number of post molds per meter of wall trench. Finally, this figure was divided by excavation block (square meters) to generate the final architectural density ratio.

4. These counts only include those structures for which the number of in situ building episodes could be accurately determined.

5. These figures are based on the assumption that houses were constructed from a combination of cedar and pine wall posts.

Chapter 5

1. In some cases vessel bases are also distinctive enough to assign to a vessel class. Vessel shape, however, may be more easily identified from the base sherds of some vessels than

others. Moreover, there is the risk of inflating counts by tabulating both the rim and base sherds from the same vessel.

2. The greater frequency of Mississippi Plain jars is partially the product of breakage and identification patterns. For example, some jar rims identified as Mississippi Plain may have derived from portions of Moundville Incised jars that did not bear incised decorations.

3. It is important to note, however, that we are missing the basal portions of these vessels, where much of this evidence would be visible.

4. Thickened-rim jars are not present in greater numbers where refuse from feasting events has been identified.

5. No complete Carthage Incised jars have been recovered from excavations. The argument for these jars having lower height-to-width ratios is based on partial vessels.

6. Both the PA and ECB tract assemblages were excluded from this study as the MNV for those assemblages was calculated in a manner that is not directly compatible with analyses in the current study.

7. The Riverbank assemblage falls in the middle of this sequence as the early Moundville I PA tract assemblage and the late Moundville I ECB tract assemblage were combined.

8. Because of their more distinct paste compositions and/or surface treatments, other Moundville serving-ware types are not as susceptible to issues of interanalyst bias and differential preservation as is Bell Plain, *var. Hale.*

9. A number of the Mississippi Plain bowls and bottles are probably Bell Plain, *var. Hale* vessels with eroded surfaces.

10. The logic of this argument rests on the ethnographically documented practice of larger social groups using larger pots to cook and serve meals than smaller social groups.

References Cited

Alt, Susan M.

2001 Cahokian Change and the Authority of Tradition. In *The Archaeology of Traditions: Agency and History before and after Columbus,* edited by T. R. Pauketat, pp. 141–156. University Press of Florida, Gainesville.

Anderson, David G.

1994 The Role of Cahokia in the Evolution of Southeastern Mississippian Society. In *Cahokia: Domination and Ideology in the Mississippian World,* edited by T. R. Pauketat and T. E. Emerson, pp. 167–189. University of Nebraska Press, Lincoln.

Ashmore, Wendy, and Richard R. Wilk

1988 Household and Community in the Mesoamerican Past. In *Household and Community in the Mesoamerican Past,* edited by R. R. Wilk and W. Ashmore, pp. 1–27. University of New Mexico Press, Albuquerque.

Astin, Robyn L.

1996 Mound M: Chronology and Function at Moundville. Unpublished Master's thesis, Department of Anthropology, University of Alabama, Tuscaloosa.

Atalay, Sonya, and Christine Hastorf

2006 Food, Meals, and Daily Activities: The Habitus of Food Practices at Neolithic Çatalhöyük. *American Antiquity* 71(2):283–319.

Bailey, Douglass W.

1996 The Life, Times and Works of House 59 from the Ovcharovo Tell, Bulgaria. In *Neolithic Houses in Northwest Europe and Beyond,* edited by T. Darvill and J. Thomas, pp. 143–156. Oxbow, Oxford.

Bareis, Charles J.

1976 *The Knoebel Site, St. Clair County, Illinois.* Circular 1, Illinois Archaeological Survey, Urbana.

Blitz, John H.

1993a Big Pots for Big Shots: Feasting and Storage in a Mississippian Community. *American Antiquity* 58(1):80–96.

1993b *Ancient Chiefdoms of the Tombigbee.* University of Alabama Press, Tuscaloosa.

1999 Mississippian Chiefdoms and the Fission-Fusion Process. *American Antiquity* 64(4):577–592.

Blitz, John H., and Karl G. Lorenz

2002 The Early Mississippian Frontier in the Lower Chattahoochee-Apalachicola River Valley. *Southeastern Archaeology* 21(2):117–135.

Bourdieu, Pierre

1977 *Outline of a Theory of Practice,* translated by R. Nice. Cambridge University Press, Cambridge.

1984 *Distinction: A Social Critique of the Judgement of Taste.* Harvard University Press, Cambridge, Massachusetts.

Bozeman, Tandy K.

1982 Moundville Phase Communities in the Black Warrior River Valley, Alabama. Unpublished Ph.D. dissertation, Department of Anthropology, University of California, Santa Barbara.

Braun, David P.

1980 Experimental Interpretations of Ceramic Vessel Use on the Basis of Rim and Neck Formal Attributes. In *The Navajo Project,* edited by D. C. Feiro, R. Munson, M. McLain, S. Wilson, and A. Zier, pp. 171–231. Paper No. 1. Museum of Northern Arizona Research, Flagstaff.

1983 Pots as Tools. In *Archaeological Hammers and Theories,* edited by J. A. Moore and A. S. Keene, pp. 107–134. Academic Press, New York.

Charles, Douglas K., and Jane E. Buikstra

1983 Archaic Mortuary Sites in the Central Mississippi Drainage: Distribution, Structure, and Behavioral Implications. In *Archaic Hunters and Gatherers in the American Midwest,* edited by J. L. Phillips and J. A. Brown, pp. 117–145. Academic Press, New York.

Chase, Philip G.

1985 Whole Vessels and Sherds: An Experimental Investigation of Their Quantitative Relationship. *Journal of Field Archaeology* 12(2):213–218.

Cobb, Charles R.

2003 Mississippian Chiefdoms: How Complex? *Annual Review of Anthropology* 32: 63–84.

Coe, Joffre L.

1995 *Town Creek Indian Mound: A Native American Legacy.* University of North Carolina Press, Chapel Hill.

Comaroff, Jean, and John L. Comaroff

1991 *Of Revelation and Revolution: Christianity, Colonialism, and Consciousness in South Africa.* University of Chicago Press, Chicago.

Cowgill, George

1972 Models, Methods and Techniques for Seriation. In *Models in Archaeology,* edited by D. Clarke, pp. 381–424. Methuen, London.

David, Nicholas

1972 On the Life Span of Pottery, Type Frequencies, and Archaeological Inference. *American Antiquity* 37(1):141–142.

Davy, Douglas M.

1982 Proximity and Human Behavior: Settlement Location Pattern Change in Prehistoric Illinois. Unpublished Ph.D. dissertation, Department of Anthropology, Southern Illinois University, Carbondale.

DeBoer, Warren R.

1974 Ceramic Longevity and Archaeological Interpretation: An Example from Upper Ucayali, Peru. *American Antiquity* 39(2):335–342.

1983 The Archaeological Record as a Preserved Death Assemblage. In *Archaeological Hammers and Theories,* edited by J. A. Moore and A. S. Keene, pp. 19–36. Academic Press, New York.

DeBoer, Warren R., and Donald W. Lathrap

1979 The Making and Breaking of Shipibo-Conibo Ceramics. In *Ethnoarchaeology: Implications of Ethnography for Archaeology,* edited by C. Kramer, pp. 102–138. Columbia University Press, New York.

DeJarnette, David L.

1952 Alabama Archaeology: A Summary. In *Archaeology of Eastern United States,* edited by J. B. Griffin, pp. 272–284. University of Chicago Press, Chicago.

DeJarnette, David L., and Christopher S. Peebles

1970 The Development of Alabama Archaeology: The Snow's Bend Site. *Journal of Alabama Archaeology* 16(2):77–119.

DeJarnette, David L., and Steve B. Wimberly

1941 *The Bessemer Site: Excavations of Three Mounds and Surrounding Village Areas near Bessemer, Alabama.* Museum Paper 17. Geological Survey of Alabama, Tuscaloosa.

Dobres, Marcia-Anne, and John E. Robb

2000 Agency in Archaeology: Paradigm or Platitude? In *Agency in Archaeology,* edited by M.-A. Dobres and J. E. Robb, pp. 3–17. Routledge Press, New York.

Dornan, Jennifer L.

2002 Agency and Archaeology: Past, Present, and Future Directions. *Journal of Archaeological Method and Theory* 9(4):303–329.

Earle, Timothy K.

1987 Chiefdoms in Archaeological and Ethnohistoric Perspective. *Annual Review of Anthropology* 16:279–308.

Emerson, Thomas E.

1997a Reflections from the Countryside on Cahokian Hegemony. In *Cahokia: Domination and Ideology in the Mississippian World,* edited by T. R. Pauketat and T. E. Emerson, pp. 167–189. University of Nebraska Press, Lincoln.

1997b *Cahokia and the Archaeology of Power.* University of Alabama Press, Tuscaloosa.

Ensor, H. Blaine

1993 *Big Sandy Farms: A Prehistoric Agricultural Community near Moundville, Black Warrior River Floodplain, Tuscaloosa County, Alabama.* Report of Investigations 68. Alabama Museum of Natural History, University of Alabama, Tuscaloosa.

Finney, Fred A.

1985 *The Carbon Dioxide Site.* American Bottom Archaeology, FAI-270 Site Reports 11, Pt. 1. University of Illinois Press, Urbana.

Ford, James A.

1962 *A Quantitative Method for Deriving Cultural Chronology.* Technical Manual. Pan American Union, Washington, D.C.

Ford, James A., and George I. Quimby, Jr.
1946 The Tchefuncte Culture, an Early Occupation of the Lower Mississippi Valley. *American Anthropologist* 48(2):246–251.

Ford, James A., and Gordon R. Willey
1940 *Crooks Site, a Marksville Period Burial Mound in La Salle Parish, Louisiana.* Anthropological Study No. 3. Louisiana State Geological Survey, Department of Conservation, Baton Rouge.

Fortes, Meyer
1958 Introduction. In *The Developmental Cycle in Domestic Groups,* edited by J. Goody, pp. 1–13. Cambridge University Press, Cambridge.

Foster, George M.
1960 Life Expectancy of Utilitarian Pottery in Tzintzuntzan, Michoacan, Mexico. *American Antiquity* 25(4):606–609.

Fowler, Melvin L.
1989 *The Cahokia Atlas: A Historical Atlas of Cahokia Archaeology.* Studies in Illinois Archaeology 6. Illinois Historic Preservation Agency, Springfield.

Giddens, Anthony
1979 *Central Problems in Social Theory.* Macmillan Press, London.

Gillespie, Susan D.
2000 Beyond Kinship: An Introduction. In *Beyond Kinship: Social and Material Reproduction in House Societies,* edited by R. A. Joyce and S. D. Gillespie, pp. 1–21. University of Pennsylvania Press, Philadelphia.

Goody, Jack
1958 The Fission of Domestic Groups among the LoDagaba. In *The Developmental Cycle in Domestic Groups,* edited by J. Goody, pp. 53–91. Cambridge University Press, Cambridge.
1972 *Domestic Groups.* Addison-Wesley Modular Publication in Anthropology, 28. Addison-Wesley, Reading, Massachusetts.

Griffiths, Dorothy
1978 Use-Marks on Historic Ceramics: A Preliminary Study. *Historical Archaeology* 12:68–81.

Hally, David J.
1983a Use Alteration of Pottery Vessel Surfaces: An Important Source of Evidence for the Identification of Vessel Function. *North American Archaeologist* 4(1):3–26.
1983b The Interpretive Potential of Pottery from Domestic Contexts. *Midcontinental Journal of Archaeology* 8(2):163–196.
1984 Vessel Assemblages and Food Habits: A Comparison of Two Aboriginal Southeastern Vessel Assemblages. *Southeastern Archaeology* 3(1):46–64.
1986 The Identification of Vessel Function: A Case Study from Northwest Georgia. *American Antiquity* 51(2):267–295.

Hally, David J., and Hypatia Kelly
1998 The Nature of Mississippian Towns in Georgia: The King Site Example. In *Mississippian Towns and Sacred Spaces: Searching for an Architectural Grammar,* ed-

ited by R. B. Lewis and C. Stout, pp. 49–63. University of Alabama Press, Tuscaloosa.

Hammerstedt, Scott W.

2000 Characteristics of Late Woodland and Mississippian Settlements in the Black Warrior Valley, Alabama. Unpublished Master's thesis, Department of Anthropology, University of Alabama, Tuscaloosa.

Hammerstedt, Scott W., and Jennifer L. Myer

2001 Outlying Mississippian Settlement in the Black Warrior Valley, Alabama. Paper presented at the 66th Annual Meeting of the Society for American Archaeology, New Orleans.

Hardin, Margaret Ann

1981 The Identification of Individual Style on Moundville Engraved Vessels: A Preliminary Note. *Southeastern Archaeological Conference Bulletin* 24:108–110.

Henrickson, Elizabeth F., and Mary McDonald

1983 Ceramic Form and Function: An Ethnographic Search and Archaeological Application. *American Anthropologist* 85(3):630–643.

Herndon, Richard L.

1995 Architectural Correlates of Mississippian Chiefdoms: A Case Study of the Moundville and Lubbub Creek Chiefdoms. Unpublished Master's thesis, Department of Anthropology, University of Southern Mississippi, Hattiesburg.

Hodder, Ian, and Craig Cessford

2004 Daily Practice and Social Memory at Çatalhöyük. *American Antiquity* 69(1): 17–40.

Holmes, William H.

1886 Pottery of the Ancient Pueblos. In *Fourth Annual Report of the Bureau of Ethnology to the Secretary of the Smithsonian Institution, 1882–83,* edited by J. W. Powell, pp. 257–360. Government Printing Office, Washington, D.C.

Hudson, Charles

1976 *The Southeastern Indians.* University of Tennessee Press, Knoxville.

Hutchinson, Dale, and Lorraine V. Aragon

2002 Collective Burials and Community Memories: Interpreting the Placement of the Dead in the Mid-Atlantic and Southeastern United States with Reference to Ethnographic Cases from Indonesia. In *The Space and Place of Death,* edited by H. Silverman and D. B. Small, pp. 26–54. Archeological Papers of the American Anthropological Association, No. 11. American Anthropological Association, Arlington, Virginia.

Jackson, Douglas K.

1980 *Final Report on Archaeological Investigations at the Sandy Ridge Farm Site (11-S-660).* FAI-270 Archaeological Mitigation Project Report 20. Department of Anthropology, University of Illinois, Urbana-Champaign.

Jackson, Paul D.

2004 Coexistence of the West Jefferson and Moundville I Phases. *Journal of Alabama Archaeology* 50(1):1–17.

Jenkins, Ned J.

1980 Ceramic Chronology in the Gainesville Reservoir. *Southeastern Archaeological Conference Bulletin* 22:69–74.

1981 *Gainesville Lake Area Ceramic Description and Chronology. Archaeological Investigations in the Gainesville Lake Area of the Tennessee-Tombigbee Waterway.* Report prepared for the U.S. Army Corps of Engineers, Mobile District. Report of Investigations 12, Office of Archaeological Research, Moundville, Alabama.

2003 The Terminal Woodland/Mississippian Transition in West and Central Alabama. *Journal of Alabama Archaeology* 49(1–2):1–62.

Jenkins, Ned J., and Jerry J. Nielsen

1974 Archaeological Salvage Investigations at the West Jefferson Steam Plant Site, Jefferson County, Alabama. Report submitted to Alabama Power, Birmingham, by the Department of Anthropology, University of Alabama, Tuscaloosa.

Kelly, John E.

1990 The Emergence of Mississippian Culture in the American Bottom Region. In *The Mississippian Emergence,* edited by B. D. Smith, pp. 113–152. Smithsonian Institution Press, Washington, D.C.

King, Adam

2003 *Etowah: The Political History of a Chiefdom Capital.* University of Alabama Press, Tuscaloosa.

Knight, Vernon James, Jr.

1986 The Institutional Organization of Mississippian Religion. *American Antiquity* 51(4):675–687.

1989 Certain Aboriginal Mounds at Moundville: 1937 Excavations in Mounds H, I, J, K, and L. Paper presented at the 46th Annual Southeastern Archaeological Conference, Tampa.

1990 Social Organization and the Evolution of Hierarchy in Southeastern Chiefdoms. *Journal of Anthropological Research* 46(1):1–23.

1992 Preliminary Report on Excavations at Mound Q, Moundville. Paper presented at the 49th Annual Southeastern Archaeological Conference, Little Rock, Arkansas.

1998 Moundville as a Diagrammatic Ceremonial Center. In *Archaeology of the Moundville Chiefdom,* edited by V. J. Knight, Jr., and V. P. Steponaitis, pp. 44–62. Smithsonian Institution Press, Washington, D.C.

2002 Chronology and Use of Public Architecture at the Moundville Site: Excavations in Mound Q. Report submitted to the National Science Foundation in fulfillment of award numbers 9220568 and 9727709.

Knight, Vernon James, Jr., Lyle W. Konigsberg, and Susan R. Frankenberg

1999 A Gibbs Sampler Approach to the Dating of Phases in the Moundville Sequence. Manuscript on file, Department of Anthropology, University of Alabama, Tuscaloosa.

Knight, Vernon James, Jr., and Vincas P. Steponaitis

1998 A New History of Moundville. In *Archaeology of the Moundville Chiefdom,* edited by V. J. Knight, Jr., and V. P. Steponaitis, pp. 1–25. Smithsonian Institution Press, Washington, D.C.

Kohler, Timothy A., and Eric Blinman
1987 Solving Mixture Problems in Archaeology: Analysis of Ceramic Materials for Dating and Demographic Reconstruction. *Journal of Anthropological Archaeology* 6(1):1–28.

Kramer, Carol
1982 Ethnographic Households and Archaeological Interpretations: A Case from Iranian Kurdistan. In *Archaeology of the Household: Building a Prehistory of Domestic Life,* edited by R. R. Wilk and W. L. Rathje. *American Behavioral Scientist* 25(6):663–675.

Kuijt, Ian
2000 Keeping the Peace: Ritual, Skull Caching, and Community Integration in the Levantine Neolithic. In *Life in Neolithic Farming Communities: Social Organization, Identity, and Differentiation,* edited by I. Kuijt, pp. 137–164. Kluwer Academic, Dordrecht, The Netherlands.

Lacquement, Cameron H.
2004 How to Build a Mississippian House: A Study of Domestic Architecture in West-Central Alabama. Unpublished Master's thesis, Department of Anthropology, University of Alabama, Tuscaloosa.

LaMotta, Vincent M., and Michael B. Schiffer
1999 Behavioral Archaeology: Toward a New Synthesis. In *Archaeological Theory Today,* edited by I. Hodder, pp. 14–64. Blackwell, Malden, Massachusetts.

Le Page du Pratz, Antoine S.
1972 [1758] *History of Louisiana or of the Western Parts of Virginia and Carolina: Containing a Description of the Countries that Lie on Both Sides of the River Mississippi: With an Account of the Settlements, Inhabitants, Soil, Climate, and Products. (translated with some notes and observations relating to our colonies).* T. Becket, London. Reprint, Claitor's, Baton Rouge.

Lewis, R. Barry, and Charles Stout
1998 The Town as Metaphor. In *Mississippian Towns and Sacred Spaces: Searching for an Architectural Grammar,* edited by R. B. Lewis and C. Stout, pp. 227–241. University of Alabama Press, Tuscaloosa.

Lewis, Thomas M. N., and Madeline D. Kneberg
1946 *Hiwassee Island: An Archaeological Account of Four Tennessee Indian Peoples.* University of Tennessee Press, Knoxville.
1995 *The Prehistory of the Chickamauga Basin in Tennessee.* 2 vols., compiled and edited by L. P. Sullivan. University of Tennessee Press, Knoxville.

Linton, Ralph
1944 North American Cooking Pots. *American Antiquity* 9(4):369–380.

McGill, Robert, John W. Tukey, and Wayne A. Larsen
1978 Variations of Box Plots. *The American Statistician* 32:12–16.

McKenzie, Douglas H.
1964a Houses of the Moundville Phase. *Tennessee Archaeologist* 20:49–58.
1964b The Moundville Phase and Its Position in Southeastern Prehistory. Unpublished Ph.D. dissertation, Department of Anthropology, Harvard University, Cambridge.

1965 Pottery Types of the Moundville Phase. *Southeastern Archaeological Conference Bulletin* 2:55–64.

1966 Summary of the Moundville Phase. *Journal of Alabama Archaeology* 12(1):1–58.

Marcoux, Jon

2000 Display Goods Production and Circulation in the Moundville Chiefdom: A Mississippian Dilemma. Unpublished Master's thesis, Department of Anthropology, University of Alabama, Tuscaloosa.

Markin, Julie G.

1994 Elite Stoneworking and the Functions of Mounds at Moundville. Unpublished Honors thesis, Department of Anthropology, University of Alabama, Tuscaloosa.

1997 Elite Stoneworking and the Function of Mounds at Moundville. *Mississippi Archaeology* 32(2):117–135.

Marquardt, William H.

1978 Advances in Archaeological Seriation. In *Advances in Archaeological Method and Theory 1,* edited by M. Schiffer, pp. 257–314. Academic Press, New York.

Maxham, Mintcy D.

2000 Rural Communities in the Black Warrior Valley, Alabama: The Role of Commoners in the Creation of the Moundville I Landscape. *American Antiquity* 65(2): 337–354.

2004 Native Constructions of Landscapes in the Black Warrior Valley, Alabama, AD 1020–1520. Unpublished Ph.D. dissertation, Department of Anthropology, University of North Carolina, Chapel Hill.

Mehrer, Mark W.

1995 *Cahokia's Countryside: Household Archaeology, Settlement Patterns, and Social Power.* Northern Illinois University Press, DeKalb.

Mehrer, Mark W., and James M. Collins

1995 Household Archaeology at Cahokia and in Its Hinterlands. In *Mississippian Communities and Households.* edited by J. D. Rogers and B. D. Smith, pp. 32–57. University of Alabama Press, Tuscaloosa.

Michals, Lauren M.

1998 The Oliver Site and Early Moundville I Phase Economic Organization. In *Archaeology of the Moundville Chiefdom,* edited by V. J. Knight, Jr., and V. P. Steponaitis, pp. 167–182. Smithsonian Institution Press, Washington, D.C.

Million, Michael G.

1975 Ceramic Technology of the Nodena Phase Peoples (ca. A.D. 1400–1700). *Southeastern Archaeological Conference Bulletin* 18:201–208.

Milner, George R.

1983 *The Turner and Demange Sites.* American Bottom Archaeology, FAI-270 Reports 4. University of Illinois Press, Urbana.

1984 *The Julien Site.* American Bottom Archaeology, FAI-270 Reports 7. University of Illinois Press, Urbana.

1998 *The Cahokia Chiefdom: The Archaeology of a Mississippian Society.* Smithsonian Institution Press, Washington, D.C.

Mistovich, Tim S.

1988 Early Mississippian in the Black Warrior Valley: The Pace of Transition. *Southeastern Archaeology* 7(1):21–38.

Morse, Phyllis A.

1990 The Parkin Site and the Parkin Phase. In *Towns and Temples along the Mississippi*, edited by D. H. Dye and C. A. Cox, pp. 118–134. University of Alabama Press, Tuscaloosa.

Muller, Jon

1984 Mississippian Specialization and Salt. *American Antiquity* 49(3):489–507.

1986 Pans and a Grain of Salt: Mississippian Specialization Revisited. *American Antiquity* 51(2):405–409.

1997 *Mississippian Political Economy*. Plenum Press, New York.

Myer, Jennifer L.

2002 Among the Fields: Mississippian Settlement Patterns in the Black Warrior Valley, Alabama. Unpublished Master's thesis, Department of Anthropology, University of Alabama, Tuscaloosa.

Naroll, Raoul

1962 Floor Area and Settlement Population. *American Antiquity* 27(4):587–589.

Netting, Robert McC.

1982 Some Home Truths on Household Size and Wealth. *American Behavioral Scientist* 25:641–662.

Nielsen, Axel E.

1995 Architectural Performance and the Reproduction of Social Power. In *Expanding Archaeology*, edited by J. M. Skibo, W. H. Walker, and A. E. Nielsen, pp. 47–66. University of Utah Press, Salt Lake City.

O'Brien, Patricia J.

1972 *A Formal Analysis of Cahokia Ceramics from the Powell Tract*. Monograph 3. Illinois Archaeological Survey, Urbana.

Pauketat, Timothy R.

1986 Predicting Occupation Span from Ceramic Refuse: A Case Study from the American Bottom. Unpublished Master's thesis, Department of Anthropology, Southern Illinois University, Carbondale.

1987 A Functional Consideration of a Mississippian Domestic Vessel Assemblage. *Southeastern Archaeology* 6(1):1–15.

1989 Monitoring Mississippian Homestead Occupation Span and Economy Using Ceramic Refuse. *American Antiquity* 54(2):288–310.

1994 *The Ascent of Chiefs: Cahokia and Mississippian Politics in Native North America*. University of Alabama Press, Tuscaloosa.

1998 *The Archaeology of Downtown Cahokia: The Tract-15A and Dunham Tract Excavations*. Studies in Archaeology No. 1. Illinois Transportation Archaeological Research Program, University of Illinois, Urbana-Champaign.

2001 Practice and History in Archaeology. *Anthropological Theory* 1(1):73–98.

2003 Resettled Farmers and the Making of a Mississippian Polity. *American Antiquity* 68(1):39–66.

Pauketat, Timothy R., and Neil H. Lopinot

1997 Cahokian Population Dynamics. In *Cahokia: Domination and Ideology in the Mississippian World,* edited by T. R. Pauketat and T. E. Emerson, pp. 103–123. University of Nebraska Press, Lincoln.

Payne, Claudine

1994 Mississippian Capitals: An Archeological Investigation of Precolumbian Political Structure. Unpublished Ph.D. dissertation, University of Florida, Gainesville.

Peebles, Christopher S.

1971 Moundville and Surrounding Sites: Some Structural Considerations of Mortuary Practices. In *Approaches to the Social Dimensions of Mortuary Practices,* edited by J. A. Brown, pp. 68–91. Memoir 15. Society for American Archaeology, Washington, D.C.

1974 Moundville: The Organization of a Prehistoric Community and Culture. Unpublished Ph.D. dissertation, University of California, Santa Barbara.

1978 Determinants of Settlement Size and Location in the Moundville Phase. In *Mississippian Settlement Patterns,* edited by B. D. Smith, pp. 369–416. Academic Press, New York.

1979 *Excavations at Moundville, 1905–1951.* University of Michigan Press, Ann Arbor.

1981 Archaeological Research at Moundville: 1840–1989. *Southeastern Archaeological Conference Bulletin* 24:77–81.

1983 Moundville: Late Prehistoric Sociopolitical Organization in the Southeastern United States. In *The Development of Political Organization in Native North America,* edited by E. Tooker, pp. 183–201. Proceedings, American Ethnological Society, Washington, D.C.

1987a Moundville from 1000 to 1500 AD as Seen from 1840 to 1985 AD. In *Chiefdoms in the Americas,* edited by R. Drennan and C. Uribe, pp. 21–42. University Press of America, Lanham, Maryland.

1987b The Rise and Fall of the Mississippian in Western Alabama: The Moundville and Summerville Phases, A.D. 1000 to 1600. *Mississippi Archaeology* 22(1):1–31.

Peebles, Christopher S., and Susan M. Kus

1977 Some Archaeological Correlates of Ranked Societies. *American Antiquity* 42(3): 421–448.

Polhemus, Richard B.

1987 *The Toqua Site: A Late Mississippian Dallas Phase Town.* Report of Investigations No. 41, Tennessee Valley Authority. Department of Anthropology, University of Tennessee, Knoxville.

Pope, Melody K.

1989 Microtools from the Black Warrior Valley: Technology, Use, and Context. Unpublished Master's thesis, Department of Anthropology, State University of New York, Binghamton.

Powell, Mary

1988 *Status and Health in Prehistory: A Case Study of the Moundville Chiefdom.* Smithsonian Institution Press, Washington, D.C.

Price, Douglas T., and Gary M. Feinman

2001 *Images of the Past.* 3rd ed. Mayfield, Mountain View, California.

Rees, Mark A.
2001 Mississippian Political Culture: Contrasting Historical Trajectories in Southeastern North America. Ph.D. dissertation, Department of Anthropology, University of Oklahoma, Norman.

Rice, Prudence M.
1987 *Pottery Analysis: A Sourcebook.* University of Chicago Press, Chicago.

Riggs, Brett H.
1999 Removal Period Cherokee Households and Communities in Southwestern North Carolina: Material Perspectives on Ethnicity and Cultural Differentiation. Unpublished Ph.D. dissertation, Department of Anthropology, University of Tennessee, Knoxville.

Rodning, Christopher B.
2005 The Cherokee Town at the Coweeta Creek Site. Unpublished Ph.D. dissertation, Department of Anthropology, University of North Carolina, Chapel Hill.

Rogers, Daniel J.
1995 Dispersed Communities and Integrated Households: A Perspective from Spiro and the Arkansas Basin. In *Mississippian Communities and Households,* edited by D. R. Rogers and B. D. Smith, pp. 81–98. University of Alabama Press, Tuscaloosa.

Rothschild, Nan A., Barbara J. Mills, T. J. Ferguson, and Susan Dublin
1993 Abandonment at Zuni Farming Villages. In *Abandonment of Settlements and Regions: Ethnoarchaeological and Archaeological Approaches,* edited by C. M. Cameron and S. A. Tomka, pp. 123–137. Cambridge University Press, Cambridge.

Ryba, Elizabeth A.
1995 Summit Architecture on Mound E at Moundville. Unpublished Master's thesis, Department of Anthropology, University of Alabama, Tuscaloosa.

Scarry, C. Margaret
1986 *Change in Plant Procurement and Production during the Emergence of the Moundville Chiefdom.* Unpublished Ph.D. dissertation, Department of Anthropology, University of Michigan, Ann Arbor.
1993a Agricultural Risk and the Development of the Moundville Chiefdom. In *Foraging and Farming in the Eastern Woodlands,* edited by C. M. Scarry, pp. 157–181. University Press of Florida, Gainesville.
1993b Variability in Mississippian Crop Production Strategies. In *Foraging and Farming in the Eastern Woodlands,* edited by C. M. Scarry, pp. 78–80. University Press of Florida, Gainesville.
1995 *Excavations on the Northwest Riverbank at Moundville: Investigations of a Moundville I Residential Area.* Report of Investigations 72. University of Alabama Museums Office of Archaeological Services, Tuscaloosa.
1998 Domestic Life on the Northwest Riverbank at Moundville. In *Archaeology of the Moundville Chiefdom,* edited by V. J. Knight, Jr., and V. P. Steponaitis, pp. 63–101. Smithsonian Institution Press, Washington, D.C.

Scarry, C. Margaret, and Vincas P. Steponaitis
1997 Between Farmstead and Center: The Natural and Social Landscape of Mound-

ville. In *People, Plants, and Landscapes: Studies in Paleoethnobotany.* edited by K. J. Gremillion, pp. 107–122. University of Alabama Press, Tuscaloosa.

Scarry, John F.

2001 Resistance and Accommodation in Apalachee Province. In *The Archaeology of Traditions: Agency and History before and after Columbus,* edited by T. R. Pauketat, pp. 34–57. University Press of Florida, Gainesville.

Scarry, John F., and Suzanne K. Fish

1999 How Great Were the Polities of the Southwest and Southeast? Areas of Comparison and Contrast. In *Great Towns and Regional Polities: Cultural Evolution in the U.S. Southwest and Southeast,* edited by J. Neitzel, pp. 75–80. Amerind Foundation New World Studies Seminar Series. University of New Mexico Press, Albuquerque.

Scarry, John F., and Bonnie G. McEwan

1995 Domestic Architecture in Apalachee Province: Apalachee and Spanish Residential Styles in the Late Prehistoric and Early Historic Period Southeast. *American Antiquity* 60(3):482–495.

Schiffer, Michael

1972 Archaeological Context and Systemic Context. *American Antiquity* 37(2):156–165.

1977 *Behavioral Archeology.* Academic Press, New York.

1985 Is There a "Pompeii Premise" in Archaeology? *Journal of Anthropological Research* 41:18–41.

1987 *Formation Processes of the Archaeological Record.* University of New Mexico Press, Albuquerque.

Schlanger, Sarah H.

1986 Population Studies. In *Dolores Archaeological Program: Final Synthetic Report,* edited by D. A. Breternitz, C. K. Robinson, and G. T. Gross, pp. 493–523. U.S. Department of the Interior, Bureau of Reclamation, Engineering and Research Center, Denver.

Schroedl, Gerald F.

1986 Structures. In *Overhill Cherokee Archaeology at Chota-Tanasee,* edited by G. F. Schroedl, pp. 217–272. Report of Investigations 38. Department of Anthropology, University of Tennessee, Knoxville.

1998 Mississippian Towns in the Eastern Tennessee Valley. In *Mississippian Towns and Sacred Spaces: Searching for an Architectural Grammar,* edited by R. B. Lewis and C. Stout, pp. 64–92. University of Alabama Press, Tuscaloosa.

Seckinger, Ernest W., Jr., and Ned J. Jenkins

1980 A Plural Society in Prehistoric Alabama. Paper presented at the 37th Southeastern Archaeological Conference, New Orleans.

Shapiro, Gary

1984 Ceramic Vessels, Site Permanence, and Group Size: A Mississippian Example. *American Antiquity* 49(4):696–712.

Shennan, Stephen

1993 After Social Evolution: A New Archaeological Agenda? In *Archaeological Theory:*

Who Sets the Agenda?, edited by N. Yoffee and A. Sherratt, pp. 53–59. Cambridge University Press, Cambridge.

Shepard, Anna O.

1971 *Ceramics for the Archaeologist.* Publication 609. Carnegie Institution of Washington, Washington, D.C.

Smith, Michael E.

1987 Household Possessions and Wealth in Agrarian States: Implications for Archaeology. *Journal of Anthropological Archaeology* 6:297–335.

Speck, Frank G.

1907 Notes on Chickasaw Ethnology and Folk-Lore. *Journal of American Folk Lore* 20:50–58.

Stanish, Charles

1999 Settlement Pattern Shifts and Political Ranking in the Lake Titicaca Basin, Peru. In *Settlement Pattern Studies in the Americas: Fifty Years since Virú,* edited by B. Billman and G. Feinman, pp. 116–130. Smithsonian Institution Press, Washington, D.C.

Steponaitis, Vincas P.

1978 Location Theory and Complex Chiefdoms: A Mississippian Example. In *Mississippian Settlement Patterns,* edited by B. D. Smith, pp. 417–453. Academic Press, New York.

1980 Some Preliminary Chronological and Technological Notes on Moundville Pottery. *Southeastern Archaeological Conference Bulletin* 22:46–51.

1981 Chronology and Community Patterns at Moundville. *Southeastern Archaeological Conference Bulletin* 24:99–104.

1983 *Ceramics, Chronology, and Community Patterns: An Archaeological Study at Moundville.* Academic Press, New York.

1984 Technological Studies of Prehistoric Pottery from Alabama: Physical Properties and Vessel Function. In *The Many Dimensions of Pottery: Ceramics in Archaeology and Anthropology,* edited by S. E. van der Leeuw and A. C. Pritchard, pp. 79–122. University of Amsterdam, Amsterdam.

1986 Prehistoric Archaeology in the Southeastern United States, 1970–1985. *Annual Review of Anthropology* 15:363–404.

1992 Excavations at 1Tu50, an Early Mississippian Center near Moundville. *Southeastern Archaeology* 11(1):1–13.

1998 Population Trends at Moundville. In *Archaeology of the Moundville Chiefdom,* edited by V. J. Knight, Jr., and V. P. Steponaitis, pp. 26–43. Smithsonian Institution Press, Washington, D.C.

Steponaitis, Vincas P., and Vernon J. Knight, Jr.

2004 Moundville Art in Historical and Social Context. In *Hero, Hawk, and Open Hand: American Indian Art of the Ancient Midwest and South,* edited by R. F. Townsend and R. V. Sharp, pp. 167–182. The Art Institute of Chicago in association with Yale University Press, New Haven, Connecticut.

Sullivan, Lynne P.

1987 The Mouse Creek Household. *Southeastern Archaeology* 6(1):16–29.

1995 Mississippian Household and Community Organization in Eastern Tennessee. In *Mississippian Communities and Households,* edited by D. R. Rogers and B. D. Smith, pp. 99–123. University of Alabama Press, Tuscaloosa.

Swan, Caleb

1855 Position and State of Manners and Arts in the Creek, or Muscogee Nation in 1791. In *Information Respecting the History, Condition and Prospects of the Indian Tribes of the United States,* vol. 5, edited by H. R. Schoolcraft, pp. 251–283. J. B. Lippincott, Philadelphia.

Swanton, John R.

1922 *Early History of the Creek Indians and Their Neighbors.* Bureau of American Ethnology Bulletin 73. Smithsonian Institution, Washington, D.C.

1928 Social Organization and Social Usages of the Indians of the Creek Confederacy. In *Forty-second Annual Report of the Bureau of American Ethnology to the Secretary of the Smithsonian Institution, 1924–25,* pp. 23–472. Smithsonian Institution, Washington, D.C.

1931 *Source Material for the Social and Ceremonial Life of the Choctaw Indians.* Bulletin 103. Bureau of American Ethnology, Washington, D.C.

Taft, Kristi Elaine

1996 Functionally Relevant Classes of Pottery at Moundville. Unpublished Master's thesis, Department of Anthropology, University of Alabama, Tuscaloosa.

Turner, Christy G., and Laurel Lofgren

1966 Household Size of Prehistoric Western Pueblo Indians. *Southwestern Journal of Anthropology* 22:117–132.

Varien, Mark D., and Barbara J. Mills

1997 Accumulations Research: Problems and Prospects for Estimating Site Occupation Duration. *Journal of Archaeological Method and Theory* 4(2):141–191.

Varien, Mark D., and J. M. Potter

1997 Unpacking the Discard Equation: Simulating the Accumulation of Artifacts in the Archaeological Record. *American Antiquity* 62(2):194–213.

Vogel, Joseph O., and Jean Allan

1985 Mississippian Fortifications at Moundville. *Archaeology* 38(5):62–63.

Walker, Lisa J., and William H. Lucero

2000 The Depositional History of Ritual and Power. In *Agency in Archaeology,* edited by M.-A. Dobres and J. E. Robb, pp. 130–147. Routledge Press, New York.

Ward, Trawick, and R. P. Stephen Davis, Jr.

1991 The Evolution of Siouan Communities in Piedmont North Carolina. *Southeastern Archaeology* 10(1):40–53.

Warrick, Gary A.

1988 Estimating Ontario Iroquoian Village Duration. *Man in the Northeast* 36:21–60.

Welch, Paul D.

1981 The West Jefferson Phase: Terminal Woodland Tribal Society in West Central Alabama. *Southeastern Archaeological Conference Bulletin* 24:81–83.

1989 Chronological Markers and Imported Items from the Roadway Excavations at Moundville. Paper presented at the 46th Annual Southeastern Archaeological Conference, Tampa.

1990 Mississippian Emergence in West Central Alabama. In *The Mississippian Emergence,* edited by B. D. Smith, pp. 197–225. Smithsonian Institution Press, Washington, D.C.

1991a Monopolistic Control over Goods and the Political Stability of the Moundville Chiefdom. Paper presented at the 56th Annual Meeting of the Society for American Archaeology, New Orleans.

1991b *Moundville's Economy.* University of Alabama Press, Tuscaloosa.

1996 Control over Goods and the Political Stability of the Moundville Chiefdom. In *Political Structure and Change in the Prehistoric Southeastern United States,* edited by J. F. Scarry, pp. 69–91. University Press of Florida, Gainesville.

Welch, Paul D., and C. Margaret Scarry

1995 Status-Related Variation in Foodways in the Moundville Chiefdom. *American Antiquity* 60(3):397–419.

Whitridge, Peter J.

1999 The Construction of Social Differences in a Prehistoric Inuit Whaling Community. Unpublished Ph.D. dissertation, Department of Anthropology, Arizona State University, Tempe.

Wilk, Richard R.

1983 Little House in the Jungle: The Causes of Variation in House Size among Modern Kekchi Maya. *Journal of Anthropological Archaeology* 2:99–116.

Wilk, Richard R., and Robert McC. Netting

1984 Households: Changing Forms and Functions. In *Households: Comparative and Historical Studies of the Domestic Group,* edited by R. McC. Netting, R. R. Wilk, and E. J. Arnould, pp. 1–28. University of California Press, Berkeley.

Wilk, Richard R., and William Rathje

1982 Household Archaeology. *American Behavioral Scientist* 25(6):617–640.

Wilkinson, L., M. A. Jill, S. Miceli, G. Birkenbeuel, and E. Vang

1992 *Systat Graphics.* SYSTAT, Inc., Evanston, Illinois.

Wilson, Gregory D.

1998 A Case Study of Mississippian Resistance in the American Bottom. Unpublished Master's thesis, Department of Anthropology, University of Oklahoma, Norman.

1999 The Production and Consumption of Mississippian Fineware in the American Bottom. *Southeastern Archaeology* 18(2):98–109.

2001 Crafting Control and the Control of Crafts: Rethinking the Moundville Greenstone Industry. *Southeastern Archaeology* 20(2):118–128.

Wilson, Gregory D., R. P. Stephen Davis, Jr.

2003 Mapping the Moundville Community: A GIS Analysis of the Moundville Roadway. Poster presented at the 60th Annual Meeting of the Southeastern Archaeological Conference, Charlotte.

Wilson, Gregory D., Jon B. Marcoux, and Brad Koldehoff

2006 Square Pegs in Round Holes: Organizational Diversity between Early Moundville and Cahokia. In *Leadership and Polity in Mississippian Society,* edited by B. M. Butler and P. D. Welch. Occasional Papers No. 33. Center for Archaeological Investigations, Southern Illinois University, Carbondale.

Wilson, Gregory D., and Christopher B. Rodning
2002 Boiling, Baking, and Pottery Breaking: A Functional Analysis of Ceramic Vessels from Coweeta Creek. *Southeastern Archaeology* 21(1):29–35.

Wimberly, Stephen B.
1956 A Review of Moundville Pottery. *Southeastern Archaeological Conference Newsletter* 5(1):17–20.

Winter, Marcus
1976 Differential Patterns of Community Growth in Oaxaca. In *The Early Mesoamerican Village,* edited by K. Flannery, pp. 227–234. Academic Press, New York.

Wright, Muriel H.
1958 American Indian Corn Dishes. *The Chronicle of Oklahoma* 36:155–166.

Index

www.ingramcontent.com/pod-product-compliance
Lightning Source LLC
LaVergne TN
LVHW051421090926
847619LV00027B/249
9780817354442